ISLAM EXPOSED
A Three-Volume Series

VOLUME I

A SIMPLE CRASH COURSE ON ISLAM

Are the Bible's God and Allah the Same?

J.P. Sloane, Ph.D.

AvingtonHouse
Publishing

ISLAM EXPOSED:
A Three-Volume Series
Volume I
A SIMPLE CRASH COURSE ON ISLAM
Second Edition Revised 2018

By J.P. Sloane, Ph.D.
© Copyright 2013, © revised edition 2024 by J.P. Sloane, Ph.D.
Printed in the United States of America

ISBN-13: 978-0692697528
ISBN-10: 0692697527

AvingtonHouse Publishing, Dallas

All Koran passages, unless otherwise designated, are taken from Marmaduke Pickthall's translation of the Koran.

All Scriptures, unless otherwise designated, have been taken from the King James Version of the Bible with "thee, "ye" and "thou" converted to Modern English. The use of "you" and the Old English words "thy" and "thine" have sometimes been translated into the contemporary word your." For further clarification, words ending in the archaic plural suffixes "t," "est," and "eth" have been deleted and substituted with the modern ending. The archaic word "Lo!" has been rendered to "See!," "Look," "Pay attention," and "Realize." Because not all verses benefit from these changes, we have left some archaic words intact for the purpose of retaining the poetic essence of the King James Bible and the various translations of the Koran, which were also, for whatever reason, rendered in the English of the seventeenth century.

The same applies to the four, twentieth-century translations of the Koran we have referenced, which were also originally rendered in the English of the seventeenth century: Marmaduke Pickthall (published 1930), Abdullah Yusuf Ali (published 1934-8 revised 1939), Arthur John (A.J.) Arberry (published 1955) and Muhammad Habib Shakir (1866–1939) (published 1981 not without some controversy).

We also consider "Heaven" and "Hell" proper nouns describing actual places; therefore, they have been capitalized in this work

The cover design is from a NASA photo of the Helix Nebula (i.e., "Eye of God") photographed using the Hubble Telescope.

CONTENTS

CHAPTER 3
THE PROPHET OF ISLAM

LIST OF ILLUSTRATIONS

CHARTS

FIGURES:

TABLES:

INTRODUCTION

THE MYSTERIOUS MIDDLE EAST

The Western world has long had a romantic fantasy surrounding the mysterious Middle East. In the 1920s, with the onset of the film industry's silent era, people fantasized about the allusive Bedouins of the Arabian Desert while watching the handsome, strong and brooding film star, Rudolph Valentino, as he rode across the silver screen in his legendary roles of The Sheik (1921) and The Son of the Sheik (1926).

Fig. 1. Rudolph Valentino on a 1926 Playbill

Who has not heard of or read mythical stories about magical genies and flying carpets, such as *Tales From a Thousand and One Arabian Nights, Scheherazade, The Thief of Bagdad, Ali Baba and the Forty Thieves* and, of course, what child did not love the story of *Aladdin and the Magic Lamp?*

People in the West knew very little about the mysterious Prophet of Islam and the Muslim religion. All we knew was what was portrayed in books and movies. We thought of handsome sheiks and wise caliphs along with veil-faced belly dancers and beautiful harem girls. The young girls fantasized about being swept up onto the back of an Arabian prince's saddle and whisked away to some remote and romantic palace beyond the silent and ever-shifting sand dunes of the Arabian Desert.

17

The young men dreamed about exotic, dark-eyed beauties drawing water at some serene and beautiful, palm-laden desert oasis.

As a result, of growing up with all these tales of Arabian nights and magical genies, most of us assumed that these fabled riders of camels and Arabian stallions were similar to us in the West. After all, they loved and desired to be loved. They all wanted nice places to live—be it a palace or just a tent—and like those of us in the West, they lived through intrigues, battles, and times of peace. They loved their children and families, and the mysterious riders of the desert believed in one God. That belief created many in the West to think then, as many do now—that the god (Allah) of the Koran and the God of the Bible are the same deities. We were (and still are) led to believe by our politicians that Allah was simply the Arabic name for God. After all, the Koran contains stories about Abraham, Moses, Pharaoh, and Jesus. The Koran teaches that Allah gave the People of the Book (Bible) including the Torah with a succession of prophets (Sûrah 2:87) the Psalms (sûrah 4:163) as well as the gospel (Sûrah 5:46), so does it not make sense that we all worship the same God?

When Muslim jihadists (al-Qaeda) attacked the Pentagon in Washington, DC, and the World Trade Center in New York City on September 11, 2001, an event now referred to as 9/11, it was not Arabians on flying carpets that had flown into the Pentagon and the Twin Towers of the Trade Center—that was no fairy tale. It was Arabians, nonetheless, who had flown three pirated American Airliners, two into the Twin Towers, and one into the Pentagon. That infamous day also included a hijacked United Airlines plane, which went down in a rural field in Somerset County, Shanksville, Pennsylvania. The reason the jihadi mission over Pennsylvania failed was due to an uprising and struggles by valiant American heroes onboard the ill-fated plane. By sacrificing their lives, the hijacked United Airlines plane crashed, thus unable to reach its unknown designated target.

Thousands of innocent men, women, and children died on that dreadful day. It was more horrendous than when the Japanese made their sneak attack on Pearl Harbor on December 7, 1941. Not too long after that event, Al-Qaeda informed the West they were preparing thousands of suicide bombers to further attack America and their allies. Most of us in the West thought this was just braggadocios; after all, people do not just strap on bombs and blow themselves up—perhaps a few mentally disturbed fanatics—but not hundreds or thousands of rational human beings. How wrong we were!

America's president at the time, George W. Bush, insisted that the Trade Center attack was just a few extreme Muslims who hijacked a peaceful religion. What did we know? Almost immediately, all those fanciful storybook ideas we had of handsome sheiks and beautiful Arabian Princesses—who loved and desired to be loved just like us—faded into a new and much more troublesome curiosity.

Who really are these people of the desert? What is driving this religion of Islam, and what does it mean? Is the Koran really, as some claim, similar to the Bible because it contains stories from the Bible? We are told that Muslims acknowledge that Jesus was born of a virgin, and the Nativity is even recorded in the Koran. Again, does this mean we all worship the same God, and what does the Koran actually say about Jesus, Mary, and the Virgin Birth?

Sadly, long after that infamous day in September of 2001, many Americans and Europeans are just as confused as they were before the events of 9/11. Many still seek answers to the difference between the Arabian fairy tales many of us grew up with and the truth regarding the Islamic countries in the Middle East. Some claim we all worship the same God, but do we? We will look at some of the basic comparisons between the traditions of the Middle East, as revealed through the Koran and the Judeo-Christian West, which are derived from the Bible. The question continues to be; did the God of the Bible—as some insist—author the Koran?

THE JESUS OF ISLAM

Those of us who are Christians believe Jesus is God who came to earth born of a virgin named Mary and, therefore, was fully God and fully human. Muslims also believe Jesus was born of a virgin named Mary, but that is where it stops. The Muslim Jesus is a second or even third-rate prophet of Islam behind that of Muhammad and their messiah, the Mahdi, and we are constantly reminded that He is not the son of Allah. (As Christians, we agree that Jesus is not the son of Allah, but He is the Son of the biblical God known as YHWH or יהוה.)

The overwhelming majority of the world's religions and cults have had to acknowledge Jesus in some way. Jesus is incorporated into many faiths, unlike Mohammad, and acknowledged as either an ascended master, a prophet, a rabbi, or as He claims Himself to be, the Son of God. Unlike other faiths, Islam seems obsessed with tearing down the claims made by Jesus Himself while trying to wrap Him in the fabric of Islam.

The Koran has a recurring theme attacking the Divinity of Christ while embracing Him as one of their most important prophets. Consider that Allah claims he gave the Christians and Jews the Torah and Gospel (Sûrah 3:3) and that "... there is none that can alter the words (and decrees) of Allah ..." (Sûrah 6:34); then contradicts itself by going against the gospel (good news) message that God came to earth in the form of a man by denying, directly or indirectly. Jesus is the Son of God, as we will see when we study the Quran and Hadith in this book. In the Koran alone, we are told 21 times that Allah has no son (sûrahs, 2:116; 4:171; 6:101; 9:30; 10:68; 17:111; 18:4; 19:35; 19:88; 19:89; 19:90; 19:91; 19:92; 21:26; 23:91; 25;2; 37:152; 39:4; 43:81; 43;82; 72:3). In order to drive the message that Allah has no son, the Koran purposefully refers to Jesus as the son of Mary (not Allah) 23 times (sûrahs 2:87, 2:253, 3:45, 4:157, 4:171, 5:17, 5:46, 5:72, 5:75, 5:78, 5:110, 5:112, 5:114, 5:116, 9:31, 19:34, 23:50, 33:7, 43:57, 57:27, 61:6, 61:14). It must also deny the Trinity because that includes God the Son (Matthew 28:19), at least 65 times (sûrahs,3:64; 4:36; 4:48; 4:116; 5:72; 6:14; 6:81; 6:88; 6:106; 6:136; 6:137; 6:148; 6:151; 9:31; 10:28; 10:29; 12:108; 13:15; 13:33; 13:36; 16:51; 16:52; 16:53; 16:54; 16:55; 16:56; 16:57; 16:73; 16:86; 17:22; 17:39; 17:40; 17:56; 17:57; 18:12; 18:110; 22:31; 23:59; 23:117; 24:55; 25:68; 28:87; 28:88; 29:8; 30:31; 31:13; 35:13; 35:14; 39:64; 39:65; 40:41; 40:42; 40:43; 40:66; 41:6; 43:15; 43:45; 46:4 46:5; 46:6; 50:26; 51:51; 60:12; 72:2; 72:18).

Finally, the Koran denies that Jesus was ever crucified for our sins, but some Muslim theologians suggest it is possible that Judas was crucified in His place. To bolster that argument, the Koran tells us Jesus died peacefully when he allegedly said, "Peace on me [Jesus] the day I was born, and the day I die, and the day I shall be raised alive!" (Sûrah 19:33.)

We also read in the Koran:

And because of their saying: "We slew the Messiah, Jesus son of Mary, Allah's messenger"—they slew him not nor crucified him, but it appeared so unto them; and see [pay attention]! Those who disagree concerning it are in doubt thereof; they have no knowledge thereof save pursuit of a conjecture; they slew him not for certain (Sûrah 4:157, bracketed clarification mine).

The problem with this is that all four gospels (which Allah says he gave and protects) tell us that Jesus *was* crucified. His mother (we are told by name in Matthew, Mark, and John, and with a group in Luke) was at the foot of the cross, and Jesus spoke directly with her. Surely, Mary would have recognized her own son, especially when He talked to her (John 19:25-27).

So how did the Koran's Jesus die? The Koran tells us that Jesus did not die (a contradiction of sûrah 19:33) but was taken up bodily (raptured) to heaven by Allah (Sûrah Quran 3:55 and 5:117)!

As we have shown, when you study Islam, you cannot help but notice its underlying theme to discredit Jesus as the Divine savior of the world (John 3:16-17), while at the same time embracing Him as a virgin born, highly regarded Prophet of Islam. If you are confused by this constant mantra attacking the Divinity of Jesus, please understand that if Jesus is who He claims to be and who the Bible tells us He is, then there is no need for a man named Muhammad to begin a new revelation some 700 years in the future in 610 A.D.

AND FINALLY

Because one volume could not possibly share all there is to know about Islam, we have prepared three separate volumes for those who want to understand Islam more fully. In Volume II of *Exposing Islam, The Koran: Selected Sûrahs, Commentary and Bible Comparisons*, you will be able to read and study for yourself 23 complete sûrahs containing 700 verses of the actual Koran. We provide commentary when studying each verse of the Koran in order to clarify and explain some of the difficult verses.

Many people have asked if we could format a book comparing the Koran's Bible versions with the actual stories from the Bible, similar to a parallel Bible. (Parallel Bibles have the King James Bible and other translations, such as the NIV version, placed side by side.) Because of the Koran's many biblically unique and historical problems, using a parallel format will not work, but when appropriate, we have placed the actual Bible passages, which the Koran attempts to retell, below the Koran's version so you can compare them and judge for yourself.

Volume III of our three-volume series, *Exposing Islam,* is titled *Islam: Science—Bible—Archaeology and Myths* and compares the Koran and Hadiths (the second holiest book in Islam) with science, myths, and historical errors. We also show how the Koran takes a third Pagan religion (Buddhism) and converts it into an Islamic-approved version of the Nativity of Christ.

It is our desire for the reader to enjoy reading these three volumes, which have been designed as a resource for studying Islam, as well as a reference library for the average person to gain a better grasp of exactly what Islam actually involves.

As we stated on the copyright page, because most of the Koran's translations were written in the King's English of the seventeenth century—like the King James Bible—we wanted to make the koranic quotes easier to read. Therefore, we have taken the liberty of converting some of the old terms, such as "thee," "ye" and "thou," etc., to the modern English usage of "you" and the Old English words "thy" and "thine" into the contemporary words "you," "your," etc. Because not all the verses benefit from these changes, a few exceptions have kept their archaic words intact. This was done in order to preserve the poetic essence of the King James Bible and the various English translations of the Koran. Both books are quite capable of speaking for themselves.

So sit back, relax, and prepare to embark on an exciting and educational journey of discovery. By the time you have completed exploring these three volumes, you will have as much knowledge or more about Islam as many Christians have about their faith. We trust you will enjoy being able to finally gain more insight into the mysterious world of the Middle East as we unravel the various mysteries of Islam, including the claims that the God of the Bible and the Koran are the same.

CHAPTER 1

RELIGION—WHAT IS IT?

In general, when most people think of the various world religions, they reason that they all hold some basics in common—the belief that there is a God or god(s) and that deities need appeasement.

Religion comes to us through the Latin word *religio*, which translates to mean "fear" or "awe" when addressing the supernatural or a deity.[1] One of the underlying themes of most religions is man's attempts to please god(s) through rituals and sacrifice, but it was through the Hebrews that the concept of pleasing God through a moral life was first introduced.[2]

Throughout history, most civilizations embraced many gods, but the concept of only one God seems to have originated with the ancient Hebrews. Monotheism is the belief that there is only one God "mono" or "one," combined with "theistic" from the Greek word *Theos* or God. As Christians, we also believe in one God through a unique entity called the Trinity—or one God revealed in three persons (Father, Son, and Holy Spirit). The Hebrews believed—based on Scripture—that God would one day send them a Messiah (Genesis 3:14; Proverbs 30:4; Isaiah 9:6, etc.). Messianic Jews of the first century accepted Jesus (YAWA) as that long-awaited Messiah.

The Greeks in Antioch, a city in Asia Minor, translated "Messiah" (anointed) into the Greek word Christos (Christ), which also means anointed. This is how those of us who believe that Jesus is the Son of

God came to be known as "Christians" (Acts 11:26). Seven centuries after the birth of Jesus, a new religion called "Islam" (i.e., submission)[3] emerged on the Arabian Peninsula, loosely incorporated the Judeo-Christian faith. Because of the incorporation of what appears to be biblical Scriptures into the revelations given to Muhammad, the Prophet of Islam, many—especially those who have never read the Koran—believe Islam is an extension of the Judeo-Christian faith and the final revelation of Allah to mankind.

To understand this complicated controversy, we will start at the beginning with the Hebrew Patriarch, Abraham, and his God. We will then focus on the transmission of Abraham's faith through his descendants. We will also address the authorship of the Bible versus the authorship of Koran, both of which, ironically enough, were produced by descendants of Abraham's own family.

The Bible and the Koran: Their Similarities and Differences

Islam: The Religion of One-Upmanship

When we were kids, it seemed that there was always one person who had to out-do all the others. We probably remember someone like Susie, who came to school one day with a new dress. In front of everyone, Amy told Susie how pretty her dress was and that she had one just like it at home—only hers had rhinestones around the neck, or the time Billy came to school and showed off the baseball his dad had just given him. Johnny responded, saying that his dad had just bought him a new baseball, too; only Babe Ruth autographed his! That is one-upmanship.

Why did we share that story with you? We shared it because Islam is a religion of one-upmanship. Just look at the alleged claim that God had to reveal Himself to a man named Muhammad to provide him with a new and improved holy book, which was even better than the Judeo-Christian Bible! Not only that, but the Koran says that Muhammad was the last and greatest prophet—even greater than

Moses and Jesus—which we will address further in our commentary for Sûrah 2:129 in Volume II of our three-volume series, *Exposing Islam, The Koran: Selected Sûrahs, Commentary and Bible Comparisons*.

How was it possible that Muhammad could become even greater than the miracle worker and Law Giver Moses? Muhammad had a dream in which he went to Heaven (the "Night Journey," Sûrah 17), which led him to reprimand the Jews, reminding them how they had their Temple destroyed in 70 A.D. and how they were finally purged from the land and scattered throughout the world in 135 A.D. Muhammad had a revelation in this night vision that the Jews could find forgiveness if they converted to Islam. In that night vision, Muhammad also condemned the Christians because they said Jesus is an associate of Allah. In Sûrah 17, there is no mention of Muhammad meeting any biblical prophets that were added later in the Hadith's version of the "Night Journey." It is in the Hadith where we see the one-upmanship on Moses, which was not recorded in the Koran:

Sahih al-Bukhari Book 4 Hadith 429

Narrated by Malik bin Sasaa

Then we ascended to the 6th heaven and again the same questions and answers were exchanged as in the previous heavens. There I met and greeted Moses who said, "You are welcomed O brother and. a Prophet." When I proceeded on, he started weeping and on being asked why he was weeping, he said, "O Lord! Followers of this youth who was sent after me will enter Paradise in greater number than my followers."

In the spirit of one-upmanship, Muhammad has Moses claiming that he was the predicted Prophet greater than Moses, who proceeds to cry like a baby because Muhammad would one-up him by bringing *even more* people to Islamic Paradise then he had been capable of doing! One could not be faulted when reading this to think that Moses seems a little jealous of Muhammad.

As we have just seen, Muhammad is alleged to be the prophet greater (one-up) than Moses, but it does not end there. Muslims also claim that Muhammad was also the one promised by Jesus Himself (even more one-upmanship) when He said:

> And I (Jesus) will ask the Father, and He will give you another... (John 14:16a, NIV, bracketed clarification mine).

Muslims point to the above verse and the Koran as proof that Jesus promised Muhammad would be the one that would follow Him:

> And when Jesus son of Mary said: O Children of Israel! Lo! I am the messenger of Allah unto you, confirming that which was (revealed) before me in the Torah, and bringing good tidings of a messenger who cometh after me, whose name is the Praised One [Ahmed or Muhammad]. Yet when he hath come unto them with clear proofs [miracles], they say: This is mere magic (Sûrah 61:1, bracketed clarifications mine).

They believe the word "another" mentioned in John 14:16a is Muhammad—the prophet Moses spoke of when he said:

> The LORD your God will raise up for you a prophet like me (Deuteronomy 18:15a, NIV).

Selective memory is when we take Scripture out of context to make it say anything we want. The selective memory of Muhammad fails to tell us—as the late media commentator and great American, Paul Harvey, used to end his radio broadcasts with—"The rest of the story."

To begin with, what Jesus actually said was:

> And I will ask the Father, and He will give you another advocate to help you and be with you forever—the Spirit of truth. The world cannot accept Him because it neither sees Him nor knows Him. But you know Him, for He lives with you and will be in you (John 14:16-17, NIV).

Jesus told His disciples that He would leave them with the Holy Spirit—not leave them with Muhammad. When we look at what Moses said in its entirety, we see a different picture emerge as well:

> The Lord your God will raise up for you a prophet like me from among you, from your fellow Israelites. You must listen to Him (Deuteronomy 18:15, NIV).

Who is the prophet spoken of in the Bible who will be greater than Moses—Muhammad, who was not a Jew—or someone else? Biblical scholars know that we can use the Bible to interpret the Bible and, therefore, all we have to do is look in the Bible for the answer:

> Jesus has been found worthy of greater honor than Moses, just as the builder of a house has greater honor than the house itself (Hebrews 3:3, NIV).

The following table shows how the religion of Muhammad—when compared to the Bible—appears to be a religion of one-upmanship:

Table 1: The One-Upmanship of the Koran

THE BIBLE	KORAN/HADITH
The Canon of Scripture closed with the New Testament. Canon is the text of the accepted books believed to be divinely inspired by God (2 Timothy 3:16).	The Koran is the final revelation superseding the Bible. The Koran acknowledges the Bible, but the Koran is the final revelation given in pure Arabic (Sûrah 46:12).
Jesus the Son—and greatest revelation of God "Salvation is found in no one else, For there is no greater name under Heaven given to mankind by which we must be saved" (Acts 4:12, NIV).	Muhammad—last and greatest revelation of Allah Muhammad is a prophet greater than Jesus because Allah has not taken a son (Sûrah 17:111). Only Muhammad bears the Seal of the Prophets (Sûrah 33:40).

THE BIBLE	KORAN/HADITH
Jesus was visited by two prophets.	Muhammad was visited by three prophets.
Elijah and Moses (Matthew 17:3). There were three eyewitnesses (2 Peter 1:16-18).	Abraham, Moses, and Jesus; however, this happened in a dream—there were no live eyewitnesses (Hadith) Sahih al-Bukhari, Volume 4, Book 55, Number 648, Narrated (by) Ibn Umar.
The Bible has three Heavens (2 Corinthians 12:2). Presumably, (1) the air or sky around the earth; (2) outer space, and (3) Heaven, the abode of God.	Islam has seven Heavens (Sûrah 67:3).
God does not change His mind for something better. "God is not a man that He should lie" (Numbers 23:19a).	Allah does change his mind (in the spirit of one-upmanship) for something better (Sûrah 2:106). Consider: If a perfect God makes perfect decisions from the beginning (because He is perfect, He could do it no other way), why would there be a need for Him to change His mind unless it is to go back on His word?
God is revealed through the Bible. The Old Testament predicted the New Testament in Jeremiah 31:31, and Jesus fulfilled that prophecy in Matthew 26:28; therefore, there is only one Bible in two volumes.	Allah is revealed through the (1) Bible; (2) Koran, and (3) Hadith. In addition to the Koran, the Hadith consists of innumerable volumes (a collection of books).

The Bible

Judeo-Christianity and Islam would not be complete without a basic understanding of the two books on which the Judeo-Christian and Islamic faiths are based.

To begin with, the Bible and the Koran are both divided into two volumes. The Bible's first volume is the Tanakh, and it primarily concerns the Jews. Christians refer to it as the Old Testament. The second volume is the New Testament, and it primarily concerns Christians. Together they are referred to as the Bible; it was written over a period of about 1500 years. The Old Testament has 39 books (the Catholic Bible has an additional eight books made up of what is called the Apocrypha), and the New Testament is comprised of 27 books for a total of 66 books in the Protestant Bible and 74 in the Catholic version. Each Testament of the Bible is broken into books (some books are also comprised of letters), which are broken into chapters, and then broken into verses.

Originally, this was not the way the Testaments were written, but for the sake of scholarly research and study, the chapter and verse system was incorporated at a later date. The books contain historical accounts ranging from the creation of the world to the patriarchal establishment of the Hebrew people and the nation of Israel. The Old Testament also concerns itself with prophetic passages that point to the Messiah, which came to fruition in the writings of the New Testament. The Bible contains over 25% prophecy, much of which has been fulfilled, with some actually being fulfilled now in our present generation, and still more to be fulfilled with the End of Days—a time that seems not so far off. We should point out here that biblical prophecy is the equivalent of God autographing His work (2 Timothy 3:16), thus validating itself—a unique phenomenon noticeably missing from the Koran and other religious works.

The New Testament was prophesied in the Old Testament in Jeremiah 31:31. It was foretold that God would one day give a new covenant to His people; that covenant is the New Testament, and it was fulfilled through a divine event on which Christians and Muslims agree—the virgin birth of Christ Jesus.[4]

Archaeology has established that the Bible has an incredible history of being accurate, and although it took over one and a half millennia and around 40 authors for it to be completed, the continuity of the Bible shows itself to be without conflict. (Some have tried to indicate conflicting passages, but on careful study, including archaeological revelations, the detractors have failed to prove their case.) The Bible explains why there is a clear thread running throughout all the Scriptures over thousands of years without contradiction:

> Above all, you must understand that no prophecy of Scripture came about by the prophet's own interpretation of things. For prophecy never had its origin in the human will, but prophets, [al]though humans spoke from God as they were carried along by the Holy Spirit (2 Peter 1:20-21, NIV, bracketed clarification mine).

The Koran

The Islamic Prophet Muhammad received the Koran over a 23-year period. Because Muhammad could not read or write, he memorized the verses given to him from Allah through the angel, Gabriel. Some of Muhammad's followers would write down the messages on pieces of rocks, bleached camel bone, palm leaves, or anything else they could find. Understandably, the Koran was not formally collected into a book until shortly after Muhammad's death in 632 A.D.

Regarding the modern translations of the Koran, we have observed that many of the English koranic translations have been laced with the Old English language of the seventeenth century, as opposed to the contemporary English grammar used during the time in which these translations were actually written. Of the four translations of the Koran, we used as references—Mohammad Marmaduke Pickthall (1875–1936), Arthur John (A.J.) Arberry (1905–1969), Abdullah Yusuf Ali (1872–1953), and Muhammad Habib Shakir (1866–1939)—they all lived well into the twentieth century, which was hardly a point in time when the Old English of the seventeenth century was spoken. It seems that those who translated the Koran wanted to give the impression of its sacred origin being as divinely inspired as possible by using the hallowed language of the King James Bible, even though the Koran was written almost a millennium before such a language was spoken. To be fair to the translators, they are not the first ones to attempt that. Creating a biblical semblance with the Koran began at its very inception when they incorporated Bible stories, albeit inaccurately, and divided the Koran into two volumes, thus echoing the Bible's Old and New Testaments.

One important aspect of the Koran is when Allah confirmed to Muhammad several times that he authored both the Bible and the Koran.

> And We caused Jesus, son of Mary, to follow in their footsteps, confirming that which was (revealed) before him in the Torah, and We bestowed on him the Gospel wherein is guidance and a light, confirming that which was (revealed) before it in the Torah—a guidance and an admonition unto those who ward off (evil).
>
> Let the people of the Gospel judge by what Allah has revealed therein. If any do fail to judge by (the light of) what Allah has revealed, they are (no better than) those who rebel (Sûrah 5:46-47, Abdullah Yusuf Ali).

In fact, not only does Allah claim to have written both the Old and New Testaments, but he also told Muhammad to challenge the Jews and Christians to judge the Koran through comparison with the Bible. If the Koran is not from Allah, then it will obviously be apparent to Bible believers. Allah told Muhammad he is confident there are no contradictions because if there are, then the Koran could be judged as false. Bearing in mind the above verse which advises, "Let the people of the Gospel judge by what Allah has revealed therein," the Koran also instructs:

31

Will they not then ponder on the Qur'an? If it had been from other than Allah they would have found therein much incongruity (Sûrah 4:82).

Yet, in the Koran, we will read over and over again how it denies the very heart of the Gospel by denying the gospel message. What is the gospel message? The Bible informs us:

By this gospel you are saved, if you hold firmly to the word I preached to you. Otherwise, you have believed in vain. For what I received I passed on to you as of first importance: that Christ died for our sins according to the Scriptures, that He was buried, that He was raised on the third day according to the Scriptures, and that He appeared to Cephas (Peter) and then to the Twelve. After that, He appeared to more than five hundred of the brothers and sisters at the same time, most of whom are still living, though some have fallen asleep. Then He appeared to James, then to all the apostles, and last of all He appeared to me (1 Corinthians 15:2-8, NIV, bracketed clarification mine).

Unlike the Bible, the Koran does not contain any books, although it does have 114 sûrahs (i.e., chapters) broken down into verses. Despite the lack of actual books in the Koran, as we previously explained, the various sûrahs and verses are divided into two volumes, not unlike the Bible. Still, there is no continuity to these verses, and at best, they are simply random collections pieced together without any specific or chronological order.

There are some familiar Bible stories appearing throughout the various sûrahs in the Koran, as well as some non-biblical, historical persons and events found in the Koran. Some of the passages are very challenging since they contain anachronisms. (An anachronism is a story with people or things out of place in the time when the events are reported to have occurred.) For example, let's say someone wrote a story about the end of the American Civil War and said that President Abraham Lincoln heard about General Lee's surrender to General Grant through an email. Because computers and the Internet would not be invented until the next century, the inclusion of the email in this story would be considered an anachronism. Remember the word "anachronism" when we examine the Koran.

A curious thing regarding the order of the sûrahs in the Koran is that the first volume contains the last verses revealed to Muhammad. One exception would be the very first sûrah, "Al-Fatihah" (i.e., "The Opening"). Most Islamic scholars believe that "Al-Fatihah," which was received by Muhammad in Mecca, was the first complete and most important sûrah given to him. The other sûrahs which follow in Volume I consist of much later sûrahs and are quite lengthy. The very first sûrahs are quite small and consist of only one run-on sentence broken into several short verses. As Muhammad became able to retain more revelations, the sûrahs became longer and more detailed. Therefore, the last and lengthier sûrahs were placed at the beginning of the Koran, while the first and shorter sûrahs were placed toward the end.[5] Regarding any conflicts found in the Koran, the last revelations given to Muhammad (which are placed at the front of the Koran) are the tie breakers.

Although the Koran is broken into two volumes, the chapters are numbered consistently. Volume I consists of Sûrahs 1 through 20, and Volume II continues with Sûrahs 21 through 114. The two-volume break is not clear, unless—because Allah claims to be the author of both the Bible and the Koran—they wanted to have the Koran's composition look similar to the Judeo-Christian Bible, which appears to have been their goal.

COMPARISON OF ATTRIBUTES AMONG THOSE WHO CLAIM DIVINITY

When comparing the Koran with the Bible, three strong personalities appear—the God of the Bible, Allah of the Koran, and Satan, who is found in both books. As we will see on the following pages, some things emerge that become quite interesting when compared side-by-side. Who has the most in common? Who is the most unique?

Table 2: A Comparison of Immortal Beings

ATTRIBUTES OF YAWA GOD OF THE BIBLE	ATTRIBUTES OF SATAN	ATTRIBUTES OF ALLAH, GOD OF THE KORAN
God Cannot Go Back on His Word, and He Never Changes His Mind	*Satan Can Lie Because He Is the Father of Lies*	*Allah Can Go Back On His Word and Does Change His Mind*
"God is not human, that He should lie, not a human being, that He should change his mind. Does He speak and then not act? Does He promise and not fulfill?" (Numbers 23:19, NIV.) "And also the Strength of Israel (God) will not lie nor repent: for He is not a man, that He should repent" (1 Samuel 15:29, clarification mine). "For I am the LORD, I change not; therefore the sons of Jacob are not consumed" (Malachi 3:6). "... *which God, who cannot lie, promised before* time began..." (Titus 1:2, NKJV, emphasis added).	"You belong to your father, the devil, and you want to carry out your father's desires. He was a murderer from the beginning, not holding to the truth, for there is no truth in him. When he lies, he speaks his native language, for he is a liar and the father of lies" (John 8:44, NIV). Satan is a schemer, which means he is a plotter and a deceiver.	While Allah claims to never go back on his word (Sûrah 6:115); he can and does change his mind for something better, giving the appearance of being a liar or making it seem that he was unable to know what was best from the start: "None of Our revelations do We **abrogate** (take back) or **cause to be forgotten, but We substitute something better or similar:** Don't you know that God Has power over all things?" (Sûrah 2:106, emphasis added.) "And they (the unbelievers) schemed, and Allah schemed (against them): and Allah is the best of schemers" (Sûrah 3:54 and Sûrah 8:30).

		"Are they then secure from Allah's scheme? None deemeth himself secure from Allah's scheme save folk that perish" (Sûrah 7:99).
YAWA (JEHOVAH) GOD of the Bible Is One	*Satan Is One Desiring to Become God*	*Allah of the Koran Is One*
"Hear, Oh Israel: The Lord our God is one Lord" (Deuteronomy 6:4). Jesus, "I and the Father are one" (John 10:30).	Satan was created a Cherub, the highest of the immortal angelic beings. He sought to be like God (Isaiah 14:14-15).	Allah of the Koran is one god. "Allah for-gives not (the heresy of) joining other gods with Him ..." (Sûrah 4:16).
Trinity: As Explained in the Bible = One God in Three Persons: God the Father, Jesus, God the Son, and God the Holy Spirit	*Trinity: As Applied to Satan = Only One Person. While Acknowledging Jesus, Satan Calls God's Word into Question*	*Trinity: As Applied to Allah = Only One Person. While Acknowledging Jesus, Allah Rejects the Trinity as Falsely Consisting of Allah, Mary, and Jesus*
The Trinity the Bible speaks about is a unique entity, which consists of one God who is expressed in three persons from the very beginning of time (Isaiah 48:16; Matthew 28:19).	Satan called God's word into question from the very beginning (Genesis 3:1). Satan is a liar and a deceiver. "... He was a murderer from the beginning, not holding to the truth, for there is no truth in him.	The Koran *completely* misinterprets the biblical Trinity: The Koran teaches that Christians believe Mary is the second person of the Trinity (Sûrah 5:116), and the Koran makes the argument against the Trinity because Allah has not

Biblical Trinity	Trinity Applied to Satan	Trinity Applied to Allah
Consider: A triangle has three corners. Remove any one of the corners, and it is no longer a triangle. The triangle's *three* corners are not associates and were added to the triangle because without any corners it would not have been a triangle to begin with; there-fore, the triangle always existed in that form; yet while the triangle is one in existence, each corner is a separate and intricate part of the whole.	When he lies, he speaks his native language, for he is a liar and the father of lies" (John 8:44, NIV).	taken a wife (Sûrah 6: 101. Depending on the translation, it could be a concubine or com-panion). This shows that in Islam, the concept of the Trinity is completely unrelated to how the Bible teaches the Trinity, which consists of "... the Father, the Son, and the Holy Spirit" (Matthew 28:19, para-phrase mine).
The God of the Bible Has a Son	**Satan Never Had Any Children**	**Allah Claims He Has No Son**
Old Testament: "Who has ascended up into Heaven, or descended? Who has gathered the wind in his fists? Who has bound the waters in a garment? Who has established all the ends of the earth? What is His name, and what is His Son's	Being an angel, Satan cannot have children or create anything. Because angels are immortal, there is no need for them to replace themselves (have children) and, therefore, when Jesus was asked about sex after the Resurrection:	"If Allah had willed to choose a son, *He could have chosen what He would of that which He has created...*" (Sûrah 39:4, emphasis added). "... How can He [Allah] have a son when He has no consort?" (Sûrah 6:101a.) **Koran contradiction**: We are told that Allah could have picked out a

Biblical God Had Son	Satan Never Had Children	Allah Claims He Has No Son
name, if you can tell?" (Proverbs 30:4.) **New Testament:** Jesus was not a created being because *nothing* that was created was created without Him. He has always existed with the Father (John 1:1-3)	"Jesus answered and said unto them, 'You do err, not knowing the Scriptures, nor the power of God. For in the Resurrection, they neither marry, nor are given in marriage, but are as the angels of God in Heaven' " (*Matthew* 22:29-30).	son from the humans he made if he wanted one. Then we are told he has no son because he has no wife—to produce a son. Which is it?
Jesus Was Crucified for Our Sins	***Satan Participated in the Crucifixion of Jesus***	***Allah Denies the Crucifixion of Jesus***
Jesus Himself refers to His crucifixion: "And when I [John] saw Him [Jesus], I fell at His feet as dead. And he laid his right hand upon me, saying unto me, 'Fear not; I am the first and the last: I am He that lives, and was dead; and, behold, I am alive for evermore, Amen; and have the keys of Hell and of death' " (Revelation 1:17-19, bracketed clarifications mine).	"Then entered Satan into Judas, surnamed Iscariot, being of the number of the twelve. And he went his way and communed with the chief priests and captains, how he might betray Him unto them" (Luke 22:3-4).	"And because of their saying: 'We slew the Messiah, Jesus son of Mary, Allah's messenger—they slew him not nor crucified him, but it appeared so unto them; and see! those who disagree concerning it are in doubt thereof; they have no knowledge thereof save pursuit of a con-jecture; they slew him not for certain" (Sûrah 4:157, Marmaduke Pickthall).

Jesus Was Crucified for Our Sins When did God die? He died on the Cross (Luke 46:46) and was resurrected from death (Luke 47:34).		
Bible: Dealing with Non-Converts	***Satan: Dealing with Non-Converts***	***Islam: Dealing with Non-Converts***
In Christianity, if those they witness to do not come to Christ, Christians are not to seek any revenge, but move on (Matthew 10:14). **Old Testament:** "You shall not avenge, nor bear any grudge against the children of your people, but you shall love your neighbor as yourself: I *am* the LORD" (Leviticus 19:18,). **New Testament:** "... But I say unto you, 'Love your enemies, bless them that curse you, do good to them that hate you, and pray for them ...' " (Matthew 5:44).	In Satanism, if you do not seek to serve the Devil, then he will surely seek you out: "Be sober, be vigilant; because your adversary the devil, as a roaring lion, walks about, seeking whom he may devour" (1 Peter 5:8). "And the great dragon was cast out, that old serpent, called the Devil, and Satan" (Revelation 12:9). "And they worshipped the dragon which gave power unto the beast: and they worshipped the beast, saying, 'Who is like unto the beast? who is able to make war with him?' " (Revelation 13:4.)	In Islam, if someone refuses to convert and follow Allah, Muslims are to cut off the heads. **Koran:** "When your Lord revealed to the angels: 'I am with you, there-fore make firm those who believe. *I will cast terror into the hearts of those who dis-believe.* Therefore *strike off their heads and strike off every fingertip* of them' " (Sûrah 8:12, Shakir) **Notice**: The above verse implores acts of *terrorism* as part of Islamic jihad.

God Is the Almighty, the Alpha and the Omega	Satan Claims That One Day He Will Be God	Allah Claims He Is Both the God of the Bible and the Koran
"This is what the Lord says—Israel's King and Redeemer, the Lord Almighty: 'I am the first and I am the last; apart from me there is no God' " (Isaiah 44:6). "I [Jesus] am the Alpha and the Omega, the beginning and the end, the first and the last" (Revelation 22:13; bracketed clarification mine)	The Bible teaches about the Satanic spirit behind the king of Tyre: "For you have said in your heart, 'I will ascend into Heaven, I will exalt my throne above the stars of God: I will sit also upon the mount of the congregation, in the sides of the north: I will ascend above the heights of the clouds; I will be like the Most High [God]' " (Isaiah 14:13-14).	By studying and comparing the Koran—as we are instructed to do (Sûrah 4:82; 5:46-47; 6:114), whose attributes are more compatible with those of Allah? Is it the one in the first or second column or neither?

39

DO SOME CHRISTIAN DENOMINATIONS AGREE WITH MUSLIMS THAT ALLAH AND JEHOVAH (YHWH) ARE THE SAME GOD?

For the first time in the history of Christianity, Pope Francis (Pietro di Bernardone) of Rome read Islamic prayers and readings from the Koran at the Vatican on Sunday, June 8, 2014. It was an effort to appease the Palestinian Muslims and work toward peace among them and their neighbors, the Jews.[6] Perhaps he was building on the Second Vatican Council of 1965—when the Roman Church made the controversial proclamation that the Allah of the Koran and the Triune God of the Bible are one and the same.[7] For the most part, Muslims are in agreement with Vatican II's proclamation, so one would think that would have settled the issue. What do the Koran and Allah have to say about this—but more importantly—what does the Bible have to say?

Until the events of September 11, 2001, when the United States was attacked by Muslim jihadists, which resulted in the loss of 2,996 lives and over 6,000 injured,[8] not much attention was given to the religion of Islam. Most people had a vague idea that the three monolithic religions—Judaism, Christianity, and Islam—believed in the same God. With the advent of those events, the world had a rude awakening as it watched Islamic jihadists, destroy the World Trade Center's Twin Towers in New York City and destroy part of the Pentagon in Washington, D.C. Thanks to those events, the religion of Islam took front and center on the world stage. Politicians quickly proclaimed that Islam was a "religion of peace"—but seeing such horrific violence—the politicians' words sounded hollow. With the events of 9/11, for the first time, many people became curious about Islam, its history, and its prophet. How did that powerful religion so quickly since its inception in the seventh century, and how has it historically interacted with Christians and Jews?

Our knowledge about the God of the Judeo-Christian religion is revealed through the Bible. To briefly recap, the Protestant Bible consists of 66 books contained in two sections and is based on revelations given to mankind through holy oracles or prophets of God. God signed His manuscript—the Bible—by making over a quarter of it prophetic, with many of the prophecies having already been fulfilled; some are currently being fulfilled and others will be manifested at some point in the future.[9]

The God of the Bible—as opposed to Allah—specifically states that He would use the prophetic Word to prove that He is God, and there is none like Him because only He can know of things that are hidden in the future. Only He can know:

> ... the end from the beginning and from ancient times the things that are not yet done (Isaiah 46:10a).

In fact, the Bible has several passages where God explains that it is through prophecies that He validates Himself and, therefore, the entire Bible. The God of the Bible gives this challenge to prophets, holy men of other faiths and the idols of men when He proclaims:

> "Present your case," says the LORD. "Set forth your arguments," says Jacob's King. "Tell us, you idols, what is going to happen. Tell us what the former things were, so that we may consider them and know their final outcome. Or declare to us the things to come, tell us what the future holds, so we may know that you are gods. Do something, whether good or bad, so that we will be dismayed and filled with fear" (Isaiah 41:21-23, NIV).

> With whom will you compare me or count me equal? To whom will you liken me that we may be compared? (Isaiah 46:5, NIV.)
> Remember the former things, those of long ago; I am God, and there is no other; I am God, and there is none like me. I make known the end from the beginning, from ancient times, what is still to come. I say, My purpose will stand, and I will do all that I please. From the east I summon a bird of prey; from a far-off land, a man to fulfill my purpose. What I have said, that I will bring about; what I have planned, that I will do (Isaiah 46:9-11, NIV).

Some might find it curious that it would be seemingly impossible to observe this type of claim or validation made in the Koran.

As we previously stated, the reason for dividing the Bible into two books is because it was prophesied in the Old Testament:

"Behold, the days come," says the LORD, "that I will make a new covenant with the house of Israel, and with the house of Judah" (Jeremiah 31:31).

Through the ages, Christians have referred to the Bible in two ways—the first being the Old Covenant and the second, a New Covenant. This is based on the passage in Jeremiah 31:31, which we just read; therefore, we would expect to find two Testaments—the Old and the New. No such promise was ever given to Muhammad—indeed, if Allah did not like something he had first given to Muhammad, he simply repealed (abrogated) it, which we see throughout the Koran. There is usually no clear separation of ideas or stories in the Koran as there is with the Bible, and there is no clear continuity as we see in the Bible; therefore, there is no clear-cut reason for the Koran to be divided into two separate volumes like the Bible. In the first volume of the Koran, there was an effort to reverse those conciliatory appeals made by Allah toward Christians and Jews when Muhammad first began receiving his revelations from Allah.

Muhammad tried to appeal to the biblical background of the Christians and Jews and even included some Bible stories in the Koran—presumably to give the Koran a sense of the same authorship—which the Christians and Jews rejected outright due to the many errors found in the so-called biblical accounts presented in the Koran. Of course, there were only three ways to deal with this problem: (1) Admit there were some errors, which would call into question Allah being the God of the Bible; (2) claim that the Bible—not the Koran—was corrupted by self-serving Christians and Jews with an agenda, or (3) simply call anyone who questions—Muhammad, Allah, or the Koran an apostate and kill them!

One interesting observation that we noticed in the Koran is that regardless of the many conflicting stories found between the Bible and the Koran, one thing they both agree on—as we pointed out earlier—while denying the divine origin of Jesus, the Koran does agree that Mary was a virgin when she gave birth to Him.[10]

Lastly, in keeping with this claim that the God of the Bible and Allah are one and the same, we have another declaration by the former President of the United States, George W. Bush, six days after the 9/11 attack on America by Muslim terrorists. President Bush claimed on September 17, 2001, "Islam is a 'religion of peace.' "[11]

> THE PRESIDENT: Thank you all very much for your hospitality. We've just had a (sic)—wide-ranging discussions on the matter at hand. Like the good folks standing with me, the American people were appalled and outraged at last Tuesday's attacks. And so were Muslims all across the world. Americans and Muslim friends and citizens, tax-paying citizens, and Muslims in nations were just appalled and could not believe what we saw on our TV screens.

> These acts of violence against innocents violate the fundamental tenets of the Islamic faith. And it's important for my fellow Americans to understand that.

The president also said in his speech:

> The face of terror is not the true faith of Islam. That's not what Islam is all about. Islam is peace. These terrorists don't represent peace. They represent evil and war. When we think of Islam, we think of a faith that brings comfort to a billion people around the world. Billions of people find comfort and solace and peace. And that's made brothers and sisters out of every race—out of every race.

On another occasion, President Bush stated, "It doesn't matter what religion you are … we all pray to the same God."[12] America's next president, Barack Hussein Obama, would also share that same opinion when President Obama spoke at a White House dinner he hosted to

43

celebrate the Islamic holy month of Ramadan.[13] In Chapter 9, we discuss the Yale University Covenant, "A Common Word between Us and You," which promotes Islam and Christianity as being compatible (i.e., Chrislam). Could this become the biblical End Times world religion? In the Appendix of this book, we have supplied some of the names of the clergy and other important figures who signed this document.

In light of these controversial claims, is it any wonder there is so much confusion surrounding who is correct? Now we must do the research to see if what the pope and presidents are implying is true: Did the God of the Bible author the Koran? Do the three monotheistic religions really worship the same God? We will compare the Bible with the Koran to find out. If the same author wrote the Bible and the Koran, there should be no contradictions—doctrinally, chronologically, geographically, or historically.

WHAT AUTHORITY DO WE HAVE TO JUDGE THE KORAN BY THE BIBLE?

Before we proceed further, it is imperative to know that Allah himself challenged the Christians and Jews to use the Bible to judge the Koran:

> Shall I seek other than Allah for judge, when He it is Who has revealed unto you (this) Scripture, fully explained? Those unto whom We gave the Scripture [Bible] (aforetime) know that it is revealed from your Lord in truth. So be not thou (O Muhammad) of the waverers [doubters/apostates] (Sûrah 6:114, bracketed clarifications mine).

> Will they not then ponder on the Qur'an? If it had been from other than Allah, they would have found therein much incongruity (Sûrah 4:82).

If there is some discrepancy, then we are told in Sûrah 28:

Say: "Then bring some (other) book from Allah which is a better guide than both of them, (that) I may follow it, if you are truthful" (Sûrah 28:49, Muhammad Habib Shakir).

Because the Bible is the first and most revered of the two holy books, the Koran will be, as suggested above in Sûrah 4:82, subjected to the biblical standard, which is the older and time-tested text. By doing so, we will be analyzing the koranic and Islamic claims in their sûrahs (chapters) that the God of the Bible is the Allah of the Koran. We have heard novices make the claim that the Koran contains Scripture. Shakespeare contains Scripture too, but just as beautifully and historically based some of his books are, they are not on an equal basis with the Bible. This is a legitimate observation, which we will address by comparing some of the biblical stories contained in the Koran to see how accurately they parallel the original ones in the Bible.

It is important to note that although the God of the Bible has several names, the name "Allah" does not appear in either the Old or New Testaments. Still, for the first time in history, accommodations have been put in place to appease Muslims at the expense of the accuracy of Scripture, despite these biblical warnings:

... that in the last days perilous times shall come (2 Timothy 3:1).

... evil men and seducers shall wax worse and worse [increase] deceiving, and being deceived (2 Timothy 3:13, bracketed clarification mine).

The Spirit clearly says that in later times some will abandon the faith and follow deceiving spirits and things taught by demons (1 Timothy 4:1, NIV).

What could be more damnable than denying that Jesus is the Christ, the Son of God? Before we continue, we will review what the Bible tells us about changing God's Word in the Old and New Testaments:

You shall not add unto the word which I command you, neither shall you diminish ought [anything] from it, that you may keep the commandments of the Lord your God which I command you (Deuteronomy 4:2, bracketed clarification mine).

For I testify unto every man that hears the words of the prophecy of this book, If any man shall add unto these things, God shall add unto him the plagues that are written in this book (Revelation 22:18).

And if any man shall take away from the words of the book of this prophecy, God shall take away his part out of the book of life, and out of the holy city, and from the things which are written in this book (Revelation 22:19).

It seems that Vatican II, the Catholic Church, and Presidents Bush and Obama's deference to the god of Islam being the same as the God of the Bible are not alone. In addition, some Christian publishers have also elected to become biblical revisionists as well. In a 2012 unapologetic violation of Deuteronomy 4:2 and Revelation 22:18-19, the publishing house, Wycliffe Bible Translators and the Summer Institute of Linguistics (SIL), took it on themselves—in an effort to pacify the sensitivities of Muslims—to remove all 9/11 references to Jesus as the Son of God.[14] They changed Jesus' own words in Matthew 28:19 from, "Go you, therefore, and teach all nations, baptizing them in the name of the Father, and of the Son, and of the Holy Ghost" to "Cleanse them by water in the name of Allah, his Messiah, and his Holy Spirit."[15] Think about it. Would it have made any sense for the writers of the New Testament—who were writing in Greek—to have appealed to the Greeks by writing, "Go you, therefore, and teach all nations, baptizing them in the name of Zeus, his Messenger, and the Holy Ghost." That would make no sense either!

What do we find in the Bible regarding taking such liberties with Scripture? What does the Bible say about changing the Gospel message of Jesus Christ? The early Church was also exposed to those who preached another Christ, as we can see in Scripture. Still, God also warns about changing His Word, which should serve as a warning to the sacrilegious publishers of Wycliffe Bible Translators and the Summer Institute of Linguistics who know better:

Now therefore hearken … You shall not add unto the word which I command you, neither shall you diminish ought from it (Deuteronomy 4:1-2).

The following shows how—even in the first century—the church had to deal with unscrupulous people who sought to pervert the real Jesus and the gospel:

I marvel that you are so soon removed from Him that called you into the grace of Christ unto another gospel:

Which is not another; but there be some that trouble you, and would pervert the gospel of Christ.

But though we, or an angel from Heaven, preach any other gospel unto you than that which we have preached unto you, let him be accursed.

As we said before, so say I now again, "if any man preach any other gospel unto you than that you have received, let him be accursed."

For do I now persuade men, or God? or do I seek to please men? for if I yet pleased men, I should not be the servant of Christ (Galatians 1:6-10).

For I testify unto every man that hears the words of the prophecy of this book, "If any man shall add unto these things, God shall add unto him the plagues that are written in this book: And if any man shall take away from the words of the book of this prophecy, God shall take away his part out of the book of life …" (Revelation 22:18-19).

The Bible continues to warn us about such heretics.

Who is a liar but he that denies that Jesus is the Christ? He is the antichrist that denies the Father and the Son.

Whosoever denies the Son, the same has not the Father: he that acknowledges the Son has the Father also (1 John 2:22-23).

The apostle Peter also observes the type of men who purposefully corrupt the Word of God when he warns:

> But there were false prophets also among the people, even as there shall be false teachers among you, who secretly shall bring in damnable heresies, even denying the Lord that bought them, and bring on themselves swift destruction (2 Peter 2:1).

In order to discover if our God is, in fact, Allah—as the Koran challenges us to do in Sûrah 4:82 and 5:47—we will need to explore both the words of YHWH (Jehovah) with the words of Allah. As Christians, we should closely compare the Bible with the Koran for possible literary and historical discrepancies.

Although we are coming from the orthodox Judeo-Christian perspective, we will endeavor to be even-handed in our examination of the Koran in light of the Bible. Because the Bible was written over a 1500-year period of time (ignoring the 400 years between the Old and New Testaments), and the Koran was written in only 23 years, we must also take into account, due to hand-written copies over the great expanse of time, some errors in copying might have occurred.

While we do not agree with the conclusions about the Bible discussed in the following commentary—possibly done as an effort on the author's part to be fair—we offer it here as an example of the fact that numerous scholars have problems with many passages found in the Koran. In this case, we have a corrupted koranic passage containing an errant translation of a word analyzed by Sir Norman Anderson found in Sûrah 2:36.

> The truth is that the textual history of the Qur'an is very similar to that of the Bible. Both books have been preserved remarkably well. Each is, in its basic structure and content, a very fair record of what was originally there. But neither book has been preserved totally without error or textual defect. Both have suffered here and there from variant readings in the early codices known to us,

but neither has in any way been corrupted. Sincere Christians and Muslims will honestly acknowledge these facts.[16]

If Allah is the author of both books, the Koran makes it abundantly clear that he is able to protect that which he reveals to mankind, which must include the Book (Bible) as well as the Koran; therefore, if we are to take Allah at his word, we do so by the authority of the Bible.

We have, without doubt, sent down the Message [Bible]; and We will assuredly guard it (from corruption) (Sûrah 15:9, Abdullah Yusuf Ali, bracketed clarification mine).[17]

At the risk of being repetitive, we must reinforce that the Koran justifies itself by citing that the Bible is the authority to judge the Koran by because the Bible was given to the Jews and Christians before Allah gave the koranic message to Muhammad, so we will heed Allah's challenge where he states:

But if you are in doubt as to what We have revealed to you, ask those [People of the Book] who read the Book [Bible] before you; certainly the truth has come to you from your Lord, therefore you should not be of the disputers [doubters] (Sûrah 10:94, Muhammad Habib Shakir, bracketed clarifications mine).[18]

IS THE KORAN CONSISTENT?

An interesting observation concerning the Koran's accuracy is found in the most basic of stories—the creation of man. The Bible has one description, which is as follows:

And the LORD God formed man of the dust of the ground, and breathed into his nostrils the breath of life; and man became a living soul (Genesis 2:7).

After God created a man from the dust of the ground, He then created a woman, but unlike the way in which He created Adam, this time, He continued the creation process by taking a rib from Adam's side.

And the LORD God caused a deep sleep to fall upon Adam, and he slept: and he took one of his ribs, and closed up the flesh instead thereof;

And the rib, which the LORD God had taken from man, made He a woman, and brought her unto the man.

And Adam said, "This is now bone of my bones, and flesh of my flesh: she shall be called Woman, because she was taken out of Man" (Genesis 2: 21-23).

On the other hand, the Koran has four methods by which God created man. One version has Allah creating man out of water, and then uses a different method to create the woman from a blood clot:

And He it is Who has created man from water, and has appointed for him kindred by blood and kindred by marriage; for your Lord is ever Powerful (Sûrah 25:54).

This verse is possibly just poorly pieced together, and by "blood kindred," it is simply referring to siblings.

In the second version, Allah created man from out of clay (dust):

And when We said to the angels: "Fall down prostrate before Adam" and they fell prostrate all save Iblis [Satan], he said: "Shall I fall prostrate before that which you have created of clay?" (Sûrah 17:61, bracketed clarification mine.)

In the Koran's third version, Allah first used dust, then mixed it with sperm (where he got the sperm is inexplicable):

His comrade, when he (thus) spoke with him, exclaimed: "Believe not you in Him Who created you of dust, then of a drop (of seed) [Abdullah Yusuf Ali's translation inserts the word 'sperm'], and then fashioned you a man?" (Sûrah 18:37, bracketed clarification mine.)

Finally, we have some creative commingling of the above techniques, bringing the creation of man into its fourth version, this time using the above ingredients, but now with the introduction of flesh as a separate component:

O mankind! if you are in doubt concerning the Resurrection, then see! We have created you from dust, then from a drop of seed, then from a clot, then from a little lump of flesh shapely and shapeless, that We may make (it) clear for you. And We cause what We will to remain in the wombs for an appointed time, and afterward We bring you forth as infants, then (give you growth) that you attain your full strength. And among you there is he who dies (young), and among you there is he who is brought back to the most abject time of life, so that, after knowledge, he knows naught [nothing]. And you (Muhammad) see the earth barren, but when We send down water thereon, it does thrill and swell and put forth every lovely kind (of growth) (Sûrah 22:5, bracketed clarification mine).

In the above verse, perhaps Allah commingled the original creation event—as also seen in the Bible—when he stated, "We have created you from dust." He then—without a clear transition—jumped to the next creation method when he said, "And We cause what We will to remain in the wombs ...," a reproduction concept more familiar by the generation he is addressing.

Allah also indicated that Adam and Eve were both made in the same way, as we will see below, foregoing the biblical revelation of Eve being made from the rib of Adam:

Allah created you from dust, then from a little fluid, then He made you pairs (the male and female). No female bears or brings forth [a child] save with His knowledge. And no one grows old who grows old, nor is anything lessened of his life, but it is recorded in a Book, See! that is easy for Allah (Sûrah 35:11, bracketed clarification mine, emphasis added).

51

To make this verse even more convoluted, the "Book" spoken of here might be confusing the Bible's reference to the "Book of Life" (Psalm 69:28; Philippians 4:3; Revelation 3:5, 13:8, 17:8, 20:12, 15, 21:27). It is a book found in Heaven where the *names* are written down of those who will spend eternity with God, unlike the Koran, which—in this instance—deals with a book that records *events* in a person's earthly life.

What is the reasoning behind these inconsistent, conception stories? We know it is not uncommon for a woman to have clotting during her period, but God knows babies are not formed from a clot of blood in the woman's womb; they are formed from a fertilized egg, yet once more in a different sûrah, we are told again that babies come from a blood clot:

> He it is Who created you from dust, then from a drop (of seed) *then from a clot, then brings you forth as a child,* then (ordains) that you attain full strength and afterward that you become old men—though some among you die before—and that you reach an appointed term, that haply [happily] you may understand (Sûrah 40:67, bracketed clarification mine, emphasis added).

As we can see, there are several different versions of the origins of man in the Koran, as well as having conflicting science regarding the ongoing reproductive event.

The Oldest Surviving Fragments of the Koran

Muslims like to argue that the Koran they have today is virtually unchanged from the original one written down after Muhammad's untimely death. This, despite the evidence that there were conflicting passages between some of the first, written down Korans. As we will see in Chapter 4, there was a problem with uniformity between different Korans. This caused the third Caliph, Uthman ibn Affan, to collect all the Korans and select the version he thought to be the purest and had the others burned.

According to the BBC: "What may be the world's oldest fragments of the Koran have been found by the University of Birmingham.

Radiocarbon dating found the manuscript to be at least 1,370 years old, making it among the earliest in existence."[18]

Yet there are not only many discrepancies between this the oldest Koran known, but even more controversial is the possibility that it might have been written *before* Muhammad was born, or at least when Muhammad was a child as was reported in the British newspaper, the Daily mail:

- Fragments of the oldest Koran were discovered last month in [the University of] Birmingham
- Carbon dating found the pages were produced between 568AD and 654AD
- But several historians now say that the parchment may predate Muhammad
- They believe that this discovery could rewrite the early history of Islam

Fragments of the world's oldest Koran, found in Birmingham last month, may predate the Prophet Muhammad and could even rewrite the early history of Islam, according to scholars.

The pages, thought to be between 1,448 and 1,371 years old, were discovered bound within the pages of another Koran from the late seventh century at the library of the University of Birmingham.

Written in ink in an early form of Arabic script on parchment made from animal skin, the pages contain parts of the Suras, or chapters, 18 to 20, which may have been written by someone who actually knew the Prophet Muhammad - founder of the Islamic faith.[19]

In fairness, we should point out that the radiocarbon dating was probably done on the parchment and not the ink. Writing material was at a premium back then, so many times, an old document would be repurposed when the old ink might have faded beyond recognition or purposefully bleached so that new wording could be reapplied.

Therefore, the parchment might have been older than Muhammad, while the writing might have been applied at a later date.

As we will demonstrate in Chapter 5 when we discuss the "Dead Sea Scrolls," some of the gospel fragments found at Qumran—written around twenty years after Jesus rose from the dead and ascended to be with the Father—show that the bible is virtually unchanged after 2,000 years, while the fragments and pages from the Koran, written about twenty years after the death of Muhammad, are inconsistent and troubling.

NOTES:

1. Lewis M. Hopfe and Mark R. Woodward, *Religions of the World* (Upper Saddle River. Pearson/Prentice Hall Publ., 2005), 5.
2. Hopfe and Woodward, 5.
3. Norman Geisler, Abdul Saleeb, *Answering Islam,* 2nd ed. (Grand Rapids: Baker Books, 2002), 338.
4. A.J. Arberry, *The Koran Interpreted* (New York: Touchstone, 1955), 9. In the preface of this translation of the Koran, there is a discussion of the koranic version of the birth of a non-divine Jesus born under a palm tree. The author points out how the Koran and Bible agree that Mary is a virgin. In both the Koran and the Bible, Mary asks, "... How can I have a Son without the touch of a man?" (Koran: Sûrah 19:20; Bible: Jeremiah 7:14; Matthew 1:18-21; Luke 1:34); however, the author of the preface avoids the difference between the Koran and the Bible. In the Bible, "... the angel said to her, 'Do not be afraid, Mary; you have found favor with God. You will conceive and give birth to a son, and you are to call Him Jesus. He will be great and will be called the Son of the Most High. The Lord God will give Him the throne of His father David, and he will reign over Jacob's descendants forever; his kingdom will never end.' 'How will this be,' Mary asked the angel, 'since I am a virgin?'" (Luke 1:30-34, NIV.) Notice that 700 years before Muhammad, God told Mary her Son would be divine. We address this in greater detail in Volume III of *Islam Exposed, Islam: Science—Bible—Archaeology and Myths.*

5. Muhammad Marmaduke Pickthall, *The Meaning of the Glorious Koran*, 7th ed. (New York: Everyman's Library, 1993), xvii.

6. *Christian Broadcasting Network*, "Historic First: Islamic Prayers Held at the Vatican," 10 June 2014. Web. 1 October 2014.

7. Hahnenberg, Edward P., *A CONCISE GUIDE TO THE DOCUMENTS OF VATICAN II* (Cincinnati: St. Anthony Messenger Press, 2007), 45, 158-159, 162.

8. Wikipedia contributors, "September 11 attacks," *Wikipedia: The Free Encyclopedia.* N.p., n.d. Web. 23 August 2013.

9. J. Barton Payne, *The Encyclopedia of Biblical Prophecy*, 674. Payne writes, "There are 1,239 prophecies in the Old Testament and 578 prophecies in the New Testament for a total of 1,817. These prophecies are contained in 8,352 of the Bible's verses. Since there are 31,124 verses in the Bible, the 8,352 verses that contain prophecy constitute 26.8 percent of the Bible's volume." There are no other holy books containing such prophetic foresight in the world. This is a sure sign of the Bible's divine origin.

10. Sûrah 19:20-21.

11. THE WHITE HOUSE, September 17, 2001, " 'Islam is Peace' says President," September 2001. Web. 3 September 2003.

12. *CBN News:* "President Bush Plans to Take Part in an 'Interfaith Session' at the United Nations. The meeting of the United Nations General Assembly was initiated by Saudi King Abdullah, who's been promoting dialogue between Islam and other world religions. Then White House Press Secretary Dana Perino says President Bush believes that we all pray to the same God." "The meeting is [was] scheduled to take place on November 13." October 30, 2008. Web. 22 August 2013.

13. Stacy A. Anderson, *"Obama Hosts Ramadan Dinner at White House"* (07/25/2013). In a Huffington Post release, Anderson writes, "Obama spoke at a White House dinner he hosted to celebrate the Islamic holy month of Ramadan. The meal, or iftar, breaks the day of fasting when Muslim families and communities eat together after sunset. Obama said, 'Ramadan is a time of reflection, a chance to demonstrate one's devotion to God through prayer and through fasting, but it's also a time for family and friends to come together.' " (Allah is not mentioned.)

   25 July 2014. Web. 4 September 2013. Baltimore Sun Transcript of President Obama's speech. "President Obama's Remarks at the Islamic Society of Balti-more. *Baltimoresun.com*, 3 Feb. 2016. Toward

his conclusion, Pres. Obama includes a quote allowing for Allah and YAWA as one; something with which no biblical historian could agree: "...the Muslim Americans in Chattanooga who honored our fallen service members, one of them saying, 'the name of God, the God of Abraham, Moses, Jesus, and Muhammad, God bless our fallen heroes.' " (Applause.) Pres. Obama ends with, "May God's peace be upon you. May God bless the United States of America. Thank you very much, everybody. (Applause.)" (Allah not mentioned.)

14. *Jack Van Impe Presents,* Episode 26, Dir., Alex Rogers Kimbrough, 29 min., Jack Van Impe Ministries, N.p. 29 June 2013. Web. 9 September 2013.

    "Son of God" Translation Controversy. *The Alliance for Biblical Integrity*. 18 Feb 2012. Web. 9 September 2013.

15. Stoyan Zaimov, " 'Father' and 'Son' Removed from Bible Translations for Muslims," January 30, 2012. Web. 2 July 2013.

16. Sir Norman Anderson, *The World's Religions* (Grand Rapids: Eerdmans, 1987), 47.

17. Abdullah Yusuf Ali trans., the *Holy Qur'an* (Hertfordshire: Wordsworth Edition Limited, 2000), 206.

18. Sean Coughlan. "'Oldest' Koran Fragments Found in Birmingham University." *BBCNews*,BBC,22July2015,

19. Jennifer Newton for. "The 'Birmingham Koran' Fragment That Could Shake Islam after Carbon-Dating Suggests It Is OLDER than the Prophet Muhammad. "*Daily Mail Online*, Associated Newspapers, 31 Aug.2015.

CHAPTER 2

THE MESSIAH OF CHRISTIANITY

Concerning the Literacy of Jesus

When contrasting the founders of two of the major monotheistic faiths, it is necessary to address their education. What was Jesus' educational background, and was He literate? In the biblical Hebrew culture, education was as important as it is today,[1] and we might be surprised to learn that the Jews ranked very high among the winners of the world-renowned Nobel Peace Prize awards during its first 101-year history.

> Out of more than 720 prizes awarded since 1901, more than 130 (or about 18 percent) have gone to Jewish laureates. Jews have won almost three times the number of awards won by either Germany or France (including their Jewish winners) and 10 times more than those won by Japan. Consider: Jews comprise only 0.3 to 0.5 percent of the world's population.[2]

In the Mishnah, Avot 5:21 ("Chapters of the Fathers,"), also called "Ethics of the Fathers" (rabbis of the Mishnaic Period), instructions are laid out for the various stages of the implementation of Hebrew literacy.[3] We read in Scripture the admonition from Solomon, who wrote, "Of making many books there is no end, and much study wearies the body" (Ecclesiastes 12:12). Education and literacy were understood to be part of every Israeli life during the Old Testament times:

> And these words, which I command you this day, shall be in your heart.

> And you shall teach them diligently unto your children, and shall talk of them when you sit in your house, and when you walk by the way, and when you lie down, and when you rise up.

> And you shall bind them for a sign upon your hand, and they shall be as frontlets between your eyes (Deuteronomy 6:6-8).

What was to be bound "upon the hand" and contained in a little box worn on the forehead were passages of written Scriptures. Notice how God stressed education and literacy. It is not only imperative to memorize, but also very important to be able to read and write:

> And you shall write them upon the doorposts of your house and upon your gates (Deuteronomy 11:20).

We see this emphasis on education in the New Testament as well. The Apostle Paul was schooled in the traditional way of the Hebrew people as we observe by his own admonition:

> I am a Jew, born in Tarsus in Cilicia, but brought up in this city, educated at the feet of Gamaliel according to the strict manner of the law of our fathers, being zealous for God as all of you are this day (Acts 22:3, NIV).

When Paul wrote to Timothy, he stated:

> All Scripture is given by inspiration of God and is profitable for doctrine, for reproof, for correction, for instruction in righteousness (2 Timothy 3:16).

Notice that Paul, a Jew, wrote to Timothy, another Jew. Paul and Timothy knew how to read and write, and the subject Paul discussed with Timothy was about the study of Scripture.

Jesus' Birth and Early Life

Let's now look at what we know about Jesus and His birth. Without delving into the theology of Christ's pre-incarnation, we will address just the events of His birth, and since the Bible is silent about His early youth, we are not able to address that portion of His life.

An accepted fact about the birth of Jesus, which is acknowledged by Muslims and Christians alike, is that He was born to a virgin named Mariam or Mary (Old Testament: Isaiah 7:14; New Testament: Matthew 1:20; Luke 1:26-35; Koran: Sûrah: 3:42-47; 19:16-22; 66:12). His mother was espoused to a man named Joseph. Little is known about Joseph except that he was a workman[4] and a descendant of King David. We know that Jesus was born in Bethlehem (Old Testament: Micah 5:2; New Testament: Luke 2:4-7). When Jesus was born, a special star appeared in the sky (Old Testament: Numbers 24:17; New Testament: Matthew 2:2, 7, 9, 10). We also know that because of a death threat against Jesus by King Herod, Jesus and His family escaped to Egypt until the demise of Herod and after it became safe to return to Israel (Old Testament: Hosea 11:1; New Testament: Matthew 2:14-15). Soon after, His parents moved back to Nazareth. Jesus was still very young, and because He was without sin (Hebrews 4:15, 9:28), His childhood must have been an agreeable, if not a very uneventful one without any negative incidences on His part. Aside from growing up like any normal child, there is nothing out of the ordinary to report about Jesus' youth.

Jesus at Age Twelve Declared He is The Son of God

However, when Jesus was 12 years old, an incident out of the norm occurred when His parents traveled to Jerusalem for the Passover Feast. Because it was the custom of people in those days to travel in large groups for safety reasons, His parents did not look for Him when they headed back toward home because they assumed, He was in the group with their family and friends.

The Bible tells us what happened next:

> Thinking He was in their company, they traveled on for a day. Then they began looking for Him among their relatives and friends. When they did not find Him, they went back to Jerusalem to look for Him. After three days they found Him in the temple courts, sitting among the teachers, listening to them and asking them questions. Everyone who heard Him was amazed at His understanding and His answers. When His parents saw Him, they were astonished. His mother said to Him, "Son, why have you treated us like this? Your father and I have been anxiously searching for you."
>
> "Why were you searching for me?" He asked. "Didn't you know I had to be in my Father's house?" (Luke 2: 44-49, NIV.)

Whose house was the Temple in Jerusalem? It was God's house. Jesus said He was in His Father's house, meaning God was Hs Father.

Jesus was not disobedient since that would have been sinful, and He never sinned. It appears that this incident was just confusion with the family's plans, and as the Bible states, Jesus' parents assumed He was with extended family members somewhere in the caravan. Although it is not stated in Scripture, the fact that several days went by without them knowing Jesus was missing, it stands to reason that He probably slept under one of the covered colonnade porches around the Temple's Outer Court. We base this on the fact that we know He stayed at the Temple and interacted with the rabbis (teachers) who were amazed that a person, who was so young, was well educated in the teachings of the Torah. It might be good to point out here that Jesus was 12 years old (Luke 2:42) and that He would have soon turned 13, which marks the beginning of adulthood for males in Judaism.

This brings up another question: How could a 12-year-old boy interact with the learned rabbis of His day and not only hold His own, but impress them by doing so? Aside from His divine intellect, Jesus was also properly schooled in the Torah and other Scriptures. Jesus could read and write as we see in an incident recorded in Luke when the synagogue, He was attending invited Him to read the Torah on the Sabbath:

> And there was delivered unto him the book of the prophet Esaias. And when He had opened the book, He found the place where it was written,
>
> "The Spirit of the Lord is upon me, because He has anointed me to preach the gospel to the poor; He has sent me to heal the brokenhearted, to preach deliverance to the captives, and recovering of sight to the blind, to set at liberty them that are bruised, to preach the acceptable year of the Lord."
>
> And He closed the book, and He gave it again to the minister, and sat down. And the eyes of all them that were in the synagogue were fastened on Him.
>
> And He began to say unto them, "This day is this Scripture fulfilled in your ear" (Luke 4:17-21).

Jesus at Age Thirty

Jesus began His ministry when he was 30 years old (Luke 3:23), which consisted of teaching the people about God and His love.[5] It was Jesus who proclaimed to Nicodemus:

> For God so loved the world that He gave His only begotten Son, that whosoever believeth in Him should not perish, but have everlasting life. For God sent not His Son into the world to condemn the world, but that the world through Him might be saved (John 3:16-17).

This is the foundational "good news" (i.e., gospel) that is presented in the New Testament; yet despite this, the curious thing is that Allah denies he has a Son, while at the same time claiming he authored the gospels—while rejecting what the gospels stand for! Should not a god be able to understand all the languages and what their words actually mean?

Three Years into Jesus' Ministry

Jesus began His ministry around the age of thirty; His ministry lasted only three years, and during that time, He brought dead people back to life, healed the sick, including lepers, and restored sight to the blind. We should also point out that Jesus' short ministry also included the forty days after He rose from the dead and before He ascended to be with the Father (Acts 1:9-11). After His resurrection from the dead, Jesus was seen by hundreds of eyewitnesses (1 Corinthians 15:6). During those three short years, Jesus gathered tens of thousands of followers, but just the men were counted (Matthew 14:13, 15:28). When you add in the wives and children, it increases the numbers by thousands. Even more amazing is just ten days after Jesus ascended into Heaven, there were another 3,000 who became His followers (Acts 2:41).

It would be impossible to expound on all the miracles Jesus performed during His very short three years of ministry. In the words of the Apostle John:

> And there are also many other things which Jesus did, the which, if they should be written every one, I suppose that even the world itself could not contain the books that should be written, Amen (John 21:25).

John also tells us that Jesus not only claims to be the Son of God but— He is God:

> Jesus heard that they (the Sanhedrin) had cast him (a man Jesus had healed) out; and when He had found him, He said unto him, "Do you believe in the Son of God?" He answered and said, "Who is He, Lord, that I might believe on Him?" And Jesus said unto him, "You have both seen Him, and it is He that talks with you." And he said, "Lord, I believe." And he worshipped Him[6] (John 9:35, bracketed clarification mine).

Continuing to refer to Himself, in another incident, Jesus asks:

> ... say of Him whom the Father has sanctified and sent into the world, "You blaspheme because I said, 'I am the Son of God?' " [Gk, *Theos*][7] (John 10:36, bracketed clarification mine.)

If that is not plain enough, Jesus states:

> I and My Father are one (John 10: 30).

This is the reason the Sanhedrin conspired to kill Jesus—because He claimed He and the Father were *one* and, therefore, claimed to be God.

Some Sought to Kill Jesus during His Ministry

After this, Jesus went mainly to the towns of the Galilee. He did not want to go near Judea because the Jewish leaders there were looking for a way to kill Him (John 7:1).

Spreading the Gospel through Love

While it is true that Jesus instructed His disciples to buy a sword (Luke 22:36), it was for self-defense—not for aggressive warfare—not even to have saved the life of Jesus Himself as we observe when the Sanhedrin came to arrest Him, and Peter drew his sword to protect Jesus.

> "Put your sword back in its place," Jesus said to him, "for all who draw the sword will die by the sword" (Matthew 26:52, NIV).

Jesus made it quite clear how His disciples should react when people refused to listen or receive the gospel message of His coming:

> And whosoever shall not receive you, nor hear your words, when you depart out of that house or city, shake off the dust of your feet (Matthew 10:14).

> But I say unto you, Love your enemies, bless them that curse you, do good to them that hate you, and pray for them which despitefully use you, and persecute you (Matthew 5:44).

The Blessing of the Jews

When a Gentile woman sought help from Jesus, "He answered, 'I was sent only to (bless) the lost sheep of Israel' " (Matthew 15:24, NIV, bracketed clarification mine). Even though Jesus was sent as a blessing to the Jews—Jesus was filled with compassion because of her faith—and delivered her daughter from demonic oppression (Matthew 15:28).

In the parable of the King, Jesus taught that the way to show love toward Him was to be a blessing to His brothers and sisters—the Jews—including the least little one (Matthew 25:40).

Jesus' Death at Age Thirty-Three

Jesus was brought to trial on made-up charges; despite that, they were still able to find Him guilty of blaspheme because He claimed to be God's Son and thereby God! (Mark 14:55-65.) Pontius Pilate, the ruling governor, believed that Jesus was innocent of any crime, so he washed his hands of the situation; however, for the sake of keeping the peace, Pilate allowed the Sanhedrin to have their way and permitted Jesus to be put to death by crucifixion.

Jesus Rose from the Dead

After Jesus was crucified, a member of the Sanhedrin went to Pilate and asked for Jesus' body. Pilate agreed. After they wrapped Jesus in fine linen, He was buried in Joseph of Arimathea's own grave (Mark 15:42-46), which fulfilled the prophecy in the Old Testament, which says:

> And He made His grave with the wicked, and with the rich in His death; because He had done no violence, neither was any deceit in His mouth (Isaiah 53:9).

After three days in the grave, Jesus was raised from the dead. The first people to see the empty tomb were Mary Magdalene and Mary, the mother of James and Salome. They were told by an angelic figure to go and tell the disciples of Jesus that He had risen from the dead (Mark 16:1-7).

Consider the possibility of Jesus being raised from the dead as a fictitious story and as a later addition to the gospel. Keep in mind that women living in the Mideast during that time were not considered credible eyewitness sources, so usually, at least two or three female witnesses were required to have the same credibility equal to one man. Therefore, it would not make any sense to have women witnesses if this story was made up; consequently, the report of the empty grave is even more credible. In addition to the eyewitness accounts of the women and Jesus' disciples, over 500 people saw Him—all at the same time (1 Corinthians 15:5-6). After 40 days, Jesus bodily ascended into Heaven in full view of eyewitnesses (Acts 1:9).

It is important to realize that Christianity stands or falls on the Divinity, life, death, burial, and resurrection of Jesus; for that reason, the Koran so vehemently and continually tries to deny it! It is hoped that if a Christian's faith in Jesus could be shaken, then there would be no obstacle for them to embrace Islam. The Christian could still have Jesus—not as their savior—rather a Jesus who was transformed into a Muslim prophet.

Knowing that the enemies of Jesus would try to refute the Divinity, life, death, burial, and resurrection of Jesus, the Apostle Paul declared:

> And if Christ has not been raised, your faith is futile [in vain]; you are still in your sins. Then those also who have fallen asleep in Christ are lost. If only for this life we have hope in Christ, we are of all people most to be pitied.
>
> But Christ has indeed been raised from the dead, the firstfruits of those who have fallen asleep. For since death came through a

man, the resurrection of the dead comes also through a man. For as in Adam all die, so in Christ, all will be made alive (1 Corinthians 15:17-22, NIV, bracketed clarification mine).

Jesus' Last Words on the Cross

"Father Forgive them..." (Luke 23:34).

NOTES:

1. *Encyclopædia Britannica,* "Ancient Hebrews." "... beginning of the first millennium B.C.E. The Jewish people learned to develop a different type of education—one that involved training a specialized, professional class of scribes in a then rather esoteric art called writing, borrowed from the Phoenicians .... The synagogue in which the community assembled became not merely a house of prayer, but also a school, with *a* 'house of the book' (*bet ha-sefer*) and a 'house of instruction' *(bet ha-midrash),* corresponding roughly to elementary and secondary or advanced levels of education." Web. 23 August 2013.
2. Shule Kopf, "Jews rank high among winners of Nobel, but why not Israelis?" 25 October 2002. N.p. Web. 1 May 2013.
3. William Berkson, Ph.D., *Pirke Avot: Timeless Wisdom for Modern Man,* Menachem Fisch, Trans. (Philadelphia: The Jewish Publ. Society, 2010), 178. Mishnah Avot 5:21. He used to say: "At five years old (one is fit) for the (study of) Scripture, at ten years for (the study of]) the Mishnah, at thirteen for [the fulfilling of] the commandments, at fifteen for the Talmud, at eighteen for the bride-chamber, at twenty for pursuing [a calling], at thirty for authority, at forty for discernment, at fifty for counsel, at sixty to be an elder, at seventy for gray hairs, at eighty for special strength, at ninety for bowed back, and at a

hundred a man is as one that has (already) died and passed away and ceased from the world."

4. James Strong, S.T.D., L.L.D., *Strong's Exhaustive Concordance of the Bible* (Peabody: Hendrickson Publ., 1988). The English Bible translates Mark 6:3 and Matthew 13:55 word *"tekton"* (Strong's word Number 5045) to mean "carpenter" however, the word derives from Strong's word "artificer," one who is specifically "a worker in wood." Joseph and Jesus probably made furniture, not houses. During that time, it would have been difficult to find a wooden house in Israel since most were made of stone. Even the ossuaries (a box which holds a person's bones) and mangers were carved out of stone.

5. William Berkson, Ph.D*., Pirke Avot: Timeless Wisdom for Modern Man,* 178, Mishnah Avot 5:21. When a Hebrew man, desiring to be a teacher (rabbi), attains the age of 30 years old, he has also attained the age of authority; it is then that he may enter into his ministry.

6. George Ricker Berry, *Interlinear Greek-English New Testament,* 4th ed. (Grand Rapids: Baker Book House, 1980). Some translations like the New International Version read, "Do you believe in the Son of Man?" but in the Greek, it reads *(εσύ πιστεύουν στο γιο του Θεού)* or in English, "Do you believe on the Son of God *(Θεού)*?"

   In the King James translation of this passage, we read: "*Say of Him whom the Father has sanctified and sent it to the world, "You blaspheme because I said, 'I am the Son of God?'"* However, some translations such as the New International Version (NIV) render this passage as "...I am the Son of Man?" In the Strong's Concordance regarding John 10:36, the word used is "God" or "Theos" in Greek and not man (*ánthrōpos*). BibleHub.com's Greek Interlinear English and Greek parallel of John 10:36 also agrees with the King James Version. It presents the Greek version alongside the English version, which states, "*eipon* (I said) *Huios* (Son) *tov Theos* (of God) *eimi* (I am)?"

CHAPTER 3

THE PROPHET OF ISLAM

Concerning the Literacy of Muhammad

Muhammad was completely orphaned by the age of six, and even though he came from a once prosperous tribe, his immediate family was poor and unable to give him a quality education. He was trained as a shepherd and later as a caravan worker. History tells us he was exceptionally intelligent, but was not able to read or write; however, he was able to work himself into what we would refer to today as a management position.

Muhammad's Birth and Early Life
Leading Up to the Koranic Revelation

Muhammad was born about 570 A.D. into the influential Quraysh tribe in Mecca. It was this prestigious clan's duty to oversee the safekeeping of the Ka'aba stone, which was used for offerings to Pagan gods, but Muhammad's father, Abdullah, died before Muhammad was born. To make matters worse for Muhammad, his mother, Amina, died by the time he was six years old. As in all cultures, family or tribal connections are very important for a couple of reasons—survival and the potential of success.

Being completely orphaned by the time Muhammad was only six years old, did not bode well for the young child, but his well-respected grandfather, Abu al-Muttalib, had been helping his mother take care of him from the time he was born.[1] Two years later, Muhammad lost his grandfather, so his Uncle Abu-Talib, chief of the Quraysh tribe, sheltered the young child. Unfortunately, it was not an easy life for orphans, even orphans born into well-respected families in those days. Muhammad was not even given a modest education, having been relegated to learning a trade without the benefit of knowing how to read and write.[2]

In general—like the early life of Jesus—Muhammad had what we would call an uneventful childhood. "Muhammad grew like any other child would in the city of Makkah (Mecca)."[3] Perhaps one of the reasons for Muhammad's lack of education was because his family lived in poverty, even though they were related to a prosperous and noble family;[4] consequently, Muhammad was consigned to working the lowly jobs of a shepherd boy.

Muhammad at Age Twelve

When Muhammad was twelve years old, he joined his uncle on a business trip. This gave him the opportunity to experience his first caravan trip to Syria and prepared him for a lucrative career.[5]

Muhammad at Age Twenty-Five

When Muhammad was a young man of twenty-five, he led a successful caravan business venture to Syria where he met his future wife, Khadija, a wealthy widow 15 years his senior. Khadija was attracted to Muhammad, so she proposed that they should be married—probably very unusual for a woman to propose at that time in history—to which he was agreeable. By all accounts, theirs was a very successful marriage.

Muhammad encountered many attractive women, any one of them he could have added as another wife since polygamy was allowed in Arabia, but she was the love of his life. Islamic sources say that he stayed true to her throughout the marriage,[6] which produced two sons and four daughters, although one of the boys died in infancy. That is basically all that is known about Muhammad during that period of his life.[7] The marriage lasted until he was 50 when his 65-year-old wife died. They were married for 25 years.[8]

Three Years into Muhammad's Ministry

Muhammad began his ministry when he was 40 years old. During the first three years of his 22-year ministry, Muhammad had a handful of followers (five or six—some put it as high as 40; there is some controversy concerning numbering and dates in Islam). Most, if not all, were family (including his wife, Khadijah) and friends. We do not go into as much detail with Muhammad's first three years in ministry compared with the brief three-year ministry of Jesus because an incredible amount of accomplishments took place with Jesus. Conversely, Muhammad's first three years were relatively benign, with only thirteen followers after ten years (some put the figure between one and two hundred). During his entire ministry, the only acknowledged miracle (according to some Muslim historians) was how Muhammad—being illiterate—had been given the Koran. However, we are not inferring that Muhammad did not also accomplish a lot during his ministry because that would be inaccurate. Muhammad did manage to accomplish a great deal throughout the remaining years of his lengthy ministry.

Muhammad at Age Forty-One

During Muhammad's 41st year, while meditating one evening in the *cave of Hira* during the month of Ramadan, he received the first five verses of the Sûrah Al-Alaque.

Unlike biblical prophets, when Muhammad first received his revelations, he thought he was possessed by a demon.[9] The angel, Gabriel, appeared to Muhammad in 610 A.D. with the following message—as told by one of Muhammad's earliest biographers,

Ibn Ishaq—from the time Muhammad fell asleep while meditating in the cave at Hira:

"He came to me" said the apostle of God, "while I was asleep, with a coverlet [cover/bedspred] of brocade whereon was some writing, and said, 'Read!' I said, 'What shall I read?'[10] He pressed me with it so tightly that I thought it was death; then he let me go and said, 'Read!' I said, 'What shall I read?' He pressed me with it the third time so that I thought it was death; then he let me go and said 'Read!' I said, 'What then shall I read?'—and this I said only to deliver myself from him, least he should do the same to me again. He said: 'Read in the name of thy Lord who created, Who created man of blood coagulated. Read! Thy Lord is the most beneficent, Who taught by the pen, Taught that which they knew not unto men' So I read it, and he departed from me. And I awoke from my sleep, and it was as though these words were written on my heart."[11]

Because the words the angel, Gabriel, wrote on Muhammad's heart stayed in his memory, he overcame his problem of illiteracy and the need for him to write what the angel revealed. At first, Muhammad thought he had been visited by a demon (i.e., jinn), but his wife, Khadija, assured him that because he was pious and a good man to his family, Allah would never allow him to be disgraced.[12]

After Muhammad's first encounter with the angel Gabriel, additional manifestations were intermittent. Some say it took three years before Muhammad heard from the angel Gabriel again. The long silence drove him into suicidal thoughts of despair. Once the revelations returned, Muhammad became reinvigorated and began preaching them again. In doing so, Muhammad initiated what would become the "religion" of Islam. Critics have asked why the Koran was not given to Muhammad all at once instead of over such a long period of time.

The Koran itself gives the explanation:

(It is) a Qur'an which We have divided (into parts from time to time), in order that you might recite it to men at intervals: We have revealed it by stages (Sûrah 17:106, Abdullah Yusuf Ali).

And those who disbelieve say: "Why is the Qur'an not revealed unto him all at once? (It is revealed) thus that We may strengthen your heart therewith; and We have arranged it in right order" (Sûrah 25:32).

Although secretly at first, among the first converts in 610 A.D. were his wife, followed by some friends and relatives, one of which was Abu Bakr.[13] Eventually, the new faith began to take root.

Muhammad at Age Forty-Nine and the End of His Monogamous Life

As stated earlier, in 619 A.D. Muhammad's only wife, Khadijah, died, followed by the death of his uncle and protector, Abu Talib. It was after the death of Muhammad's first wife when he became very aggressive in establishing his new religion.

Around 620 A.D., when Muhammad was still 50, he asked his good friend and the first non-family member who converted to Islam, Abu Bakr, permission to marry Abu's six-year-old daughter. (Some argue that Aisha was five years old when she was betrothed and eight when the prophet consummated their marriage. This is based on the Oriental or Eastern tradition at that time, which reckoned that a person was already a year old when they were born, unlike the West, where we begin with age zero at birth).[14] Bakr agreed, so Aisha became Muhammad's second betrothed.[15]

Three years later (around age 8 or 9) in 623 A.D., she became Muhammad's youngest wife;[16] however, in that same year, he also married Sawda. By the time Muhammad reached the age of 54, his lustful appetite had grown, and his harem increased—partially due to his carnal appetite and the need to establish politically valuable, family ties, which furthered his prestige among the people.[17] Muslim men, on the other hand, were only allowed to have up to four wives;[18]

however, there were no limits regarding how many women Muhammad could take as his wives, including close cousins.[19] Muhammad even convinced his adopted son, Zyad, to give up his wife so he could have her.[20] As his child bride, Aisha sarcastically observed—regarding how Allah made an exception for Muhammad's sexual appetite and the number of wives he could have—stated:

Sahih al-Bukhari, Volume 6, Book 60, Number 311

Narrated [by] Aisha:

I used to look down upon those ladies who had given themselves to Allah's Apostle and I used to say, "Can a lady give herself (to a man)?" But when Allah revealed: "You (O Muhammad) can postpone (the turn of) whom you will of them (your wives), and you may receive any of them whom you will; and there is no blame on you if you invite one whose turn you have set aside (temporarily)." **I said (to the Prophet), "I feel that your Lord (Allah) hastens in fulfilling your wishes and desires"** [i.e., "Allah can refuse you nothing!"], (Bracketed clarification mine, bolded emphasis added.)

It is believed that Muhammad had a total of thirteen wives, with the possible exception of two who might have been concubines.[21] He was survived by nine of them when he died.[22]

Some Sought to Kill Muhammad during His Ministry

The Arab tribes were numerous and constantly warring. In fact, "Mecca possessed a central shrine of the gods, the Ka'aba, a cube-shaped building that housed the 360 idols of tribal patron deities; it was the site of a great annual pilgrimage and fair."[23] It is not difficult to understand why these varying Arabian tribesmen resented Muhammad for trying to elevate and replace their tribal god with his own tribal god. This upstart from Mecca was very infuriating to the various tribes because, for generations, their gods had always been a very important part of their tribal heritage. They reasoned that

Muhammad had no right to elevate his tribal god above theirs, thus forcing his god on them as a supreme deity.

By the time the Prophet of Islam was 55 years old, those tensions had reached such a peak that Mecca was no longer a safe haven for Muhammad, and rumors of a plot to assassinate him began to surface. That was not unexpected since trouble between Muhammad's followers and the various Arab tribes had been brewing for some time.

Around that same time in 620 A.D., a committee of six men was sent to Mecca from Yathrib to discuss the possibility of Muhammad relocating there to become a judge. Yathrib (later renamed Medina) had several Jewish tribes and a Christian tribe who were at odds with each other. Muhammad was known as a monotheist with a strong, commanding image and had a reputation as being a reasonable, just, and honest person. Those men wanted Muhammad to relocate to Yathrib to act as a mediator or judge for its citizens.[24] The problem Muhammad was having with the good citizens of Mecca was not because the Arab tribes had become intolerant of Allah; on the contrary, it was because Muhammad was preaching intolerance against their gods.[25]

During September of 622 A.D., strained relations between the varying factions came to a boil, and an actual plot to assassinate the Prophet of Islam was uncovered. At that point, Muhammad took advantage of Yathrib 's invitation and managed to secretly slip out of Mecca and retreat with 70 of his followers to Yathrib.[26]

The Spreading Islam through the Sword

Since the death of his wealthy wife, Khadija, Muhammad found himself in financial reversals; however, what he saw as a divine revelation justifiably allowed him to use the sword to rob nonbelievers to help further the cause of Islam. In the Koran, we can see this validation of warfare against non-Muslims:

> Warfare is ordained for you, though it is hateful unto you; but it may happen that you hate a thing which is good for you, and it

may happen that you love a thing [avoiding war] which is bad for you. Allah knows, you know not. (Sûrah 2:216)

They question you (O Muhammad) with regard to warfare in the sacred month. Say: Warfare therein is a great (transgression), but to turn (men) from the way of Allah, and to disbelieve in Him and in the Inviolable [sacred] Place of Worship, and to expel His people thence, is a greater sin with Allah; for persecution is worse than killing. And they will not cease from fighting against you till they have made you renegades from your religion, if they can. And Whosoever became a renegade and dies in his disbelief: such are they whose works have fallen both in the world and the Hereafter. Such are rightful owners of the Fire: they will abide therein (Sûrah 2:216-217, bracketed clarification mine).

But when the forbidden months are past, then fight and slay the Pagans wherever you find them, and seize them, beleaguer them, and lie in wait for them in every stratagem (of war); but if they repent, and establish regular prayers and practice regular charity, then open the way for them: for Allah is Oft-Forgiving, Most Merciful (Sûrah 9:5, Abdullah Yusuf Ali).

Because of this new revelation, Muhammad's small band of men were encouraged. It was not long before he convinced many more to join him in his quest to spread Islam and share in the spoil."... for his next expedition, Muhammad was able to collect 300 men, at least more than any other previous occasion."[27]

In 624 A.D. at age 54, Muhammad allowed for seven attacks on Meccan caravans headed up by Pagan traders; however, Abu Sufyan, being a formidable leader as well as a profitable trader, arranged to meet Muhammad's forces with 950 Meccan troops—they outnumbered Muhammad's forces by three to one. Despite the odds—because of Muhammad's superior military savvy—he met them in battle at a place called Badr and soundly defeated the Meccan's larger army. To Muhammad, that victory against overwhelming odds confirmed Allah's divine favor for him on the battlefield.[28]

76

The next military encounter was the following year in 625 A.D. at Uhud, headed up once again by the defeated leader of Badr, Abu Sufyan. Muhammad was outnumbered by three to one a second time with Sufyan's army consisting of over 3,000 men from the Quraysh tribe against Muhammad's forces of approximately 1,000 men. At first, it seemed history was going to repeat itself as Sufyan's forces began retreating. Despite Muhammad's orders, his forces were overcome with greed for the spoils-of-war, broke ranks, and left their vantage point. Sufyan seized the opportunity and rallied his cavalry. They attacked Muhammad's troops from the rear, so the tide of battle had changed. In the fog of war, rumors spread that Muhammad had been killed. Fearing that to be true, his remaining forces withdrew and left the Quraysh to savor their victory. They returned victoriously to Mecca.[29]

The Killing of Jews

Polytheism was very prevalent in Mecca, so Muhammad was not well received there. It was in Medina where he was more readily accepted, partly because the Medinas were familiar with the concept of monotheism due to the influence of three large Hebrew tribes and a Christian community in the area. Muhammad was initially accepted as a mediator between all the Medina tribes. His temperance and wisdom endeared him to the people of Medina, which aided him in uniting the various tribes into one cohesive unit; consequently, he was able to incorporate a new constitution that required the varying tribes of the area to work together for the common good. Unfortunately, the weak link in this newly forged chain was with the three Jewish tribes who, after listening to Muhammad's koranic proposal, refused to accept his commingling of their beliefs with his new revelations of Islam. As a result, a schism developed between the Jews and the Muslims, which forced Muhammad to change his policy of tolerance toward them.

Because of Muhammad's defeat at Uhud, the Meccan army decided to make an end of Muhammad at Medina, but at the suggestion of a Persian convert, Muhammad had ditches dug in the parts of Medina that were vulnerable to attack. He also made secret alliances with some of the other outlying tribes; consequently, the army from Mecca found Muhammad's Medina stronghold better fortified. Combined with poor weather conditions, they decided to return to Mecca, leaving their military adventure more of a draw than a victory. Of course, this outcome greatly enhanced Muhammad's prestige, and as a result, he drew many more supporters to him and his cause.

Muhammad had previously driven out two of the three Jewish tribes from Yathrib because they mocked him and his new religion; however, after that, Muhammad decided to attack the last remaining Jewish tribe (Qurayza) of Medina under the guise that they aided his Meccan enemies. He rounded up approximately 800 Jewish men and pubescent boys (some historians put the figure at 900 [30]) and began beheading them—one by one—at the edge of one of the trenches. This bloody work took Muhammad all day and went well into the evening.[31]

Tor Andræ wrote about this bloody business:

> One must see Muhammad's cruelty toward the Jews against the background of the fact that scorn and rejection was the greatest disappointment of his life, and for a time they threatened completely to destroy his prophetic authority; therefore, for Muhammad it was a fixed axiom the Jews were the sworn enemies of Allah and His revelation. Any mercy toward them was out of the question.[32]

Presumably, Allah agreed with his prophet and validated Muhammad's disdain for Jews when he gave him the following koranic revelations:

> And you know of those of you who broke the Sabbath, how We said unto them: Be you apes, despised and hated! (Sûrah 2: 65.)

> Say [Muhammad]: "O People of the Scripture! Do you blame us for anything else than that we believe in Allah and that which is

revealed unto us and that which was revealed in a former time, and because most of you are evil-livers?"

"Shall I tell you of a worse (case) than theirs for retribution with Allah? (Worse is the case of him) whom Allah has cursed, him on whom His wrath has fallen and of whose sort Allah has turned some to apes and swine, and who serves idols. Such are in worse plight and further astray from the plain road" (Sûrah 5:59-60 bracketed clarification mine).

So when they took pride in that which they had been forbidden, We said unto them: "Be you apes despised and loathed!" (Sûrah 7:166.)

Soon after that incident in 630 A.D., when Muhammad was around 60 years old, he proceeded to conquer Mecca; those he did not kill, he converted to Islam. Muhammad continued to clean out the Ka'aba of its idols (as stated earlier, Arabs had 360 different gods at that time), all except Allah. Muhammad also pardoned his old nemesis, Abu Sufyan, and bestowed many fine gifts and presents on him and those he had spared. Two years later, Muhammad died at the age of 62 in Medina under suspicious circumstances. Many, including Muhammad, believe the Prophet of Islam was poisoned.[33]

While this is not an in-depth expose', but rather a general overview regarding the lives of Jesus and Muhammad, it nonetheless serves to contrast these dynamic personalities who were responsible for two of the largest religions on the planet today.

With Jesus, we see a short and simple life of 33 years, a literate man of healing and peace who never married and proclaimed Himself to be the Son of God as well as God's revelation to man.

Muhammad also claimed to bring God's revelation to man, but only as the last and greatest prophet. He lived 62 years, and although he was illiterate, he married Khadija, a woman above his station in life. He was true to her and lived peacefully for the first 49/50 years of his life until she died. It was during a 23-year time period—which extended beyond his first wife's death—when Muhammad began to receive what he believed to be revelations from God; however, during the last 12 years of his life, until he died at the age of 62, he was embroiled with many wives, robberies and religious wars.

Consider: Muhammad and Jesus (Isa) were as different as night and day, yet both of them claimed to have loved and served the only one, true God.

Death of Muhammad at Sixty-Two

Because the date of Muhammad's birth is not certain, the date of his death and how old he was when he died is arguably anywhere from 61 to 63, according to some accounts; however, most Islamic scholars agree that Muhammad was 62 when he died. In addition, there is also some controversy regarding what caused the death of Muhammad. While some Muslims either play down the possibility Muhammad was assassinated by a Jewish woman he had forcibly taken for his harem— or outright deny it—there are some credible, early Islamic sources which state otherwise.

The story goes that when Muhammad conquered the Jews at the Battle of Khaybar in 629 A.D. (93 miles north of Medina), one of the Jewish warriors he killed was Zaynab Bint al-Harith, who had a sister known as Marhab. Muhammad was attracted to her and forcibly placed her in his harem; however, before Muhammad had any sexual relations with her, she poisoned him. Muhammad died in Medina June 8, 632 A.D. It took a while for him to die, which brings up another coincidence. If Marhab did actually feed Muhammad poisoned meat (lamb), it might have very well been on June 4 of that year, which was the date celebrated by the Jews as the day God gave Moses the Torah.[34] However, some Muslim sources (from biographers, not from the Hadith or koranic sources) report the poisoning event might have occurred as long as three of four years before Muhammad actually died. While that seems highly unlikely from a medical point of view— in the spirit of fairness—it is our obligation to report that there are controversies surrounding the death of Muhammad; nevertheless, while several Hadith passages refer to Muhammad's death was caused by poisoning, we can find no time frame mentioned as to when the poisoning occurred and the time he died—only that it did occur. Objectively, should the alleged span of years be accurate regarding when Muhammad consumed the poisoned lamb, we must take into account that he was well aware of how it felt to be poisoned. Since Muhammad recognized the symptoms of being poisoned, he was the best judge of what was happening to him and leaving no reason for us to doubt that he was most likely poisoned again.

In Islam, there are two collections of holy books—the Koran and the Hadith. The Hadith (which Muhammad forbade being published[35]) consists of six major Sunni collections gathered by the Persian scholar, Muhammad al-Bukhari who, some 200 years after the death of Muhammad, "... traveled widely throughout the Abbasid Empire from the age of 16, collecting the traditions he believed were trustworthy. It is said that al-Bukhari collected over 300,000 The Hadith and included only 2,602 traditions in his Sahih;"[36] therefore, we are able to find in the Islamic al-Bukhari Hadith credibility for Muhammad being poisoned [37] where we read:

(Hadith) Sahih al-Bukhari, Volume 3, Book 47, Number 786

Narrated [by] Anas bin Malik:

A Jewess brought a poisoned (cooked) sheep for the Prophet who ate from it. She was brought to the Prophet and he was asked, "Shall we kill her?" He said, "No." I continued to see the effect of the poison on the palate of the mouth of Allah's Apostle.

We also have this story in more detail:

(Hadith) Sahih al-Bukhari, Volume 4, Book 53 Number 394:

Narrated [by] Abu Huraira:

When Khaibar was conquered, a roasted poisoned sheep was presented to the Prophet as a gift (by the Jews). The Prophet ordered, "Let all the Jews who have been here, be assembled before me." The Jews were collected and the Prophet said (to them), "I am going to ask you a question. Will you tell the truth?"

81

They said, "Yes." The Prophet asked, "Who is your father?" They replied, "So-and-so." He said, "You have told a lie; your father is so-and-so." They said, "You are right." He said, "Will you now tell me the truth, if I ask you about something?" They replied, "Yes, O Abu Al-Qasim; and if we should tell a lie, you can realize our lie as you have done regarding our father." On that he asked, "Who are the people of the (Hell) Fire?" They said, "We shall remain in the (Hell) Fire for a short period, and after that you will replace us." The Prophet said, "You may be cursed and humiliated in it! By Allah, we shall never replace you in it." Then he asked, "Will you now tell me the truth if I ask you a question?" They said, "Yes, O Abu Al-Qasim." He asked, "Have you poisoned this sheep?" They said, "Yes." He asked, "What made you do so?" They said, "We wanted to know if you were a liar in which case we would get rid of you, and if you are a prophet then the poison would not harm you"

We also find this story told in Ibn Sa'd al-Baghdadi's,[38] *The Book of the Major Classes,* where al-Baghdadi writes:

Verily a Jewish woman presented poisoned (meat of) a she goat to the apostle of Allah. He took a piece from it, put it into his mouth, chewed it and threw it away. Then he said to the Companions: "Halt! Verily, its leg tells me that it is poisoned." Then he sent for the Jewish woman and asked her, "What induced you to do what you have done?" She replied, "I wanted to know if you are true; in that case Allah will surely inform you, and if you are a liar I shall relieve the people of you."[39]

A few pages later, we read:

... When the apostle of Allah conquered Khaibar and he had peace of mind, Zaynab Bint al-Harith the brother of Marhab, who was the spouse of Sallam Ibn Mishkam, inquired, "Which part of the goat is liked by Muhammad?" They said, "The foreleg." Then she slaughtered one from her goats and roasted it (the meat). Then she wanted a poison which could not fail .... The apostle of Allah took the foreleg, a piece of which he put into his mouth. Bishr took another bone and put it into his mouth. When the apostle of Allah ate one morsel of it, Bishr ate his and other people also ate from it. Then the apostle of Allah said, "Hold back your hands! because this foreleg; ... informed me that it is poisoned. Thereupon Bishr said, "By Him who has made you great! I discovered it from the morsel I took. Nothing prevented me from emitting it out, but the idea that I did not like to make your food unrelishing. When you had eaten what was in your mouth, I did not like to save my life after yours, and I also thought you would not have eaten it if there was something wrong."

Muhammad's Last Words

> *"Allah cursed the Jews and the Christians ...."*[40]

NOTES:

1. Norman L. Geisler and Abdul Saleeb, *Answering Islam: The Crescent in Light of the Cross* (Grand Rapids, MI, Baker Books, 2003), 70.
2. Hopfe & Woodward, *Religions of the World*, 335. "Islam makes much of the fact that Muhammad was illiterate. Thus the revelation of the Qur'an to him was even more miraculous."
3. Muhammad Husayn Haykal, *The Life of Muhammad* (American Trust Publications, 1976), 55.
4. Ibn Ishaq; Sirat Rasul Allah, *The Life of Muhammad*, trans., A. Guillaume (New York: Oxford University Press, 1980), 81.
5. Ishaq, Ibn, *Sirat Rasul Allah* 81.
6. Hopfe & Woodward, *Religions of the World*, 336.
7. Geisler & Saleeb, *Answering Islam*, 71.
8. Caner, Ergun & Emir Fethi Caner, *Unveiling Islam* (Grand Rapids: Kregel Publ., 2002), 40-41.

9. Muhammad Ibn Ishaq. *The Life of Muhammad: Sirat Rasul Allah* Trans A. Guillaime (New York: Oxford Press., 2002), 106.[i] 2002), 106.

10. -In Arabic, this passage can be translated, "I do not know how to read" or "What shall I read?" ([Hadith] al-Bukhari, Volume 1, Book 1, Number 47, bracketed clarification mine.)

11. Sahih Bukari Vol. 1 Ch. 1 No. 3

12. Sahih Bukhari Book 9 Volume 87 No. 111b

13. Geisler and Saleeb, *Answering Islam*. 73.

14. Abdullah ibn Abi Quhafa was his given name, and Abu Bakr was later bestowed on him, which means "Father of the virgin" because Muhammad married Abu Bakr's six (5) year old daughter; however, Muhammad did not consummate this marriage until several years later. Web. 6 May 2013.

15. East Asian age reckoning (2015 September 10). *In Wikipedia, The Free Encyclopedia*. Web. October 7, 2015.

16. Edwin H. Palmer, et al. *The Holy Bible, New International Version: Containing the Old Testament and the New Testament* (Grand Rapids: Zondervan, 1985), 1441. Footnote Matthew 1:18. "In the Judea and the *Middle East*, a betrothal was a pledge to be married. There were no sexual relations ... but it was a much more binding relationship than a modern engagement and could be broken only by divorce" (italics added).

17. This is similar to Hinduism, where it is not unusual for parents to have prearranged marriages for their children. It was not uncommon for parents during the time of Muhammad to promise children in marriage at a young age. Muhammad and Aisha did not consummate their marriage until they had been married for about three years (8 or 9 years old).

18. Haykal, Muhammad Husayn. *The Life of Muhammad*, (n.p., American Trust Publications, 1976), 243-244.

19. The Koran allows a Muslim up to four wives. "And if you fear that you will not deal fairly by the orphans [because you become sexually attracted to them], marry of the women, who seem good to you, two or three or four; and if you fear that you cannot do justice (to so many) then one (only) or (the captives) that your right hands possess. Thus it is more likely that ye will not do injustice" (Sûrah 4:3, bracketed clarification mine).

20. "O Prophet! Lo! We have made lawful unto you your wives unto whom you have paid their dowries, and those whom your right hand possesses of those whom Allah hath given you as spoils of war, and the daughters of your uncle on the father's side and the daughters of your aunts on the father's side, and the daughters of your uncle on the mother's side and the daughters of your aunts on the mother's side who emigrated with you, and a believing woman if she give herself unto the Prophet and the Prophet desire to ask her in marriage—a privilege for you only, not for the (rest of) believers—We are Aware of that which We enjoined upon them concerning their wives and those whom their right hands possess—that you may be free from blame, for Allah is ever Forgiving, Merciful" (Sûrah 33:50).

21. "...So when Zeyd [Muhammad's adopted son] had performed that necessary formality (of divorce) from her, We gave her unto thee [Muhammad], so that (henceforth) there may be no sin for believers in respect of wives of their adopted sons, when the latter have performed the necessary formality (of release) from them. The commandment of Allah must be fulfilled" (Sûrah 33:37b, bracketed clarifications mine).

22. Ergun Mehmet Caner, Emir Fethi. Caner, *Unveiling Islam: An Insider's Look at Muslim Life and Beliefs* (Grand Rapids: Kregel Publications, 2002), 56, Figure 2: The Wives of Muhammad.

23. W. Montgomery Watt, *Muhammad at Medina* (Oxford: Clarendon Press, 1956), 395.

24. John L Esposito. *Islam: The Straight* Path (New York: Oxford University Press, 1988), 3.

25. Saifiur Rahman Al-Mubarakpuri, *The Sealed Nectar: The Life of the Prophet Muhammad (P.B.U.H.)* (Fortress Publications, 2013), 114-115.

26. The myth of Muhammad's tolerance vs. the intolerance of the Meccans (and the Pagan Arab tribes) is typical of taqiyya (Islamic deception). We have only to read the early historiographers of Islam writings and their various papers and the Hadith to disprove this revisionist history:

   "When the apostle openly displayed Islam as Allah ordered him, his people did not withdraw or turn against him, so far as I have heard, until he spoke disparagingly of their gods. When he did that, they took great offence and resolved unanimously to treat him as an enemy" (Ibn Ishaq, Ibn Hisham 167). "[Muhammad] declared Islam publicly to his fellow tribesmen. When he did so, they did not withdraw from him or reject him in any way, as far as I have heard, until he spoke of their gods and denounced them" (al-Tabari, Volume VI, p. 93, bracketed clarification mine). "[The Meccans] said they had never known anything like the trouble they had endured from this fellow. He had declared their mode of life foolish, insulted their forefathers, reviled their religion, divided the community and cursed their gods" (Ibn Ishaq, Ibn Hisham 183). "We [the Meccans] have never seen the like of what we have endured from this man [Muhammad] (bracketed clarification mine). He has derided our traditional values, abused our forefathers, reviled our religion, caused division among us, and insulted our gods. We have endured a great deal from him" (al-Tabari, Volume VI, page 101).

27. Hamilton Alexander Rosskeen Gibb and J.H. Kramer, eds., *Shorter Encyclopedia of Islam* (Ithaca: Cornell University Press, 1953), 397.
28. Watt, *Muhammad at Medina*, 10.
29. Watt, 14.
30. Watt, 15-16.
31. Ishaq, Ibn, *The Life of Muhammad*, 464.
32. Caner & Caner, *Unveiling Islam*, 52.
33. Tor Andræ, Mohammed: *The Man and his Faith*, trans., Theophil Menzel (New York: Harper & Row Publishing, 1955), 155-156. Born, Tor Julius Efraim Andræ, in 1885 into a clerical family. He was a noted Swedish scholar, as well as the Bishop of Linköping, from 1936 until his death in 1947. Bishop Andræ studied Theology and comparative religions at the Uppsala University, where in 1917, he completed his Ph.D.
34. Hopfe & Woodward, *Religions of the World*, 338-339. Like Alexander the Great, Muhammad made no provisions for a successor to rule in his place. It was agreed that abu-Bakr, the father of Aisha, Muhammad's youngest wife (who by that time was 18 years old and, in whose arms Muhammad, died), become the new caliph. Muhammad told Aisha as he lay dying, "...I feel as if my aorta is being cut from that poison." ([Hadith] Sahih al-

Bukhari, narrated by 'Aisha: Volume 5, Book 59, Number 713; (also, *Sahih al-Bukhari*, Volume 3, Book 47, Number 786; *Sahih Muslim*, Book 026, Number 5430; *Sunan Abu Dawud*, Book 39, Number 4498.)

35. "Jewish Holidays for 632," Jewish Holidays for 632, n.p., n.d. Web. 8 June 2014. The day the Torah (Ten Commandments) was given to Moses fell on Tuesday, June 4, which falls on the Hebrew calendar of the seventh [day] of Sivan, 4392 (6/4/632 Monday, seventh [day] of Sivan, 4392 English calendar, 6/4/632 Mon, Shavuot II).

36. In Islam, there are two Holy Books, the Koran (Qur'an), and the Hadith (which is actually many volumes of books); yet something most people are unaware of is when Muhammad found out that some of his followers were writing down the Hadith, he prohibited their publications! Muhammad reminded his followers that Allah repeated several times—the Koran was perfect and complete in every detail, so why would there be a need for anything else—not directly given by Allah, but only hearsay—to be written down as a supplement to the Koran:

    "Abu Sa'id Khudri reported that Allah's Messenger (peace be upon him) said: 'Do not take down anything from me, and he who took down anything from me except the Qur'an, he should efface that [delete it] and narrate from me [only repeat what I have said] there is no harm in it [unless you write it down] and [likewise], he who attributed any falsehood to me'—and Hammam said: I think he also said: 'deliberately' - he should, in fact, find his abode in the Hell-Fire" (Sahih Muslim, Book 42 No. 7147). Al-Bukhari, Sahih (May 16, 2014). *In Wikipedia: The Free Encyclopedia.* Web. 18 June 2014.

37. Jonathan Brown, *The Canonization of al-Bukhr and Muslim* (Islamic History and Civilization) (N.p.: Brill Publ., 2007). Sunni Muslims consider the al-Bukhari Hadith as one of the three highly trusted collections of the Hadith besides Sahih Muslim and Muwatta Imam Malik. Many respected Muslim scholars consider the al-Bukhari Hadith the most reverent holy book after the Koran.

38. Ibn Sa'd Al-Baghdadi (2013 December 25). *In Wikipedia: The Free Encyclopedia.* Web. 18 June 2014. "Muhammad ibn Sa'd ibn

Mani' al-Baghdadi or Ibn Sa'd (Arabic: ابن سعد), often called Katib ul-Waqidi: Ibn Sa'd was born in the year 784 A.D. and died in 845 A.D. He was a Sunni Muslim scholar of Islam and an Arabian biographer, received his training in the tradition from al-Waqidi and other celebrated teachers. He lived for the most part in Baghdad, and had the reputation of being both trustworthy and accurate in his writings, which, in consequence, were much used by later writers." Ibn Sa'd authored *The Book of The Major Classes* (Arabic: *Kitab Tabaqat al-Kubra*), which is a collection of historical information regarding famous Muslims. "This eight-volume work contains the lives of Muhammad, his Companions and Helpers, including those who fought at the Battle of Badr as a special class, and of the following generation, the Followers, who received their traditions from the Companions."

39. Al-Baghdadi, Ibn Sa'd, *The Book of the Major Classes*, page 249.
40. Al-Baghdadi, Ibn Sa'd, 251-252.
41. Narrated by Aisha, Muhammad's child bride, now around 18 years old whose lap his head rested on when he breathed his last words as recorded in Hadith Sahih Bukhari, Volume 2, Book 23, Number 472.

CHAPTER 4

A BRIEF OVERVIEW OF THE KORAN

How the Koran Came to Be

To begin with, Koran (Arabic, *Qur'an*) is usually understood to mean "read" or "recite."[1] It is compiled into two sections totaling a little less in size than the New Testament. It consists of 114 sûrah's, 20 in the first section and 94 in the second. The Koran tells us it was first delivered to Muhammad by the angel, Gabriel, while he was meditating in the cave at Hira. These revelations spanned over a 23-year period of Muhammad's life during what was called the Meccan and Medinan periods, and because the Koran was not compiled until after Muhammad's death, its continuity was a challenging effort.

When we read the Koran, we are struck by its lyrical, yet disjointed style.[2] We should point out that Arabs, during the time of Muhammad, used poetry as a learning aid to help memorize, similar to the way we use poetic, lyrical rhythms to teach our children the alphabet in English. That was an effective and very productive method of teaching when many people, like Muhammad, could not read or write.

Twentieth-century Iranian rationalist, scholar, and Iranian Senator (1954-1979), Ali Dashti, explains:

The Qur'an contains sentences which are incomplete and not fully intelligible without the aid of commentaries; foreign words, unfamiliar Arabic words, and words used without other than the normal meaning; adjectives and verbs inflected without observance of the concord gender and number; illogically and ungrammatically applied pronouns which sometimes have no referent; and predicates which in rhymed passages are often remote from the subjects. These and other such aberrations in the language have given scope to critics who deny the Qur'an's eloquence.[3]

As we previously indicated, the Koran endorses the Bible—if for no other reason than to validate itself as being from the "same God" and desiring to give itself credibility. However, because there are numerous, glaring contradictions between the Bible and the Koran, many Islamists have attempted to deflect from those troubling biblical Scriptures by claiming that either the Christians or Jews practiced taḥrīf (the corruption of Scripture, or at the very least some of the books of the Bible were fabricated and more was added at a later date). This was done to give Muslims a way out of having to deal with those troubling passages in the Bible that conflict with the teachings of Muhammad. The problem with this is that the Bible is not only the most scrutinized book of antiquity, but it is the best-documented book closest to the original source.

One method used by Islamic apologists is to show that the Koran only mentions the Torah[4] and the gospels. This is a straw-man argument because the Koran draws from the apocryphal Syriac Gospels. As for the Torah and the Bible, in general, the Koran does not refute the other books of the Bible, which were considered canon Scripture long before the time of Muhammad. Of course, down through the years, the passages of Scripture that contradicted those biblical stories incorporated in the Koran needed to be discredited by Islamic scholars for the sake of Islam. Claims that the Bible contradicts itself were laid to rest long ago by most Christian apologists, especially those confusing Scriptures naming people and places which, until recently, could not be proven as having existed.

Remember, the Bible was written over a period of 1,500 years—not 23 years like the Koran! Thanks to archaeology, we are now are able to see how incredibly accurate Scripture really is. Conversely, as some point out, there are documented problems with the accuracy of the Koran. For example, where Muhammad allowed the words that were given to him by Allah to be rearranged or changed without any divine authority, as the following quote testifies—and because Muhammad's scribe, Abdollah, exposed the fact he was given a death sentence by the prophet of the "religion of peace:"

> The Prophet gave orders for killing six persons ... They were [1] Safwan b. Omayya; [2] Abdollah b. ol-Khatal; [3] Meqyas b. Sobaba; [4] Ekrema b. Abi Jahl; [5] ol-Howayreth b. Noqaydh b. Wahb, and [6] Abdullâh Ibn Sâd Ibn Abî Sarh. The last named, for some time, had been one of the scribes employed at Madina [Medina] to write down the revelations (bracketed clarifications mine).

> On a number of occasions he had, with the Prophet's consent, had changed the closing words of verses. For example, when the Prophet had said, "And God is mighty and wise" ['aziz hakim], 'Abdollah b. Abi Sarh suggested writing down "knowing and wise" ('alim hakim), and the Prophet answered that there was no objection. Having observed a succession of changes of this type, 'Abdollah renounced Islam on the ground that revelations, if from God, could not be changed at the prompting of a scribe such as himself. After his apostasy, he went to Mecca and joined the Qorayshites.[5]

Many Muslim scholars believe that the Koran is not capable of being accurately translated because, in doing so, it loses much of its meaning. They say that only those who are able to read and understand Arabic are capable of acquiring the true and sometimes subtle meanings offered to mankind through Allah's words in the Koran.[6]

While we have no reason to disagree with this argument, and as poetically translated as the Koran is in English, it does leave us scratching our heads on occasion! However, it appears that this is not just limited to non-Arabic translations of the Koran, but is also a criticism of the construct of the transmission of it in its Arabic composition.

We briefly touched on this in Chapter 1 when we discussed how the Koran was compiled by unorthodox means. Some memorized the passages as Muhammad repeated them, and others wrote them down on anything available to them at the time. That encouraged innovative means of writing on "... pieces of paper, stones, palm leaves, shoulder blades (of camels), ribs, and bits of leather."[7] It became a challenge when compiling and writing down the many revelations given to Muhammad the year after his unexpected death. Because the militant nature of Islam continued, many followers of Muhammad—who had committed the koranic verses to memory— were killed at the Battle of Yamama.[8] That necessitated Umar bin Al-Khattab to make the decision to formally have the Koran published in book form for posterity's sake. Umar challenged a close and confidant scribe of Muhammad's, Zayd ibn Thabit to:

> ... search for (the fragmentary scripts of) the Qur'an and collect it (in one book). By Allah! If they had ordered me to shift one of the mountains, it would not have been heavier for me than this ordering me to collect the Qur'an .... So I started looking for the Qur'an and collecting it from (what it was written on) palm-leaf stalks, thin white stones and also from men who knew it by heart.[9]

Historically, the Koran was not compiled into a coherent one-book collection at the end of its 23-year revelation. This is also true of the writing of the Bible, but for different reasons since the Bible was compiled over a 1500-year period after Moses received the initial Pentateuch (first five books of the Bible). The various books of the Bible were complete chronological events recorded as they happened. On the other hand, the Koran was loosely written down—piecemeal— only to be collected later, after the death of Muhammad, and rearranged the best as possible. Remember, with the Koran, there was no order or filing system developed to allow for a cohesive train of thought to be filed away in the order it was delivered to Muhammad. This is the reason why, at times, the Koran appears so fragmented and rambling.

At first, there were several early versions of the Koran, although many Islamic scholars deny that, insisting that the Koran today is the same as the Koran produced during the time of Muhammad, which they maintain was codified exactly as the angel, Gabriel, dictated it to Muhammad.[10]

On the other hand, al-Bukhari documents that there was more than one koranic version in circulation among some of the tribes. Of course, that caused obvious problems because many Muslims began to question the Koran, and by extension, questioned their faith. They reasoned that if Allah gave Muhammad the incorruptible Koran, why were there so many different versions saying different things? It was under the caliphate of the third successor to Muhammad, Uthman ibn Affan, that a decision was made to eliminate the problem by pulling together the various koranic versions and compiling everything into one Koran, which would be acceptable to all. It was Hudhaifa bin Al-Yaman, who—after seeing firsthand, various tribes reciting the Koran differently—expressed his dismay and concern to Uthman:

> "O the chief of the Believers! Save this nation before they differ about the Book [Qur'an] as Jews and the Christians did before." So Uthman sent a message to Hafsa saying, "Send us the manuscripts of the Qur'an so that we may compile the Qur'anic materials in perfect copies and return the manuscripts to you." Uthman then ordered Zayd bin Thabit, Abdullah bin Az-Zubair, Sa'id bin Al-As, and Abdur-Rahman bin Hyarith [Harith] bin Hisham to rewrite the manuscripts in perfect copies. Uthman said to the three Quraishi men, "In case you disagree with Zayd bin Thabit on any point in the Qur'an, then write it in the dialect of Quraish tribe (of Muhammad) as the Qur'an was revealed in their tongue" (bracketed clarifications mine).

Consequently, Uthman authorized the gathering of the many copies of the koranic versions to be assimilated, at the discretion of highly respected scribes and Islamic scholars, into a uniform, if not commingled version of the Koran. He then declared it to be the true version and had the newly compiled official version sent throughout the land to all the chief Islamic centers. Uthman then commanded that all the other versions of the Koran be gathered up and sent to him to be burned.[11] The burning of the various Korans, including the original one held by Muhammad's wife, Hafsah (which became known as Hafsah Codex), occurred sometime around 644-656 A.D., but most likely occurred in 651 A.D. The Hafsah Codex survived destruction until Hafsha's death in 667 A.D.[12]

One of the curiosities of the Koran is that the last section of the book (Volume II, Sûrahs 21 through 114) generally contains the first and shortest revelations given to Muhammad, while the first section (Volume I, Sûrah 1-20) generally consists of the last revelations, which were the larger verses given to Muhammad. Therefore, as we have discussed, the compilations of the chapters (e.g., sûrahs) in the Arabic language are not necessarily in any particular order, and no doubt vary in different koranic versions since they are the product of numerous means of acquisitions spanning various periods of time. As Arberry writes in his "Koran, Interpreted," we read in the Preface:

> The Sûrahs, collected into a volume after the death of Muhammad, are not arranged in any chronological order; indeed, most of those reproduced in this volume were revealed to the Prophet in later years of his mission … The Sûrahs themselves are in many instances—and this has been recognized by Muslim students from the earliest times—of a composite character, holding embedded in them fragments received by Muhammad at widely differing dates.[13]

Likewise, the numerical order of the verses might differ as well (not the actual arrangement of the verses). One example would be comparing the numbering of verses, as found in the Arberry and Pickthall translations. Sometimes the same verse in various translations of the Koran might be up to a five-number sequence apart. In order to compensate for this problem, we will be using a more recently adapted koranic numbering system.

Another item of interest is that the titles of each sûrah (chapter) do not always reveal what the main subject or body of the sûrah consists of, but some suggest that the titles might have been recruited from some words used in the text. Sûrah 19, "Mary," and Sûrah 17, "The Night Journey," are exceptions; however, in Pickthall's translation, the chapter usually titled "The Night Ride (Journey)," is instead titled, "Children of Israel."[14] As we have noted, titles of each sûrah might vary from one koranic version to another, although that is not common

Myth: Islam is a "Religion of Peace"

Former President Obama said, "No religion is responsible for terrorism,"[15] but is that the truth? In the very pages of the Koran, we find teachings to the contrary. Because so much ignorant misinformation, as well as lies, have been spewed by our political and some religious leaders, as well as Islamic organizations, we will let the readers decide the truth for themselves rather than debate the merits of such claims. Below are the verses from the Koran which promote fear and terror. The first one refers to those who refuse to accept Islam and stay in the faith and gives examples of how they will be dealt with by Allah or Muslim terrorists acting on his behalf.

> ... (another similitude) is that of a rain-laden cloud from the sky: In it are zones of darkness, and thunder and lightning: They press their fingers in their ears to keep out the stunning thunderclap, [all] the while **they are in *terror* of death**. But Allah is ever [a]round the rejecters of Faith! (Sûrah 2:19, Abdullah Yusuf Ali, bracketed clarification mine, bolded emphasis added).

> **We shall cast *terror* into the hearts** of those [Christians] who disbelieve because they ascribe unto Allah partners, for which no warrant has been revealed. Their habitation is the Fire, and

95

hapless the abode of the wrong-doers (Sûrah 3:151, bracketed clarification mine, bolded emphasis added).

Remember the Lord inspired the angels (with the message): "I am with you: give firmness to the Believers: **I will instill terror into the hearts of the Unbelievers**: smite you above their necks and smite all their finger-tips off them" (Sûrah 8:12, Abdullah Yusuf Al, bolded emphasis added).

Against them make ready your strength to the utmost of your power, including steeds of war, **to strike *terror* into (the hearts of) the enemies,** of Allah and your enemies, and others besides, whom you may not know, but whom Allah does know. Whatever you shall spend in the cause of Allah, be repaid unto you, and you shall not be treated unjustly (Sûrah 8:60, Abdullah Yusuf Ali, bolded emphasis added).

And those of the People of the Book who aided them—Allah did take them down from their strongholds **and cast *terror* into their hearts**. (So that) some you slew, and some you made prisoners (Sûrah 33:26, Abdullah Yusuf Ali, bolded and italicized emphasis added).

He it is who has caused those of the People of the Scripture who disbelieved to go forth from their homes unto the first exile. You deemed [thought] not that they would go forth, while they deemed that their strongholds would protect them from Allah. But Allah reached them from a place whereof they reckoned not, **and cast *terror* in their hearts** so that they ruined their houses with their own hands and the hands of the believers. So learn a lesson, O you who have eyes! (Sûrah 59:2, bracketed clarification mine, bolded and italicized emphasis added).

(Hadith) Sahih al-Bukhari, Book 4, Volume 52, Number 220

Narrated [by] Abu Huraira:

Allah's Apostle said, "I have been sent with the shortest expressions bearing the widest meanings, **and I have been made victorious with *terror*** (cast in the hearts of the enemy), and while I was sleeping, the keys of the treasures of the world were brought to me and put in my hand." Abu Huraira added: Allah's Apostle has left the world and now you, people, are bringing out those treasures (i.e., the Prophet did not benefit by them (bolded and italicized emphasis and added).

Terror is a vital part of Islamic psychological warfare against all unbelievers and is to be utilized until the whole world succumbs to Islam:

And fight them on until there is no more tumult or oppression, and there prevail justice and faith in Allah altogether and everywhere [everyone in the whole world]; but if they cease, verily Allah does see all that they do (Sûrah 8:39, Abdullah Yusuf Ali, bracketed clarification mine).

The Doctrine of Taqiyya: Allah-Approved Lying to Advance the Cause of Islam

We will also briefly discuss deception in Chapter 9, under the subtitle *Sharia: The Shadow Government,* regarding how Allah can and does change his mind (Sûrah 2:106), as opposed to the God of the Bible who can never change his mind (Malachi 3:6). It is worth revisiting again.

One of the tenants of the Judeo-Christian faiths is that Christians and Jews consider it a sin to lie. In fact, the Ninth Commandment—which Allah takes credit for giving to Moses—tells us not to lie (Exodus 20:16), and the Bible even goes so far as to identify Satan as the father of lies (John 8:44).

Consider: If someone makes a pronouncement concerning something and people act on that information, only to be told later what was said is no longer valid, they should not be faulted for having done something approved by Allah if he later changes his mind. If an authority told you something was permissible and then went back on his or her word—we call that lying.

Unlike the God of the Bible, who never lies (Numbers 23:19), Allah can change his mind as it suits him. This, of course, has become a major problem for those who defend the Muslim faith. There is also a related doctrine in Islam that is based on Allah's ability to say one thing one day and renege on it another day—it is called "taqiyya" (pronounced tuh-**kee**-yuh)—which allows a Muslim to lie as a way of saving face to protect the honor and status of Islam and Allah.[16] Through the use of taqiyya, the end (protecting and promoting Islam) is justified by the means.[17] Examples of taqiyya are lying, breaking treaties you never planned to keep (*Treaty of the Prophet*), manipulating the truth regarding Islam, and citing Gnostic gospels to support claims in the Koran. Taqiyya goes a step further by fabricating its own gospel titled *The Gospel of Barnabas*,[18] which pretends to be the writings of Barnabas, a first-century apostle. However, it is a counterfeit Barnabas making the claim that Jesus is not the Son of God and incorporates other false Islamic propaganda. We know that *The Gospel of Barnabas* is a forgery because of its contents. One example is the number of years between Jubilees:

> And then through all the world will God be worshipped, and mercy received, insomuch that the Year of Jubilee, which now cometh every hundred years, shall by the Messiah be reduced to every year in every place ....[19]

In the Bible, God tells Moses:

> A jubilee shall that fiftieth year be unto you: ye shall not sow, neither reap that which grows of itself in it, nor gather the grapes in it of thy vine undressed (Leviticus 25:11).

A biblical Jubilee comes every 50 years, but around 1300 A.D. Pope Boniface VIII changed the Year of Jubilee so it would occur once a century, only to be reversed by Pope Clemens VI in 1343 A.D. Therefore, it seems likely that the so-called, *The Gospel of Barnabas* (which we will address again in the next chapter) was a fourteenth-century forgery, although some put it in the sixteenth century. A reason to place it in the fifthteenth or sixteenth century is because *The Gospel of Barnabas* has Jesus using the term "false and lying gods" (Latin, *dei falsi e bugiardi*, page 99) and also describes King Herod as serving "false and lying gods" (page 267), an expression which is missing from both the Bible and the Koran. However, it is used in Dante's classic novel, *Divine Comedy*, which was written between 1308 A.D. and his death in 1321 A.D. As previously shown in Table 1, the Bible has three Heavens (2 Corinthians 12:2), while the Koran claims seven Heavens (Sûrah 41:12), but Dante has nine Heavens with Paradise as the tenth level just like Dante's Empyrean, which is also above the nine levels of Heaven. It is curious that in *The Gospel of Barnabas*, Jesus states:

> Paradise is so great that no man can measure it. Verily I say unto thee that the Heavens are nine … I say to thee that paradise is greater than all the earth and all the Heavens together.[20]

Another example of Muslim misinformation is how they take verses from the Koran out of order—verses which have been abrogated (reversed) by Allah in an effort to deflect attention away from the Koran's violent teachings. It becomes apparent when an unsuspecting person searches the Internet and discovers that there are so many jihad passages, along with anti-Christian and Jewish verses in the Koran and the Hadith. They might also question the fairness of Islam based on Sûrah 14:4, which says that a person has no choice in deciding whether or not to become a Muslim because it is Allah who decides. Then you come across a website regarding Sûrah 14:4 in which the website's Muslim administrator acknowledges it, but claims that it is a very "misunderstood" quote and then, for the sake of discussion, display it for the viewer to read:

> And We never sent a messenger save with language of his folk, that he might make (the message) clear for them. Then Allah sends whom He will astray, and guides whom He will, He is the Mighty, the Wise (Sûrah 14:4).

The website's administrator offers several proof texts during Muhammad's earlier ministry in Mecca for us to consider (as we will share below) in an attempt to contradict this passage. By doing so, he is trying to prove that those who reject Islam do so out of their own free will. We are then instructed that in order to be fair, we should read the entire Koran and weigh the positive and conciliatory verses against the negative and hostile verses—which supposedly outweigh the negative ones—and that is how we are supposed to deal with all the negative verses we find in the Koran. Let's look at those passages from the Koran which the Muslim administrator provides us with as proof texts to show that people do have free will without Allah's interference:

> Lo [Listen]! This is a Reminder. Let him who will, *then choose* a way unto his Lord (Sûrah 73:19, bracketed clarification mine).

> Say: I ask of you no reward for this, save that whoso will, *may choose* a way unto his Lord (Sûrah 25:57, emphasis added).

> Nay, but verily it is an Admonishment, *So let whosoever will pay heed to it* (Sûrah 80:11-12, emphasis added).

The conclusion we are supposed to draw from this is that one negative verse (Sûrah 14:4) should not really trouble us.[21] What is conveniently avoided and more important, is that Islam is a religion of abrogation (revisionism/change). So what does that mean, and how does a gullible reader of the Koran really know which verse is correct when he or she comes across conflicting verses? Do they weigh them against each other as the Muslim instructor suggests? The answer is simple—whatever the last revelation given to Muhammad was—that is the teaching/law the Koran tells its readers they are to go with in case of a contradiction.

As a review, the last revelations begin with Sûrah 2 in Volume I of the Koran, so the lower the numbers are, the more important the sûrahs; the larger the sûrah numbers are, the less relevant they are. Notice that the proof texts on the previous page are mostly from Volume II of the Koran (Volume I, Sûrahs 1-20 and Volume II, Sûrahs 21-114). All the proof texts offered to us by this Islamic site are older ones; therefore, the negative passage, Sûrah 14:4, is the last and final word on the matter and the one to be enforced by Allah. We go into greater detail in Volume II: *The Koran: Selected Sûrahs, Commentary and Bible Comparisons*. We even supply you with a table outlining where each sûrah appears in the Koran and the order in which they were actually received by Muhammad.

Another deliberate falsehood (*taqiyya*) is the lie that Jerusalem is the third holiest site in Islam. The truth is—that claim was born in the 20th century for political reasons as a means to discredit Israel's claim to the Temple Mount. Consider: if Jerusalem is Islam's third holiest city then why is it not mentioned in the Koran even once? We will address that in greater detail in Volume III of *Islam Exposed: Science-Bible-Archaeology and Myths,* Chapter 3, where we discuss Sûrah 17, "The Night Journey: Is Jerusalem the Third Holiest City in Islam?"

In conclusion, while we would call the explanation given by this Muslim website administrator deceptive, regarding the inconsistencies found in the Koran, a Muslim would proclaim that the administrator is merely using the technique of taqiyya.

NOTES:

1. Michael Nazir-Ali, *Frontiers in Muslim-Christian Encounter* (Oxford: Regnum Books, 1987), 124.
2. Ali Dashti, *Twenty-Three Years: A Study of the Prophetic Career of Muhammad* (London: George Allen & Unwin, 1985), 48-49.
3. Dashti, 49.
4. The Torah, or Jewish Written Law, is the first five books of the Tanakh, also known as the Old Testament.
5. Ergun Mehmet Caner and Emir Fethi Caner, *Unveiling Islam: An Insider's Look at Muslim Life and Beliefs* (Grand Rapids: Kregel Publications, 2002), 45.

6. Seyyed Hossein Nasr, *Ideals and Realities of Islam* (London: George Allen & Unwin, Ltd., 1975), 44.

7. Abdullah Yusuf Ali, *The Holy Koran: Translation and Commentary* (Damascus: Uloom Al Qur'an, 1934). (Ali mentions this in the introduction of his translation of the Koran.) We also have Stanton, H. U. Weitbrecht, *The Teaching of the Qur'an* (New York: Biblo & Tannen, 1969), 10.

8. Dr. Muhammad Khan, trans., *Al-Bukhari*, Volume 6 Book 61 Number 509 (Grand Rapids: Eerdmans, 1981), 478-479.

9. *Al-Bukhari,* Vol. 6, Number 477-78.

10. Badru D Kateregga and David W. Shenk, *Islam and Christianity: A Muslim and a Christian in Dialogue* (Grand Rapids: Eerdmans, 1981), 29-30.

11. Dr. Muhammad Khan, trans., *Al-Bukhari*, Volume 6, Book 61 Number 510.

12. John Zachary, *Is the Qur'an Pure?* Based on his book, *Gabriel's Faces: Voice of the Archangel,* n.p. (Harvard House, 2004). Web. 12 May 2013.

13. A.J Arberry, *The Koran Interpreted*, 25.

14. The title of Sûrah 17 in Arabic is "Al-Isra" or "Bani Isra'il," which translates, "Children of Israel."

15. David Jackson, "Obama: No Religion Responsible for Terrorism," *USA Today*, Gannett, 18 Feb. 2015. Web. 19 Feb. 2015.

16. Ibn-an-Naqīb Aḥmad; Ibn-Lu'lu', *Reliance of the Traveller: The Classic Manual of Islamic Sacred Law*, 'Umdat al-salik, trans., Nuh Ha Mim. Keller (Beltsville: Amana Publ., 1997), section r8.2, page 745. "Speaking is a means to achieve objectives. If a praiseworthy aim is attainable through both telling the truth and lying, it is unlawful to accomplish through lying because there is no need for it. When it is possible to achieve such a claim by lyin[g], but not by telling the truth, it is permissible to lie if attaining the goal is permissible" (bracketed clarification mine, emphasis added).

17. WikiIslam contributors, "Taqiyya." *WikiIslam, The Online Resource on Islam*, n.pag. Web. 3 Aug. 2015.

18. Jon Sorensen, "Why the *'Gospel of Barnabas' Is a Medieval Fake."* Why the *'Gospel of Barnabas'* Is a Medieval Fake. Catholic Answers, 30 June 2014. Web. 12 June 2015.

19. *Gospel of Barnabas.* The (Brooklyn: A&B Publishers Group, 1993), Ch. 85. There are 27 pages of introduction Islamic propaganda followed by chapters that are no more than one or two paragraphs each; however, the book is over 270 pages.

20. The Bible acknowledges only three heavens: (1) The earth's atmosphere (where birds fly); (2) space, where the stars are, and (3) the heavenly abode of God (Reference: 2 Corinthians 12:2).

21. There are dozens of verses in the Koran that tell us Allah chooses who will become Muslims and rejects others. Here is one example:

    "Thy Lord brings to pass what He wills and chooses. They have never any choice. Glorified be Allah and Exalted above all that they associate (with Him) [Jesus and Mary]!" (Sûrah 28:68, bracketed clarification mine, bolded and italicized emphasis added.)

    To be fair, there are also verses that contradict what this verse says:

    "Say: '(It is) the truth from the Lord of you (all). Then *whosoever will, let him believe, and whosoever will, let him disbelieve.'* Lo! We have prepared for disbelievers Fire. Its tent encloses them. If they ask for showers, they will be showered with water like to molten lead which burn their faces. Calamitous the drink and ill the resting-place!" (Sûrah 18:29, bolded and italicized emphasis added.)

    As we show in Volume II *of Islam Exposed, The Koran: Selected Sûrahs, Commentary and Bible Comparisons*, many defenders of the Koran will use proof texts that have been abrogated or are no longer valid. This passage is one of them. As previously stated, the rule of thumb is when there are conflicting passages in the Koran, the one that is revealed last replaces the one given earlier. Normally, Chapter one supersedes Chapter 2, and in this case, Sûrah 18, allowing for free choice, would supersede Sûrah 28, which does not allow a person the choice to accept Islam and salvation or reject Islam and be condemned to Hell. The problem for most people who are not familiar with the teachings of Islam. is that they can be duped by Muslim scholars. These Muslim apologists know that the order of sûrahs and verses placed in the Koran are not in the order received. Sûrah 28 (the free will verse) was received 49th, while Sûrah 18 (the no free will verse) was received 69th; thus, it takes precedence over Sûrah 28 (the free will verse), making that conciliatory passage null and void!

CHAPTER 5

THE KORAN EXPOSED IN LIGHT OF THE BIBLE

Koranic Arabic Exclusivity Contrasted
with Biblical Universality

At the outset of this chapter, we will revisit the Islamist argument that the Koran cannot be accurately translated into any other language because only Arabic is capable of transmitting the true nature and revelation of Allah to his people.[1] Seyyed Nasr explains it this way:

> The form of the Qur'an is the Arabic language which religiously speaking is as inseparable from the Qur'an as the body of Christ is from Christ Himself. Arabic is sacred in the sense that it is an integral part of the Quranic revelation whose very sounds and utterances play a role in the ritual acts of Islam.[2]

This in and of itself gives us cause to question the single authorship of both the Bible and Koran since the God of the Bible transmitted His Word through four languages: (1) Chaldees; (2) Aramaic, the official language of the Babylonian Court[3] (which ruled a large part of the early known world, and very similar to Chaldees);[4] (3) Hebrew, and (4) Konia Greek, the most far-reaching international language of the world from the fourth century Before Christ through the time of the writing of the New Testament in the first century A.D. The reason the God of the Judeo-Christian Bible transmitted His communication to the whole world via four languages is because He did not want to keep His Word secreted away for just a select few. He was desirous for all people everywhere to be able to read it and come to know His will and love for mankind. To make His word even more accessible, on the day of Pentecost, the God of the Bible had Jesus' disciples preach His Word in even *more* foreign languages:

> When the day of Pentecost came, they were all together in one place. Suddenly a sound like the blowing of a violent wind came from Heaven and filled the whole house where they were sitting. They saw what seemed to be tongues of fire that separated and came to rest on each of them. All of them were filled with the Holy Spirit and began to speak in other tongues [languages] as the Spirit enabled them.
>
> Now there were staying in Jerusalem God-fearing Jews from every nation under Heaven. When they heard this sound, a crowd came together in bewilderment because each one heard their own language being spoken (Acts 2:1-6, NIV, bracketed clarification mine).

Regarding the historical accuracy of the Bible, most Muslim scholars today have taken a note from the liberal/progressive Christian scholars of the nineteenth century onward, who claim that the Bible is corrupt and has many contradictions.[5] This is not as far-fetched as we might think, as evidenced from the very beginning of the New Testament writings of the first century, which address the fact the early church also had to deal with apostates and false teachers. In order to protect the gospel and teachings of the early church, the apostles warned the early believers to be on guard and only follow those Scriptures developed and committed to pen by the apostles. They also warned the body of believers about the attempts by false prophets and Gnostics who were endeavoring to corrupt the holy oracles and all the work they had accomplished;[6] yet it is the discredited Gnostic writings, one is *the Gospel of Thomas*,[7] which the Koran draws heavily on, and which Muslim scholars have historically cited to bolster their claims to discredit the canonical Judeo-Christian Scriptures.

As we saw in the previous chapter, Muslims use *The Gospel of Barnabas* to prove the koranic view of their Islamic Jesus *(Isa)* as opposed to the New Testament's conventional teachings of Christ. An example of this use would be appropriating the name of the historical Barnabas,[8] a contemporary of Jesus, and known by Christ's apostles. (We go into more detail regarding this false gospel in the Appendix of Volume III of *Islam Exposed: Science—Bible—Archaeology and Myths* under the subheading, "The Koran Contains Apocrypha and Gnostic Writings"). "The biblical Barnabas was also very instrumental in the Apostle Paul's ministry;[9] however, some Muslim scholars admit that *The Gospel of Barnabas* is most likely a Muslim forgery of the sixteenth century. Cyril Glassé, a Muslim Islamic researcher, describes it this way:

> As regards *The Gospel of Barnabas* itself, there is no question that it is a medieval forgery. A complete Italian manuscript exists, which appears to be a translation from a Spanish original (which exists in part), written to curry favor with Muslims of the time. It contains anachronisms which can date only from the Middle Ages and not before, and shows a garbled comprehension of Islamic doctrines, calling the Prophet "the Messiah," which Islam does not claim for him. Besides its farcical notion of sacred history, stylistically it is a mediocre parody of the gospels, as the writings of Baha' Allah are of the Koran.[10]

One example, which shows that *The Gospel of Barnabas* is contrived, can be seen in the heading of Chapter 6 in that book. It reads:

> Three magi are led by a star in the east to Judea, and, finding Jesus, make obeisance to him and gifts.[11]

Neither the Bible nor any historical account of the first century states how many magi there were; that became a later tradition. However, we do know from the Bible that there were three gifts.

And when they were come into the house, they saw the young child with Mary His mother, and fell down, and worshipped Him: and when they had opened their treasures, they presented unto Him gifts; gold, and frankincense and myrrh (Matthew 2:11).

Another problematic passage with this supposedly first-century publication is the following quote found in Chapter 42, where we read:

Jesus confessed and said the truth, "I am not the Messiah."[12]

Even more incredible is the dialogue in Chapter 97, where the priest is questioning Jesus:

Then said the priest: "How shall the Messiah be called?" ... (Jesus answered) "Muhammad is his blessed name."[13]

Yet Muhammad was not known in the first century and would not exist until a half a millennium in the future—and then not from the descendants of Israel—but rather from the descendants of Israel's enemies, which, of course, makes no sense at all! What is interesting about this dialogue is that in the Koran, it is Jesus who is called the Messiah (Sûrah 3:45), and no place in the Koran is Muhammad ever called the Messiah. We will explore more contrived Islamic arguments when we discuss specific verses from the Koran.

On What Basis Do Muslims Claim That Christians and Jews Rewrote Or Corrupted the Bible?

Before we begin, we need some background about the Bible. Catholic and Eastern Orthodox Bibles, which unlike the current Protestant Bibles, include several Apocrypha (mythical or inaccurate) books consisting of Tobit, Judith, First and Second Maccabees, Wisdom of Solomon, Sirach (Ecclesiasticus), Enoch and Baruch.[14] Additionally, at the end of the Book of Daniel in the Catholic version, there are added chapters titled, "Susanna" and "Bel and the Dragon".[15] This material was never acknowledged as sacred writings by the Hebrews of the Old Testament or the early Hebrew Church, nor was it ever mentioned by

Jesus. The Apocrypha (ancient books of unknown and doubtful origin) was not added to the Catholic Bible until the Council of Trent in 1546 A.D. when the Catholic Church incorporated the *Apocrypha* as a part of the inspired Word of God. This might have contributed to the post-koranic claims that the Judeo-Christian Bible was corrupted and rewritten,[16] despite proof to the contrary, and to bolster the koranic claim that Jesus was never crucified, died, and buried, much less having risen from the dead.[17] Other reasons Muslim scholars make the claim the Bible was corrupted, in spite of Allah's approval of it, might be because of the blatant discrepancies between the two books. It stands to reason if one book is to be discredited—from the Muslim's point of view—it has to be the Bible, or Islam crumbles under the weight of biblical and koranic contradictions.

Some Islamic scholars argue, as the Koran was dictated to Muhammad, he memorized its content, which was later transcribed by followers. As Muhammad's followers grew, he acquired a scribe to write down the revelations as he received them. This caused Islamic scholars to claim that the gospels, which were written down later, were not as accurate as the koranic revelations and, therefore, allowed for some of the discrepancies between the Bible and the Koran. (We would be neglectful if we did not point out—despite what some Islamic scholars might argue—that Allah takes credit in Sûrah 3 for equally authoring both the gospels as well as the Koran).

> He [Allah] hath revealed unto you (Muhammad) the Scripture with truth, confirming that which was (revealed) before it, even as He revealed the Torah and the Gospel (Sûrah 3:3, bracketed clarification mine).

Consider: If Muhammad was able to memorize the Koran as Allah gave it to him and retain it as long as he needed to, what was to prevent Allah from doing the same for Jesus *(Isa)* and all the other so-called biblical Muslim prophets who were literate? Yet even with this, was the Koran written down verbatim, as many Islamic scholars believe? There are some who would take issue with that belief. One documented example, as we discussed in the previous chapter regarding the accuracy of the Koran, shows how Muhammad allowed the words given to him by Allah to be rearranged by his scribe, Abdollah b. Abi Sarh, without any divine authority. We also pointed out—when Abdollah exposed that fact—the prophet of the "religion of peace" gave him a death sentence.

Allah challenged Christians in Sûrah 5:47 and 4:82 to compare the Koran, insisting that there were no discrepancies; therefore, it would not make any sense for Allah to have Christians use a corrupted Bible in critiquing the Koran because it would not be an accurate or compatible source. However, because the Koran was dictated over a period of 23 years, the Christians and Jews had plenty of time to compare the Koran with the Bible, which allowed them to discover the many discrepancies between the two.

Allah needed to abrogate or somehow overcome those earlier verses, which challenged the People of the Book to find problematic passages in the Koran. That is one of the reasons the doctrine of abrogation came into play because it allowed for Allah to change his mind as needed and thereby giving cover—through new revelations—which refuted or nullified those earlier problematic verses. In this case, new revelations were given regarding the accuracy of the Bible, which could then be used by Islamists to account for those differences.

> Have you any hope that they will be true to you when a party of them used to listen to the word of Allah, then used to change it, after they had understood it, knowingly? (Sûrah 2:75.)

Change the words in the Bible that conflict with the Koran? This certainly does appear to be an attempt to explain away the conflicts we have observed in the Koran; nevertheless, three verses later the Koran continues to suggest biblical alterations in order to explain away the many koranic discrepancies:

> And Lo [Watch]! there is a party of them who distort the Scripture with their tongues, that you may think that what they say is from the Scripture, when it is not from the Scripture. And they say: It is from Allah, when it is not from Allah; and they speak a lie

concerning Allah knowingly (Sûrah 3:78, bracketed clarification mine).

Apparently—when Muhammad was shown how the Bible undermines the credibility of the Koran—Allah once again came to Muhammad's aid with new koranic revelations which attacks the Christians and Jews who read the Bible and point out those discrepancies:

> Therefore woe [affliction] be unto those who [re]write the Scripture with their hands and then say, "This is from Allah," that they may purchase a small gain therewith. Woe [Grief] unto them for what their hands have written, and woe [anguish] unto them for that they earn thereby (Sûrah 2:79, bracketed clarifications mine).

It is interesting to realize that Sûrah 2:79 and Sûrah 3:78 were the 87th and 89th revelations given to Muhammad, respectively, out of 114 revelations. Those were revealed to Muhammad after he relocated to Yathrib (Medina). Muhammad's attempts to evangelize the local inhabitants as he did in Mecca were only natural. Because Christians and Jews were not like the Pagans of Mecca, Muhammad probably thought it would be easy to convince them that Allah was just another name for YAWA (Jehovah). Naturally, the monotheists of Yathrib would debate the Muslims and point out the discrepancies between the Bible and the Koran.

Muhammad gave the three previous verses when the oasis village he was living in was still known as Yathrib. As previously explained, he was forced to flee to Yathrib because it had become too dangerous for him to stay in Mecca. During his time there, Muhammad gained great respect and credibility by arbitrating between the Jewish tribes of the *Aws* and the Jewish tribe of the *Khazraj*. (Yathrib had over 20 other Jewish tribes,[18] as well as some Christian residents and Arabs.) Not only was Muhammad accepted, he also became a judge and a respected go-between among the various religious factions and tribes. His new religion of Islam began to grow, which enabled him to gain influence in the community. Because of his acceptance and his

111

reputation for being even-handed in settling disputes, Muhammad's credibility and Islam continued to grow—so much so that Muhammad was allowed to rename the City of Yathrib after himself. He named it "Medinat (City) al-Nabi (of the Prophet)."[19] It eventually became known simply as Medina.

As we previously explained, the literate Jews knew Scripture, so they were not convinced that the supposed biblical evidence being passed off on them—allegedly from Allah—was the real thing. As opportunities arose, they began to openly debate the Muslims in public and other places. Naturally, Muhammad did not want to lose his Muslim converts through convincing arguments made by those who had originally been given the Bible—the Jews. He needed new revelations from Allah to deal with the conflicting problem. Of course, Allah would not let Muhammad down, so once again came to his rescue:

> And because of their breaking their covenant, We have cursed them and made hard their hearts. They change words from their context and forget a part of that whereof they were admonished. Thou wilt not cease to discover treachery from all save a few of them. But bear with them and pardon them. Lo [Listen]! Allah loves the kindly.

> And with those who say: "Lo [Look]! we are Christians." We made a covenant [what covenant spoken of here is not clear], but they forgot a part of that whereof they were admonished [this passage is also unclear by not describing the reprimand]. Therefore, We have stirred up enmity and hatred among them till the Day of Resurrection, when Allah will inform them of their handiwork (Sûrah 5:13-14, bracketed clarification and commentary mine).

> Those were the (prophets) who received Allah's guidance: Copy the guidance they received; Say: "No reward for this do I ask of you: This is no less than a message for the nations."

No just estimate [guessing] of Allah do they make when they say: "Nothing does Allah send down to man (by way of revelation)" Say: "Who then sent down the Book which Moses brought?—a light and guidance to man: But you make it into (separate) sheets for show, while you conceal much (of its contents) [this seems to be suggesting that Christians withhold some of the Scriptures as opposed to rewriting the Scriptures]: therein were you taught that which you knew not—neither you nor your fathers." Say: "Allah (sent it down)": Then leave them to plunge in vain [foolish] discourse and trifling [frivolous] (Sûrah 6:90-91, Abdullah Yusuf Ali, bracketed clarifications and commentary mine).

Although the Koran suggests that Christians and Jews lied about the Bible's message to Muslims—in an effort to convert them away from Islam—it contradicts itself by stating that Allah makes it quite clear the Scriptures found in the Bible are from him. Rather than accuse the People of the Book of physically rewriting the Scriptures, as some verses in the Koran imply, this time Allah reinforces the fact that the Book (Bible) is accurate. We are told in Sûrah 6:90-91, that the true failing of the Christians and Jews is that they should have paid more attention to it. (In Volume III of *Islam Exposed: Science-Bible-Archaeology and Myths,* we go into more detail from a historical, archaeological, and scientific perspective regarding the incredible accuracy of the Bible.).

Because we are comparing the claims of Allah with the Bible's revelations—as we are challenged to do in Sûrah 5:47 and 6:114—we need to establish that the Koran acknowledges the inerrancy of Scripture. Accordingly, we have provided some of the important passages from the Koran, which prove Allah considers the Bible to be accurate! Yet in lieu of the preceding verses, one might wonder, if God is all-knowing, almighty and everywhere at once and is not bound by time—knowing the beginning from the end and the end from the beginning — (Isaiah 46:10; Revelation 1:17, 21:6), surely, He would have known in advance who would pervert His Word and prevent (protect) that from happening! Of course, He would! Even Allah (who claims to have given the Bible) makes that claim:

We have, without doubt, sent down the Message; and We will assuredly guard it (from corruption) (Sûrah 15:9, Abdullah Yusuf Ali).

If Allah has given us the Bible and the Koran, how can he make the claim that the Bible—but not the Koran—was corrupted? If Allah cannot protect the Bible from corruption, how is he now able to protect the Koran from corruption? What has changed? One might wonder how an all-knowing God could become confused and inconsistent. The following koranic passage is an important one to remember when judging the Koran in light of the Bible—especially when we find discrepancies between them—since Allah makes the claim that he wrote the Bible, which the Koran is supposed to complement:

O Children of Israel! Remember My favor wherewith I favored you, and fulfill your (part of the) covenant, I shall fulfill My (part of the) covenant, and fear Me.

And believe in that which I reveal, confirming that which you possess already (of the Scripture), and be not first to disbelieve therein, and part not with My revelations for a trifling price, and keep your duty unto Me (Sûrah 2:40-41).

Allah is telling Christians and Jews because he gave them the Bible, its covenant is true—and he has kept his part of the covenant—they need to keep their part as well. They have no excuse to be disobedient to him because they have the Scripture and should accept his revelations (old and new) under the name of Allah.

Is the Koran Compatible with the Bible as It Claims?

When comparing the Koran with the Bible, as the Koran tells us to do (Sûrah 5:47; 6:114), we have even more questions than answers. While the Koran makes the claim that the Bible is reliable and readers should use it as a means of judging the validity of the Koran, we find that by doing so, many koranic problems arise. One example is how

114

the Koran incorrectly incorporates an important passage from the biblical Chapter of Acts. The basis of the story is that God rescinded the kosher dietary laws, which were given to the Jews in Leviticus, Chapter 11 and Deuteronomy, Chapter 14:

> He [Peter] became hungry and wanted something to eat, and while the meal was being prepared, he fell into a trance. He saw Heaven opened and something like a large sheet being let down to earth by its four corners. It contained all kinds of four-footed animals, as well as reptiles and birds. Then a voice told him, "Get up, Peter, kill and eat."
>
> "Surely not, Lord!" Peter replied. "I have never eaten anything impure or unclean."
>
> The voice spoke to him a second time, "Do not call anything impure that God has made clean."
>
> This happened three times, and immediately the sheet was taken back to Heaven (Acts 10: 10-16, NIV, bracketed clarification mine).

The Koran seems to have incorporated this familiar Bible story into itself with some significant changes—ignoring completely the fundamental purpose of the story. In the next sûrah, we revisit the Banquet from Heaven story from Acts 10:10-16, only this time as it is portrayed in the Koran. In the koranic version, Jesus replaces the Apostle Peter:

> Jesus, son of Mary, said: "O Allah, Lord of us! Send down for us a table spread with food from Heaven, that it may be a feast for us, for the first of us and for the last of us, and a sign from Thee. Give us sustenance, for you are the Best of Sustainers" (Sûrah 5:114).

This is another example of how the Koran sometimes incorporates similar Bible verses out of context in a manner that seems biblical, but in reality, it is not. Again—so there is no misunderstanding—here is Allah's endorsement of the accuracy of Scripture by invoking no less a person than Jesus Himself to make the point:

And We caused Jesus, son of Mary, to follow in their footsteps, confirming that which was (revealed) before him in the Torah, and We bestowed on him the Gospel wherein is guidance and a light, confirming that which was (revealed) before it in the Torah—a guidance and an admonition unto those who ward off (evil) (Sûrah 5:46).

Here we read that Jesus supposedly knew the revelations of Allah by reading the Book, and thus, Allah is saying the Bible is trustworthy and approved by Jesus. The Koran continues:

Let the People of the Gospel judge by that which Allah has revealed therein. Whosoever judges not by that which Allah has revealed: such are evil-livers.

And unto you have We revealed the Scripture with the truth, confirming whatever Scripture was before it, and a watcher over it. So judge between them by that which Allah has revealed, and follow not their desires away from the truth which has come unto you. For each We have appointed a divine law and a traced-out way. Had Allah willed He could have made you one community. But that He may try you by that which He has given you (He has made you as you are). So vie one with another in good works. Unto Allah you will all return, and He will then inform you of that wherein you differ.

So judge between them by that which Allah has revealed, and follow not their desires, but beware of them lest they seduce you from some part of that which Allah has revealed unto you. And if they turn away, then know that Allah's Will is to smite them for some sin of theirs. Lo [Listen]! many of mankind are evil-livers.

Is it a judgment of the time of (Pagan) ignorance that they are seeking? Who is better than Allah for judgment to a people who have certainty (in their belief)?

O you who believe! Take not the Jews and the Christians for friends. They are friends one to another. He among you who takes them for friends is (one) of them. See! Allah guides not wrongdoing folk (Sûrah 5:47-51, bracketed clarification mine).[20]

Allah is telling the Muslims that even though the Christians and Jews have the "Book," which Allah revealed to them as his word, they ignored its teachings; therefore, because the Jews and Christians have not heeded Allah and recognized that the "Book" and the Koran are compatible, it will be to their own destruction. It does not benefit Muslims to become friends with Christians and Jews because they have rejected all that Allah has offered them, and they might lead them astray.

And this Qur'an is not such as could be forged by those besides Allah, but it is a verification of that which is before it and a clear explanation of the book, there is no doubt in it, from the Lord of the worlds (Sûrah 10:37, Mohammad Habib Shakir).

Once again, Allah is endorsing the Bible as having come from him and stating it is accurate because it was the first of his revelations for mankind before the Koran; yet the Bible only refers to one world— earth. We would not be faulted if we were to ask where the other worlds are and who inhabits them.

And argue not with the People of the Scripture unless it be in (a way) that is better, save with such of them as do wrong; and say: We believe in that which has been revealed unto us and revealed unto you; our Allah and your Allah is One, and unto Him we surrender (Sûrah 29:46).

According to this verse, Muslims should not be combative or argumentative with Jews and Christians because what is revealed in the Bible and Koran is from the same source. Their God is the Muslim god. This admonition of single authorship of the Bible and the Koran bestows the authority of the Bible by which to judge the Koran. Once again, we must remind ourselves that while the Bible and the God of the Bible never changes (Malachi 3:6), the Koran and Allah do change/abrogate (Sûrah 2:106).

How Do We Know Today's Bible Has Not Changed?

Many detractors of the Bible have suggested that because of the thousands of years involved in copying and translating Scriptures, many discrepancies must have occurred. This is a very valid argument and holds the judging of the Koran by what the Bible claims might not be a valid way to judge koranic passages. (The Koran is also subject to the same argument regarding its historical accuracy.) How do we know after all this time and the thousands of handwritten copies of the Bible that have been passed down to us are accurate or contain errors?

We know that before the advent of the printing press, Scriptures—and all books for that matter—had to be hand-copied by scribes and monks who might have misspelled a word or leave out a letter—including letters that are also words (e.g., "I" and "a") that would be the unintended reason for such minor and rare discrepancies. In no way do they alter the intended meaning. To be fair, there are some words that could have been translated better from the original inerrant sources, but they still preserve the overall narrative; and even though it may alter or lose some of its original nuance it still does not alter the basic concept of the dialogue.

Dead Sea Scrolls

With the discovery of the Dead Sea Scrolls, we have been afforded the opportunity to have actual ancient Scriptures and historical accounts, which, like a measuring stick, gives us the information to compare and measure the accuracy of biblical documents that have come down to us through the years. What have we learned? How do the Scriptures we have today compare with the writings from the third century before the birth of Christ, and how do the Scriptures we have today compare with writings from the early church of the first century A.D.?

In 1947, in a place called Qumran near the Dead Sea, manuscripts were discovered, which included copies of various fragments from virtually every book in the Old Testament except Esther.[21]

Fig. 2. Author doing research at Qumran

The discovery of these manuscripts has reduced the gap separating the [existing] copies by about a thousand years and is of great importance for the history of the OT. In addition to copies of the type of Hebrew texts used by the Septuagint translators, pieces of their actual Greek translation have also been found (emphasis added).[22]

The Dead Sea Scrolls have provided us with the assurance of the uncanny accuracy of the transmission of Scripture down through the ages. Norman Geisler points out how the information in Table 3 (see the next page) "... is important in showing that the predictive prophecies of the Old Testament were indeed made centuries before they were literally fulfilled."[23] We also know that the New Testament writers produced their works in the first century, most of which were written before 70 A.D. There are now fragments from the Gospel of Mark which were actually written in the first half of the first century not long after the time those events took place.[24]

Researchers found, some mostly fragmented Dead Sea Scrolls, in 11 different caves near Wadi Qumran along the northwest shore of the Dead Sea, 13 miles east of Jerusalem during the years of 1946 to 1957. They assigned identities to the scrolls according to which cave they were found in, numbered from Cave 1 through Cave 13. The majority of the scrolls were mostly written in Hebrew on lambskin parchments, but more were found written in Aramaic.

The writings from the Gospel of Mark were found in Cave 7. They were written on Papyrus, a very strong type of paper created from the papyrus plant, which had become very brittle after 2,000 years.

The scrolls found in Cave 7 are the only ones written in the Greek language. In some of the scroll remnants from this cave, researchers found several references to Jesus. In the gospels, including the Gospel of Mark, where Jesus told the disciples—regarding the Temple—that not one stone would be left standing. Some critics suggest that this was written after the destruction of the Temple in 70 A.D., yet the preserved fragments from Mark contain the writing style exclusive to Mark preserved in those fragments which support the totality of Mark's gospel. While some suggest that those writings are post-Temple destruction; we know the Romans destroyed that area in 68 A.D. and the Temple in 70 A.D.; yet the pieces of Mark, which the researchers found, are dated around 50 A.D., providing strong evidence that Jesus predicted the destruction of the Temple decades before the actual event.

Table 3: Earliest Copies of Existing Fragments of Scripture

TEXT	QUMRAN FRAGMENT IDENTIFICATION	APPROXIMATE DATE WRITTEN
Mark 4:28	7Q6	A.D.50
Mark 6:48	7Q15	A.D. ?
Mark 6:52, 53	7Q5	A.D.50
Mark 12:17	7Q7	A.D.50
Acts 27:38	7Q6	A.D. 60+
Romans 5:11, 12	7Q9	A.D. 70+
1 Timothy 3:16	7Q4	A.D. 70+
1 Timothy 4:1-3	7Q4	A.D. 70+
2 Peter 1:15	7Q10	A.D. 70+
James 1:23, 24	7Q8	A.D. 70+

Fragments from the Gospel of Mark are not the only New Testament fragments found at Qumran. A Spanish Jesuit paleographer identified the aforementioned fragments from Mark found in Cave 7, but also found "… nine fragments belonging to one gospel—Acts—and a few epistles, some of which were dated slightly later than 50 A.D., but extremely early."[25]

The Bible is the most documented book of antiquity. In the following table, we have selected just a few of the many famous books, which have been passed on to us from ancient times. Because of the volume of ancient authors and space constraints, we chose to select five of the more readily recognized authors of antiquity. Our examples, along with the New Testament, include such notables as Julius Caesar, Aristotle, Plato, etc. This is also comparable to all the other noted authors of antiquity not listed here due to space constraints.

Table 4: Comparison of Surviving Works of Antiquities

BOOK OF ANTIQUITY	AUTHOR	DATE WRITTEN	OLDEST COPIES	YEARS SEPARATING OLDEST COPIES FROM ORIGINAL BOOK	NUMBER OF COPIES SURVIVING
New Testament	Holy Spirit	50-100 A.D.	Fragments 50 A.D.	Approximately 20 years	5,366 copies
Gallic Wars	Julius Caesar	51 B.C.	900 A.D.	950 years	10
Documents regarding dialogues: Philosophy, Math and Science	Aristotle	384-322 B.C.	1100 A.D.	1,400 years	49
Historian who Cicero called "The Father of History"	Herodotus	480-425 A.D	900 A.D.	1,350 years	8
Documents regarding dialogues: Philosophy, Math & Science	Plato	400 B.C.	900 A.D.	1,300 years	8 copies
The Iliad and the Odyssey	Homer	800 B.C.	400 B.C.	400 years	643 copies

Most Muslim scholars believe that the Bible had become corrupted by the time of Muhammad, while the Koran has been accurately preserved. "But while the Qur'an is a medieval book from the seventh century, the New Testament is the most accurately copied book from the ancient world."[26]

To be clear, the purpose of this expose' is not to attack Islam or the Koran, but to respectfully allow ourselves to take the koranic challenge as found in Sûrah 5 which states:

> Let the people of the Gospel judge by what Allah has revealed therein. If any do fail to judge by (the light of) what Allah has revealed, they are (no better than) those who rebel (Sûrah 5: 47, Abdullah Yusuf Ali).

Allah is asking those who are either Jewish or Christian, "Why not consider the Koran? If it did not come from Allah (like the Bible), then you would have found problems with it," implying that there are no contradictions between the Koran and the Bible. Thus, through this three-volume series, we continue to take up the challenge to see if the Bible and the Koran are compatible, allowing biblical Scriptures to address those problematic claims made by the Koran, which will reveal if there are one or two authors involved in the creation of both books.

How Do We Know Today's Koran Has Not Changed?

Muslims believe that Allah protected the Koran, unlike the Bible, from corruption and cite this passage to prove it:

> We have, without doubt, sent down the Message; and We will assuredly guard it (from corruption) (Sûrah 15:9, Abdullah Yusuf Ali).

Nevertheless, as we learned in Chapter 4, within the first two decades after Muhammad's death, there were several different versions of the Koran circulating around the Middle East.[27] Muhammad al-Bukhari (810-870) documents how General Hudhayfah ibn al-Yaman, while observing soldiers in Iraq and Syria, reciting passages from their various copies of the Koran, noticed how they conflicted with each other. Realizing that if those soldiers would ever compare their copies of the Koran—which were supposed to be infallible as we just saw in

122

Sûrah 15:9—they might come to distrust the Koran as well as the religion of Islam. This could not be allowed, so General Hudhayfah ibn al-Yaman believed it was his duty to report this discrepancy to Caliph Uthman ibn Affan, the third caliph who succeeded Muhammad as head of the Muslim faith after the Prophet's death. Bukhari writes in the Hadith:

Sahih al-Bukhari, Volume 6, Book 61, Number 510

Narrated [by] Anas bin Malik:

... So Uthman sent a message to Hafsa saying, "Send us the manuscripts of the Quran so that we may compile the Quranic materials in perfect copies and return the manuscripts to you." Hafsa sent it to Uthman. Uthman then ordered [1] Zayd bin Thabit, [2] Abdullah bin Az-Zubair, [3] Sa'id bin Al-As and [4] Abdur Rahman bin Harith bin Hisham to rewrite the manuscripts in perfect copies. Uthman said to the three Quraishi men, "In case you disagree with Zayd bin Thabit on any point in the Quran, then write it in the dialect of Quraish, the Quran was revealed in their tongue." They did so, and when they had written many copies, 'Uthman returned the original manuscripts to Hafsa. 'Uthman sent to every Muslim province one copy of what they had copied and ordered that all the other Quranic materials, whether written in fragmentary manuscripts or whole copies, be burnt. Zayd bin Thabit added, "A Verse from Surat Ahzab was missed by me when we copied the Quran and I used to hear Allah's Apostle reciting it. So we searched for it and found it with Khuzaima bin Thabit Al-Ansari. (That Verse was): 'Among the Believers are men who have been true in their covenant with Allah' " (bracketed clarifications mine).

Therefore, the version settled on by Caliph Uthman was not the original, but merely a compilation of various koranic versions. In light of this fact, the Koran produced by Caliph Uthman would have to contain some unavoidable discrepancies from the original revelations given to Muhammad by the angel Gabriel; consequently, this contradicts the claim the Koran has remained exactly as it was given to Muhammad without any corruption.

In Volume II of *Islam Exposed: The Koran: Selected Sûrahs with Commentary and Bible Comparisons*, we compiled from Volume I of the Koran some of the longer chapters (sûrahs) we believe are of particular interest to Christians and Jews. It is interesting to realize that the Koran—unlike other religious books—cancels out or changes Allah's commandments. Therefore, what might have once been a conciliatory passage, was later canceled when it became necessary for Muhammad to deal with those troubling difficulties he encountered from time to time. That's the reason many confused people have asked, "How do we know which passage is the correct one to follow"? (Answer: The last one given cancels all the ones that were before it.)

In Volume II, we compare the pseudo-biblical history the Koran presents as being factual with those of the actual biblical sources, allowing us to review the Koran in light of the Scriptures. We will also share some of the chapters found in Volume II of the Koran, which represent the earlier, first, and shorter revelations given to Muhammad at the beginning of his ministry. That was done in accordance with the recommendations made by Allah, who challenged us to do so in Sûrahs 4:82; 5:47 and 2:23.

NOTES:

1. Muhammad Marmaduke Pickthall, *The Koran*, Introduction xxii.
2. Seyyed Hossein Nasr, *Ideals and Realities of Islam* (London: George Allen & Unwin, 1975), 44.
3. Zdravko Stefanovic, *Aramaic of Daniel in the Light of Old Aramaic* (Sheffield: Sheffield Academic Press, 1992), 32.
4. Dr. Ghassan Hanna Shathaya, "Who Are the Chaldeans?" Chaldeans online, 1999. Web. 16 January 2015. The language of the Chaldean people is Syriac, which is essentially Aramaic (a different dialect than that spoken by Jesus Christ), with a dose of Akkadian, the original language of the Assyrian, Babylonian and Chaldean tribes.

5. Ergun Mehmet Caner and Emir Fethi Caner, *Unveiling Islam* (Grand Rapids: Kregel Publ., 2002), 229.

6. "But there were false prophets also among the people, even as there shall be false teachers among you, who privy [secretly] shall bring in damnable heresies, even denying the Lord that bought them, and bring upon themselves swift destruction" (2 Peter 2:1, bracketed clarification mine). We also have warnings from the Apostle Paul: "Now I beseech you, brethren, mark them which cause divisions and offenses contrary to the doctrine which you have learned; and avoid them" (Romans 16:17); "Beloved, believe not every spirit, but try the spirits whether they are of God: because many false prophets are gone out into the world" (I John 4:1); "For many deceivers are entered into the world, who confess not that Jesus Christ is come in the flesh. This is a deceiver and an antichrist" (2 John 1:7); "Beware lest any man spoil you through philosophy and vain deceit, after the tradition of men, after the rudiments of the world, and not after Christ" (Colossians 2:8); "If there come any unto you, and bring not this doctrine, receive him not into Your house, neither bid him God speed" (2 John 1:10). Jesus Himself warned: "Beware of false prophets, which come to you in sheep's clothing, but inwardly they are ravening wolves" (Matthew 7:15); "And many false prophets shall rise, and shall deceive many" (Matthew 24: 11); "For there shall arise false Christs, and false prophets, and shall show great signs and wonders; insomuch that, if it were possible, they shall deceive the very elect" (Matthew 24:24).

7. "Gospel of Thomas," *Wikipedia: The Free Encyclopedia*. Web. 15 December 2014.

8. "And Joses, who by the apostles was surnamed Barnabas (which is, being interpreted, the son of consolation), a Levite *and* of the country of Cyprus..." (Acts 4: 36).

9. "Then tidings of these things came unto the ears of the church which was in Jerusalem: and they sent forth Barnabas that he should go as far as Antioch ... For he was a good man, and full of the Holy Ghost and full of faith: and much people was added unto the Lord. Then departed Barnabas to Tarsus, for to seek Saul: And when he had found him, he brought him unto Antioch. And it came to pass, that a whole year they assembled themselves with

125

the church, and taught much people. And the disciples were called Christians first in Antioch" (Acts 11:22-26).

10. Cyril Glassé, *The Concise Encyclopedia of Islam* (New York: Harper & Row, 1989), 64.

11. *The Gospel of Barnabas* (Brooklyn: A&B Publishers Group, 1993), 6. There are 27 pages of the Introduction to Islamic propaganda, followed by chapters that are no more than one or two paragraphs each; however, the book has over 270 pages.

12. *The Gospel of Barnabas*, 54.

13. *The Gospel of Barnabas*, 123.

14. *New American Bible*, Saint Joseph Edition (New York: Catholic Book Publishing Co., 1970), Old Testament: 469, 485, 513, 546, 750, 771, 964.

15. *New American Bible*, Old Testament (toward the end of the book of Daniel): 1039-1041.

16. Norman L. Geisler, *Encyclopedia of Christian Apologetics* (Grand Rapids: Baker Books, 2000), 31. "At the Councils of Florence and Trent ...the infallible proclamation was made accepting the *Apocrypha* as part of the inspired Word of God. Some Catholic scholars claim that the earlier Council of Florence (1442 A.D.) made the same pronouncement; however, this council claimed no infallibility and neither council's [Council of Florence 1442 A.D. or the Council of Trent, 1546 A.D.] decision has any real basis in Jewish history, the New Testament or early Christian history."

17. As we discussed in the Introduction, the Koran claims Jesus never was crucified. (Sûrah 4:157).

18. Abdullah Rahim, "Jews of Yathrib," *Exploring Islam*, n.p., n.d. Web. 17 Sept. 2015. "Altogether, the Jews were already well established in Yathrib with over 20 tribes and around 60 castles when the Arab tribes of Aus and Khazraj migrated to Yathrib. In other words, Jews were in a very healthy political and economic condition when the ancestors of Ansar (Helpers) of Yathrib reached and settled in the centre. Jews were split into a number of tribes, the strongest ones near the time of the Prophet (PBUH) being Banū Qurayza, Banū Nazeer and Banū Qaynuqa."

19. *World Heritage Encyclopedia*, "Yathrib," n.p., n.d., Web. 22 Feb. 2015. "The Arabic word, *madinah* simply means 'city' Before the

advent of Islam, the city was known as 'Yathrib' and was personally renamed by Muhammad."

"Medina," *UK Hajj Umrah | UK Hajj Umrah Medina*. Web. 22 December 2017. "Yathrib was this city's former name and later it was renamed to Medina by Muhammad (PBUH) himself."

20. Regarding the last sentence in Sûrah 5:51 where it states, "Allah guides not the wrongdoing folk," we have only to look at Sûrah 6:35 where we are told just the opposite—if he wanted to—Allah "could gather them together unto true guidance:" (Sûrah 6:35b). In context: "If their spurning is hard on your mind, yet if you were able to seek a tunnel in the ground or a ladder to the skies and bring them a sign, — (what good?). If it were Allah's will, He could gather them together unto true guidance: so be not thou amongst those who are swayed by ignorance (and impatience)!" (Sûrah 6:35, Abdullah Yusuf Ali.)

21. Walter A. Elwell, *Evangelical Dictionary of Theology*, 13th ed. (Grand Rapids: Baker Books, 1997), 297.

22. Elwell, 298.

23. Geisler, *Baker Encyclopedia of Christian Apologetics*, 189.

24. John Farrell, "Fragments of Mark's Gospel May Date to 1st Century," *Forbes*. Forbes Magazine, 27 Feb. 2012. Web. 13 May 2013.

25. Geisler, *Baker Encyclopedia of Christian Apologetics*, 533.

26. Geisler, 332.

27. Jane Dammen McAuliffe, *The Cambridge Companion to the Qur'an* (Cambridge [UK]: Cambridge Univ. Press, 2006), 31-33; 45, 59.

CHAPTER 6

THE KORAN AND THE BIBLE:
FOUNDERS, FUNDAMENTALS, PROBLEMS,
AND HERESIES

It is essential for those who want to learn about Islam—as compared to Judaism and Christianity—to understand that in Islam, all the important people in the Bible—from Adam on—are considered Muslim prophets. While the Christians and Jews have the Bible, Muslims not only claim the Bible was given to them by Allah—and thereby included in Islam—but in addition, Muslims have the Koran (Qur'an) and the Hadith. The Koran is believed to be Allah's last and final revelation to mankind. The Hadith, Islam's second holiest writings, were collected by several respected Muslims and are contained in many volumes of what is considered by Muslims to be second only in importance to the Koran. The (i.e., Hadith, which means "statement" or "talk,") is sometimes referred to as Sunnah, although Sunnah is more in line with the deeds of Muhammad. The six most well-respected compilers of the Hadith are (1) Sahih (i.e., genuine or authentic); al-Bukhari; (2) Sahih Muslim (3) Sunnah Abu Dawood; (4) Sunnah Nasai; (5) Sunnah (i.e., way or road) Tirmidhi, and (6) Sunnah ibn Majah. Besides using the Koran, we will also be citing passages from the Hadith because of their important influence over practicing Muslims and their clergy.

FUNDAMENTALS GENERALLY AGREED ON BY THE THREE MONOTHEISTIC RELIGIONS

Genesis 1:1: The Beginning

In the beginning God created the Heavens and the earth (Genesis 1:1). We read that God created everything, including the stars, animals, people, plants, and the oceans. Next, God created light and then separated the light from the darkness. In the third chapter of Genesis, we see how sin came into the world almost at the very beginning. It was through Eve—the first woman—who fell from grace (Genesis 3:1-7), not because of a desire to become wealthy, not because she desired another man other than her husband, or that she lusted over power or possessions. She was deceived into the sin of rebellion against God by listening to the serpent who convinced her to question God's Word, and Adam—who was responsible for his family of two—went along with Eve. That original sin lies at the heart of most problems today, including various religions that have come down through time.

> Now the serpent was more subtle than any beast of the field which the LORD God had made. And he said unto the woman, "Yea, has God said ..." [at this point, you may insert any biblical challenge from the Koran you have read, heard or called into question] (Genesis 3:1, bracketed clarification mine).

EXAMPLE:

> Now the serpent was more subtle than any beast of the field which the LORD God had made. And he said unto the women, "Yea, has God said..." *"that Jesus said take me and my mother for two gods beside Allah?"* (Genesis 3:1 + Sûrah 5:116a)

We know from the Bible that Adam and Eve believed in only one God, and before the flood, many others also acknowledged one God, including a man named Enoch, who was Adam's grandson from his son, Cain (Genesis 4:17). Cain was the first man to bring murder into the world when he killed his brother, Abel (Genesis 4:8). We also know that Enoch acknowledged only the one God of the Bible because he walked with God and was taken up to Heaven by Him before he died (Genesis 5:24). We are also aware of another man who lived almost a thousand years after Enoch and walked with God—his name was Noah. By the time of Noah, the world had become extremely wicked and violent—people were constantly plotting to do evil (Genesis 6:5-6), so God told Noah to build an ark to save himself, his wife, sons, and their wives, along with seven pair of clean animals and one pair of unclean animals (Genesis 7:2).

After the flood, we read about a descendant of Noah's son, Shem, who also believed and walked with the one true God of creation. His name was Abram, which God later changed to Abraham (Genesis 17:5). Before Abraham's name was changed, God prophesied that He would bless him and his wife, Sarah, and through her, Abraham would be the father of many nations (Genesis 12:2); however, during her childbearing age, Sarah never became pregnant and believed that God had closed her womb. Nevertheless, God does not judge time like we do (Psalm 90:4; 2 Peter 3:8), so Abraham and Sarah continued to grow older and still no child for Sarah.

Sarah had a handmaiden she acquired when they went to Egypt (Genesis 12:10). Because Sarah believed God had closed her womb, she invoked a Middle Eastern tradition of allowing one's slave to bear a child for her and gave Hagar, her Egyptian handmaiden, to her husband Abraham (Genesis 16:1-4). Hagar conceived, and her child was named Ishmael.

Even though Sarah doubted God's Word, God never lies or misleads (Numbers 23:19), nor is He mocked (Galatians 1:8). When He says He is going to do something, He does it. Years later, when Abraham and Sarah were very old, God sent His angels to reconfirm His covenant that Sarah would indeed bear Abraham a son (Genesis 18:10-11), but Sarah laughed:

"Where is your wife, Sarah?" they asked him.

"There, in the tent," he said.

Then one of them said, "I will surely return to you about this time next year, and Sarah, your wife, will have a son."

Now Sarah was listening at the entrance to the tent, which was behind him. Abraham and Sarah were already very old, and Sarah was past the age of childbearing. So Sarah laughed to herself as she thought, "After I am worn out, and my lord [Abraham] is old, will I now have this pleasure?"

Then the LORD said to Abraham, "Why did Sarah laugh and say," 'Will I really have a child, now that I am old?' "Is anything too hard for the LORD? I will return to you at the appointed time next year, and Sarah will have a son" (Genesis 18: 9-14, bracketed clarification mine).

God reminded Abraham He promised Sarah would conceive and bear a son:

And I will bless her, and give you a son also of her: yea, I will bless her, and she shall be a mother of nations; kings of people shall be of her.

Then Abraham fell upon his face, and laughed, and said in his heart, "Shall a child be born unto him that is an hundred years old? and shall Sarah, that is ninety years old, bear?"

And Abraham said unto God, "O that Ishmael might live before You!"

And God said, "Sarah your wife shall bear you a son indeed; and you shall call his name Isaac: and I will establish my covenant with him for an everlasting covenant, and with his seed after him" (Genesis 16:19).

God understood that Abraham also loved his son, Ishmael, whose mother was Sarah's Egyptian handmaiden, Hagar. God promised Abraham:

And as for Ishmael, I have heard you: Behold, I have blessed him, and will make him fruitful, and will multiply him exceedingly; twelve princes shall he beget [reproduce], and I will make him a great nation (Genesis 17:20, bracketed clarification mine).

So there is no misunderstanding about who the son of the covenant is, God made it very clear to Abraham:

But my covenant will I establish with Isaac, which Sarah shall bear unto you at this set time in the next year (Genesis 17:21)

Chart 1: Abraham's Sons and Intermarriages. Covenant Line Thick Gray on Right.

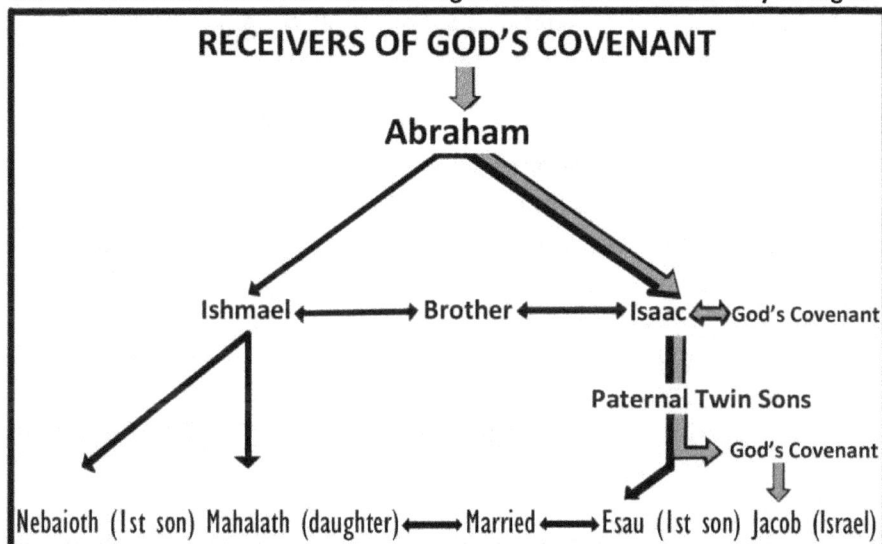

RECEIVERS OF GOD'S COVENANT

Abraham

Ishmael ⟷ Brother ⟷ Isaac ⟺ God's Covenant

Paternal Twin Sons

God's Covenant

Nebaioth (1st son) Mahalath (daughter) ⟷ Married ⟷ Esau (1st son) Jacob (Israel)

Abraham was told that the land of Canaan (i.e., Israel) would be given as a covenant blessing to his and Sarah's descendants through Isaac for forever, but first, the Jews would be held as slaves in Egypt for 400 years (Genesis 15:13; Exodus 12:40-41). Neither Ishmael nor his children were ever enslaved as an ethnic group.

We can see in the above chart how the covenant line of Abraham was through Isaac and his grandson, Jacob, whom God later renamed "Israel" (Genesis 35:10). It was Israel and his children (the Patriarchs of the twelve tribes of Israel) who had to leave the Promised Land because it was undergoing a famine, which forced them to seek refuge in Egypt. That was made possible because one of Israel's sons, Joseph, had become Egypt's Prime Minister under the Hyksos Dynasty. The children of Israel remained there as free people until the Hyksos dynasty fell, and a new Pharaoh arose who was not familiar with Joseph (Exodus 1:8). It was then that the Hebrews became enslaved, forcing them to fulfill the prophecy given to Abraham in Genesis 15:13.

It would be good for us to pause here for a moment and make the observation that while a prophecy of this nature is common in the Bible, it is noticeably missing from the Koran. This brings up the question if Allah and the God of the Bible are supposed to be the same as Muslims insist, then what happened to Allah's ability to predict the future in the Koran?

After the Jews' approximate 400 years in Egypt, God raised up a great prophet—Moses. He became famous because of his walk with God. As a result, Moses was able to free his people from slavery (Exodus 12:31-41). After their escape from Egypt, Moses went up to the mountain of Sinai (Exodus 19:20-25), where God gave the Law (Ten Commandments) to him (Exodus 20:1-17). In Matthew 5:17, the Law was fulfilled through Jesus.

We must point out that from the time of Abraham, Isaac, and Jacob, throughout the generations of Moses, King David, and Jesus, Abraham's promised children, through Sarah, only believed in one God. It is also important to note that until the time of Muhammad, the children of Ishmael were polytheists. This is not to say that Ishmael was a polytheist; because of his upbringing in the house of Abraham,[1] he probably believed in one God.

On the other hand, Hagar, Ishmael's mother, was born in Egypt, which was a Pagan polytheistic culture. We are never told if she ever converted to the belief in only one God or not; if not, she would have remained a polytheist. She could have been a monotheist, but her selection of a wife for Ishmael from among the Pagan women in her country leaves us doubtful.

We do know that Abraham chose his wife Sarah from among his family, as did Isaac and Jacob, as well as knowing that Abraham's son, Isaac, and his descendants were monotheists, while the Arab descendants of Ishmael were polytheists. It was the Arab descendants of Ishmael who believed in 360 different gods, of whom Allah was one.

Regarding Ishmael and his mother, Hagar, the Bible only states:

> Early the next morning Abraham got some food and a bottle of water. The bottle was made out of animal skin. He gave the food and water to Hagar. He placed them on her shoulders. Then he sent her away with the boy. She went on her way and wandered in the desert of Beersheba [in the land of Israel].
>
> When the water in the bottle was gone, she put the boy under a bush. Then she went off and sat down nearby. She was about as far away as a person can shoot an arrow. She thought, "I cannot stand to watch the boy die." As she sat nearby, she began to sob.
>
> God heard the boy crying. Then the angel of God called out to Hagar from Heaven. He said to her, "What is the matter, Hagar? Do not be afraid. God has heard the boy crying as he lies there. Lift the boy up. Take him by the hand. I will make him into a great nation."
>
> Then God opened Hagar's eyes. She saw a well of water. So she went and filled the bottle with water. And she gave the boy a drink.
>
> God was with the boy as he grew up. He lived in the desert and learned to shoot with a bow. While he was living in the Desert of Paran [possibly Mecca], his mother got him a wife from Egypt (Genesis 21:14-21, NIV, clarifications mine).

Yet, strangely enough, seven centuries after the advent of Christ, Muhammad had a revelation, which varies quite a bit from the Bible's history of recorded events as we will read in Volume II of *Islam*

Exposed: The Koran: Selected Sûrahs with Commentary and Bible Comparisons, and Volume III, *Science-Bible-Archaeology and Myths.*

DEPARTURE POINT OF ISLAM
FROM THE JUDEO-CHRISTIAN SCRIPTURES

Revising Biblical History in Order to Promote Prophetic Credibility Through Ishmael and His Descendant, Muhammad

Abraham lived until approximately 2,000 B.C. It was not until the seventh century A.D., over two and a half millennia in the future, when Muhammad made the startling statement—for the first time in history—that his ancestor, Ishmael, was offered as a sacrifice to God in Mecca (as opposed to Isaac in Jerusalem as the Bible states in Genesis 22:1-12). It is one of the observances Muslims make during the month of the pilgrimage (see **Eid al-Adha** in the glossary located under **Eid**).

A 16th-century miniature painting in an Ottoman Turkish manuscript showing Abraham sacrificing his son, Ishmael and Abraham tossed into the fire by Nimrod.

In an excerpt from the Koran, we read that Abraham asked Allah if Ishmael was a righteous son, so Allah tested Ishmael to see if he was righteous enough to allow himself to be offered as a human sacrifice to Allah. Abraham had to share in this trial to prove his loyalty to Allah. Because they both passed the test, Allah rewarded Abraham with another son, Isaac:

"O my Lord! Grant me a righteous (son)!"

So We gave him the good news of a boy ready to suffer and forbear. Then, when (the son) reached (the age of) (serious) work with him, he said: "O my son! I see in vision that I offer you in sacrifice: Now see what your view is!" (The son) said: "O my father! Do as you are commanded: you will find me, if Allah so wills one practicing Patience and Constancy!" So when they had both submitted their wills (to Allah), and he had laid him prostrate on his forehead (for sacrifice), We called out to him "O Abraham!"

"You have already fulfilled the vision!"—thus indeed do We reward those who do right.—For this was obviously a trial—And We ransomed him with a momentous sacrifice:

And We left (this blessing) for him among generations (to come) in later times:

"Peace and salutation to Abraham!"

Thus indeed do We reward those who do right for he was one of our believing Servants (Sûrah 37:100-111, Abdullah Yusuf Ali).

Now we read how Allah gave Abraham the news that he was going to have another son, Isaac, as a reward for being so obedient and his willingness to sacrifice Ishmael:

And We gave him the good news of Isaac—a prophet,—one of the Righteous (Sûrah 37:112, Abdullah Yusuf Ali).

Pickthall clarifies the meaning better for us when he translates this passage:

And we gave him tidings of the birth of Isaac, a prophet of the righteous (Sûrah 37:112, Marmaduke Pickthall).

The Koran's conclusion is that it was Ishmael, not Isaac, who was the intended sacrifice by his father, Abraham.

However, for the past 4,000 years, the Bible has told a different story than the relatively more recent koranic version. In Genesis 21, Hagar and Ishmael were told to leave Abraham and his family—before the sacrificial event recorded in Genesis 22:

> But Sarah saw that the son whom Hagar the Egyptian had borne to Abraham was mocking, and she said to Abraham, "Get rid of that slave woman and her son, for that woman's son will never share in the inheritance with my son Isaac."

> The matter distressed Abraham greatly because it concerned his son. But God said to him, "Do not be so distressed about the boy and your slave woman. Listen to whatever Sarah tells you, because it is through Isaac that your offspring will be reckoned. I will make the son of the slave into a nation also because he is your offspring" [child]

While the birth order is correct in both the Koran and the Bible, it stops there as the sacrificial event happens "sometime later" in the Genesis account. It precedes the koranic account by some twenty-seven centuries after Ishmael had been sent away and only Isaac remained:

> Sometime later God tested Abraham. He said to him, "Abraham!" "Here I am," he replied.

> Then God said, "Take your son, your only son, whom you love— Isaac—and go to the region of Moriah. Sacrifice him there as a burnt offering on a mountain I will show you" (Genesis 22:1-2, NIV).

Why It Matters Whether Abraham Offered Isaac Or Ishmael as a Sacrifice

Why does it matter which son—Ishmael or Isaac—was offered as a sacrifice? It is because Abraham's sacrifice of his only son of the covenant was a dramatic foreshadowing of God's sacrifice through His Son for the salvation of mankind—a fact rejected by the Koran (Sûrah 4:157).

The story of Ishmael is important in the Koran, but only as a means of deflecting from the biblical importance of Jerusalem and Mount Moriah, where both Abraham and Jesus made their sacrifices. The Koran redirects it toward Mecca and the land of Muhammad. By the Koran claiming that Abraham offered Ishmael as a sacrifice, the lineage of Ishmael takes on the impression of more importance with the intent of establishing Ishmael, not Isaac, firmly in God's prophetic plan. Had this actually happened, it would have made possible for Ishmael and his descendants, of which Muhammad is one, to have become revered as the prophets of the one true God (monotheism) in a nation of 360 Pagan gods (polytheists).

Historically, it is also very important which son Abraham intended to sacrifice—Isaac or Ishmael—because of the prophetic relevance between Isaac and Jesus, which has everything to do with the prophetic continuity of the Bible. It could not have been Ishmael because the Bible clearly states that the oracles (prophecies) of God are solely committed to Israel (Romans 3:1-3).

ABRAHAM OFFERED ISAAC ON MOUNT MORIAH

Table 5. The Relationship between the Sacrifice of Isaac in the Old Testament and the Sacrifice of Jesus in the New Testament

ISAAC	JESUS
Background: Isaac had a miraculous birth. His mother, Sarah, was 90 years old, *way past menopause* and, therefore, impossible to become pregnant—yet she did (Genesis 17:17).	Background: Jesus had a miraculous birth. His mother, Mary, was a virgin who had never known a man and, therefore, impossible to become pregnant—yet she did (Luke 1:34; Isaiah 7:14).
The Patriarch, Abraham, offered his only son to God (Genesis 22:9-10).	God offered His only Son for mankind (John 3:16-17).
Isaac carried wood to his place of sacrifice (Genesis 22:6).	Jesus carried wood to His place of sacrifice (John 19:17).
The lamb's head (i.e., horns), which God provided, was trapped in a thicket (Genesis 22:13).	Jesus, the Lamb of God, had a crown made from a thicket of thorns on His head (Matthew 27:29).
Isaac called out to his father (Genesis 22:7).	Jesus called out to his Father (Matthew 27:46; Mark 15).
The threat of death hung over Isaac for three days until he was delivered from death on the third day (Genesis 22:4).	Death was on Jesus for three days until He was delivered from death on the third day (Matthew 16:21; Mark 16:2-4; Luke 18:33, 23:33, 24:5-6; John 20:1-9).
Because God provided a sacrificial male lamb, Isaac was spared death (Genesis 22:4).	Because God provided Jesus as a sacrificial male lamb, all who believe in Him will be spared death (Isaiah 53:7; John 1:29, 36; Revelation 5:8-14, 7:9-17).

THE HISTORY OF THE MANDATORY HAJJ
(OR PILGRIMAGE)
TO THE KA'ABA IN MECCA

Muslim tradition dates this event beginning with Adam, whom they claim, built the Ka'aba as the first house of worship on earth, an event noticeably missing from the Bible. This veneration of the Ka'aba and the pilgrimage (or Hajj) to it has allegedly continued throughout the ages.

The story says that Abraham traveled to the area known as Mecca with Hagar, his Egyptian slave, and their son, Ishmael, where he left them with very little food and water. (It must be pointed out that those events are not found in the Bible.) Desperate for food, Hagar began running back and forth between two small hills known as "Safa" and "Marwa," which is played out again and again by Muslim pilgrims every year. Finally, the angel Gabriel—who gave Muhammad the Koran—answered Abraham's prayer for the safety of Hagar and Ishmael by providing a spring of water as they were frantically digging at the ground with only their fingers, thereby saving them.

The Koran also states that it was Abraham and Ishmael who built the Ka'aba in Mecca (Sûrah 2:127). While this makes for an amusing story, the historical facts—which we will explore later in greater detail—tell us otherwise.

The Hajj: A Pagan Tradition [2]

As for the Hajj, the inhabitants of Mecca had the annual event of a "Holy Month" that was a very profitable means of income before Muhammad conquered the city. We even read in the Koran about the Pagan holy month, which was eventually replaced by the Muslim Holy month of Ramadan—when Muhammad waged war against the Quraish in what has become known as *the Battle of Badar*—which occurred either on March 13th or the 17th of Ramadan 2 A.H.[3] (Ramadan was a holy tribal truce month.) This particular battle is interesting because Muhammad killed someone during the battle, a very serious offense to Pagan worshippers. It was not permissible to kill anyone during the Pagan holy month. This certainly should not have presented a problem to someone claiming not to be a Pagan, but a monotheist who only worshiped Allah, yet Muhammad had to justify his murderous actions and seek some kind of dispensation from Allah for defaming the Pagan holy month. Once again, Allah came to Muhammad's rescue by providing him with another koranic abrogation:

> They question thee (O Muhammad) with regard to warfare in the sacred month. Say: "Warfare therein is a great (transgression), but to turn (men) from the way of Allah, and to disbelieve in Him and in the Inviolable Place of Worship, and to expel His people thence, is a greater sin with Allah; for persecution is worse than killing. And they will not cease from fighting against you till they have made you renegades from your religion, if they can. And whoso becomes a renegade and dies in his disbelief: such are they whose works have fallen both in the world and the Hereafter. Such are rightful owners of the Fire: they will abide therein" (Sûrah 2:217).

Prior to Muhammad's conquest of Mecca, the Ka'aba was a shrine with many stone idols, which honored the 360 Arabian pagan gods and housed the Black Stone, which was to become sacred to the worship of Allah. It must be pointed out here that there is much controversy regarding the Black Stone and its origins (many believe it is a meteorite [4]). Some Muslims date the Black Stone back to Adam and Eve[5] and the building of the Ka'aba by Abraham and his son Ishmael.[6] Nevertheless, although the Black Stone is mentioned as having existed before Islam, we are unable to find any specific veneration of the stone itself outside of Muslim sources. Some say that Muhammad placed the Black Stone in the Ka'aba, but, as with Islam, that too is murky.

After Muhammad conquered Mecca on Ramadan 18, he sought to make the transition easier for the Pagan Meccans not unlike the Catholic Church had done to broaden its appealed to their Pagan converts when it blended the veneration of Ishtar (Easter) Saturnalia

(Christmas) and the Celtic festival of Samhain (All Saints Day/Halloween). Muhammad re-commissioned the building known as the Ka'aba, along with the Black Stone, which represented Allah, and renamed the Pagan holy month, Ramadan, thus transforming them into symbols of Islam. (Many Arabs of the day worshiped stones or had stones as representations of their Pagan gods.)

Muhammad's accommodations did not stop there. Because the city of Mecca depended so heavily on the revenues generated by the yearly Hajj—an event which predated Muhammad and Islam—the Prophet of Islam not only agreed to allow the continuation of the Hajj, but made it the second pillar of Islam. Therefore, it became mandatory for every Muslim, who was able to make the Hajj to Mecca at least once in his or her lifetime.

The Koran States It Was Abraham and Ishmael Who Built the Ka'aba in Mecca

The Koran puts a high priority on Ishmael because it is believed by Arabs, as well as by Jews and Christians, that Muhammad and the Arabs are his descendants. It is also central to Islam—as we previously saw—to downplay the significance of Isaac by redefining the importance of Ishmael because it was fundamental to Muhammad's new religion—Islam. For that reason, the Koran alleges that Abraham and his son, Ishmael, were the ones who originally constructed the ancient place of Meccan worship known as the Ka'aba as we read below:

> And when We made the House (at Makkah) [Mecca] a resort for mankind and sanctuary, (saying): "Take as your place of worship the place where Abraham stood (to pray)." And We imposed a duty upon Abraham and Ishmael, (saying): "Purify My house for those who go around and those who meditate therein and those who bow down and prostrate themselves (in worship)" (Sûrah 2:125).

We are told Abraham and Ishmael were together in the region of Mecca, where they were praying when Allah told them to purify the

Ka'aba, a box-like building where Muslims respectfully walk around in a circle. The confusing part of this is that the Koran implies that the Ka'aba already existed and instructed Abraham to "Purify My house ...;" yet in the very next verse below, we are told Abraham and Ishmael are the ones who built the Ka'aba from the ground up. Which is it?

And when Abraham and Ishmael were raising the foundations of the House, (Abraham prayed): "Our Lord! Accept from us (this duty)." Lo! [Look!] (Sûrah 2:127.)

Dr. Rafat Amari states that when researching the Black Stone of the Ka'aba, his team's research proves that Abraham and Ishmael could not have built the temple (Dr. Amari's term) in Mecca. There is no archaeological evidence indicating that Abraham or his son were ever together at the alleged site where the Ka'aba stands, which they are supposed to have jointly built. Dr. Amari acknowledges that Muhammad's biographer, Ibn Ishaq, gives credit for the building of the Meccan temple directly to Abraham and its subsequent operation by Ishmael, followed by Nabaioth.[7] The Tribe of Nabaioth supposedly inhabited Mecca when Abraham was supposed to have served at the temple in Mecca.

The saga continued. The Yemenite tribe of Khuza'ah defeated Jurhum, who then hid the Black Stone in a spring called "Zamzam." Jurhum and his companions then covered the spring with dust. It is understood that Jurhum lived in Mecca until the dam at Marib was damaged when he and his adversaries, the Khuzaahites, had to flee around 150 A.D.[8]

Dr. Amari goes into a great amount of detail regarding the spring and the events leading up to its use as a hiding place for the Black Stone. He is troubled by the claim that it laid hidden for some 300 years unnoticed, covered by mere dust as claimed. As Dr. Amari states:

To claim that a spring existed in a city for 2,500 years before Jurhum succeeded in covering it for another three centuries is an impossible assentation, since the springs of Arabia were significantly more important to the Bedouins than the Red Sea itself. You may hide the sea from the eyes of thirsty tribes, but you cannot hide a spring and its location for that amount of time.

Writers of the eighth century, who depended on information from the time of Muhammad, indicated that a Himyarite Pagan built the Ka'aba at the beginning of the fifth century, along with Yemeni leader, Asa'd Abu Karb. (Historical documentation has provided the construction date of the Ka'aba in Mecca toward the beginning of the fifth century.) Asa'd Abu Karb was also known as Abu Karb Asa'd and reigned in Yemen from 410 to 435 A.D.[9] The fact Islamic historians admit that Asa'd Abu Karb was the first ruler in history to "dress the Ka'aba," is a significant indicator that he was the true builder of the Ka'aba.[10]

Dr. Amjari continues to address the claim that the Black Stone was hidden for three or four centuries. The "stone" is-considered the main sacred element in the *Ka'aba* (the black, cube like structure in the center of the Great Mosque in Mecca). It represents the moon and is considered to be divine. The worship of the Arabian Star Family with the moon god, Allah, at their head, revolved around the Black Stone. (Perhaps this is how the symbol of Islam—☾—came to be and why it is displayed on their flags, as well as on the top of mosques.) Ellat, Allah's wife, is represented by the sun. Allah's daughters, al-Uzza and Manat (see Sûrah 53:19, 20), are represented by the morning and evening stars (even though they are only the one planet, Venus). In fairness, we should point out that some Middle East historians ascribe both the morning and evening stars to only one goddess, al-Uzza, who was considered the most powerful goddess. As we can see, the crescent symbol of Islam "☾" has only one star. There are some Muslims who believe that the Black Stone was divinely sent by Allah, who was the moon god before the planet Venus replaced it in Allah's title. Consider: How could a Black Stone, greatly worshipped and revered by the Muslims, be hidden for centuries while they were fighting to preserve the prestige they found serving it? [11]

THE NEVER-ENDING WARFARE (JIHAD)

The Ongoing and Vindictive Persecution of a Particular Group or Groups without Limitations of Time or Circumstances

Some argue that Allah is the God of War as is the God of the Old Testament; therefore, they are the same.

In the Bible, we read about wars, along with persecutions of both the children of Israel and the Christians. It is important to be aware that God never tells His people they must forever be enemies against certain groups of people. There are instances where Israel has differences with some people or groups and might be in a state-of-war periodically like they were with the now extinct Philistines, but nowhere in Scripture does it say that it is pleasing to God for a particular group—religious or ethnic—to be forced to convert or otherwise be completely wiped out. When we read about such offensive people in the Bible, God destroyed or scattered them—and that includes Israel.

The God of the Bible went out of His way to prevent warfare. He sent Jonah to Nineveh (a group akin to ISIS in its aggressiveness and militaristic cruelty) to warn them to repent, or God would allow them to be destroyed (Jonah 1:1). When Jonah finally decided to obey God and go to Nineveh and warn them, to his surprise, the Ninevites repented and were not destroyed (Jonah 3:6-10).

God told Abraham it would be 400 years before his children and their descendants would be able to inhabit the Promised Land of Canaan because the sin of the Amorites had not risen to the point where a just God would allow them to be destroyed (Genesis 15:13—16).

Even after the flood, when mankind was given a second chance to survive, they rebelled against God once again. God did not destroy them—but scattered them by confounding their languages so that each family (tribe) understood each other—but not the language of others. In that manner, God caused the people who were the descendants of Noah and his children to leave the city of Babylon, where the event occurred (Genesis 11:1-9).

When it came to the sins of Sodom and Gomorrah, God told Abraham He was going to destroy the offensive cities, but Abraham pleaded with God to spare them:

> Then the LORD said, "The outcry against Sodom and Gomorrah is so great and their sin so grievous that I will go down and see if what they have done is as bad as the outcry that has reached me. If not, I will know."
>
> The men turned away and went toward Sodom, but Abraham remained standing before the LORD. Then Abraham approached him and said: "Will you sweep away the righteous with the wicked? What if there are fifty righteous people in the city? Will you really sweep it away and not spare the place for the sake of the fifty righteous people in it? Far be it from you to do such a thing—to kill the righteous with the wicked, treating the righteous and the wicked alike. Far be it from you! Will not the Judge of all the earth do right?"
>
> The LORD said, "If I find fifty righteous people in the city of Sodom, I will spare the whole place for their sake."
>
> Then Abraham spoke up again: "Now that I have been so bold as to speak to the Lord, though I am nothing but dust and ashes, what if the number of the righteous is five less than fifty? Will you destroy the whole city for lack of five people?"
>
> "If I find forty-five there," he said, "I will not destroy it."
>
> Once again he spoke to him, "What if only forty are found there?"
>
> He said, "For the sake of forty, I will not do it."
>
> Then he said, "May the Lord not be angry, but let me speak. What if only thirty can be found there?"

He answered, "I will not do it if I find thirty there."

Abraham said, "Now that I have been so bold as to speak to the Lord, what if only twenty can be found there?"

He said, "For the sake of twenty, I will not destroy it."

Then he said, "May the Lord not be angry, but let me speak just once more. What if only ten can be found there?"

He answered, "For the sake of ten, I will not destroy it."

When the Lord had finished speaking with Abraham, he left, and Abraham returned home (Genesis 18:20-33, NIV).

Unfortunately, for Sodom and Gomorrah, only Lot and his family, who consisted of his wife and two daughters, were found to be acceptable before God, so the cities of the plain were destroyed (Genesis 19:24-25). If the God of the Old Testament were somehow different from the God of the New Testament, then we would have a problem because the Bible clearly states that God never changes (Malachi 3:6).

As we pointed out earlier, because the sin of the Amorites had not risen to the point where a just God would allow them to be destroyed (Genesis 15:13—16), Abraham and his family would not be allowed to take possession of Canaan for 400 years.

Finally, when Joshua entered what was to become the Holy Land of Israel after the 400 years of slavery for the children of Israel in Egypt, he was fooled into making a treaty with one of the Canaanite tribes called the Gibeonites. They had heard of God's command to destroy the inhabitants of Canaan and pretended to have traveled a long distance for the purpose of making a peace treaty with Joshua and the children of Israel (Joshua 9:3-9). It worked:

Then Joshua made a treaty of peace with them to let them live, and the leaders of the assembly ratified it by oath (Joshua 9:15, NIV).

148

Because Joshua made a treaty with the Gibeonites, God allowed them not to be killed:

> Three days after they made the treaty with the Gibeonites, the Israelites heard that they were neighbors, living near them. So the Israelites set out and on the third day came to their cities: Gibeon, Kephirah, Beeroth and Kiriath Jearim. But the Israelites did not attack them, because the leaders of the assembly had sworn an oath to them by the LORD, the God of Israel.
>
> The whole assembly grumbled against the leaders, but all the leaders answered, "We have given them our oath by the LORD, the God of Israel, and we cannot touch them now. This is what we will do to them: We will let them live, so that God's wrath will not fall on us for breaking the oath we swore to them." They continued, "Let them live, but let them be woodcutters and water carriers in the service of the whole assembly." So the leaders' promise to them was kept (Genesis 9:16-21, NIV).

As we can see by these examples, the God of the Bible prefers to save people—not destroy them. It is only when their sins become unbearable to a Holy God that He acts against them; however, Israel was not exempt from God's wrath either. As we saw with Joshua, God uses nations to punish other nations—so it was with the children of Israel:

> In the twelfth year of Ahaz king of Judah, Hoshea, son of Elah became king of Israel in Samaria, and he reigned nine years.
>
> He did evil in the eyes of the LORD, but not like the kings of Israel who preceded him.
>
> Shalmaneser king of Assyria came up to attack Hoshea, who had been Shalmaneser's vassal and had paid him tribute [money].
>
> But the king of Assyria discovered that Hoshea was a traitor, for he had sent envoys to So [Osorkon], king of Egypt, and he no longer paid tribute to the king of Assyria, as he had done year by year. Therefore Shalmaneser seized him and put him in prison.

The king of Assyria invaded the entire land, marched against Samaria and laid siege to it for three years.

In the ninth year of Hoshea, the king of Assyria captured Samaria and deported the Israelites to Assyria. He settled them in Halah, in Gozan on the Habor River and in the towns of the Medes.

All this took place because the Israelites had sinned against the LORD their God, who had brought them up out of Egypt from under the power of Pharaoh, King of Egypt. They worshiped other gods and followed the practices of the nations the LORD had driven out before them, as well as the practices that the kings of Israel had introduced (2 Kings 17:1-8, NIV, bracketed clarifications mine).

God made an everlasting covenant with Abraham through Isaac and his children (Genesis 17: 13, 19), but that does not mean God does not discipline His own (Ezekiel 36- 37; Luke 21:24). God uses discipline for a season, but He never intended for it to be permanent.

Muslims also argue that Allah remains the same, and once he says something, it cannot be changed:

Perfected is the Word of your Lord in truth and justice. There is naught [nothing] that can change His words. He is the Hearer, the Knower (Sûrah 6:115).

Despite this claim, the Koran does contradict itself by allowing Allah to change his mind and break his promises:

Nothing of our revelation (even a single verse) do we abrogate [change] or cause [to] be forgotten [erase], but we bring (in place) one better or the like thereof. Know you not [do you not know] that Allah is Able to do all things? (Sûrah 2:106, bracketed clarifications mine.)

In researching to see if the author of the Koran could also have authored the Bible, we have to ask the provocative question, "If God is all-knowing, then surely He would make the correct decision from the very beginning. Therefore, He would not have a need to change His mind for something even better because the best choice would be the first choice." Could it really be that an all-knowing God would make such a mistake of not knowing what is best from the very start? Of course not!

The God of the Bible does not hold grudges. On the other hand, as observed by the many passages in the Koran, Allah does hold grudges and continually calls the Jews bad names as well as calling for their destruction—even up to and on the Day of Judgment:

> Judgment Day will come only when the Muslims fight the Jews and kill them, until the Jew hides behind the tree and the stone, and the tree and the stone say: "Oh Muslim, oh servant of Allah , there is a Jew behind me, come and kill him"—except for the Gharqad tree [Boxthorn tree] because it is one of the trees of the Jews. ([Hadith] Sahih Muslim, Kitab al-Fitan, Book 41, No. 6985, bracketed clarification mine.)

If Allah is supposed to be the God of the Bible, is it not curious he has not taken it on himself to eliminate all the Jews—if they are so horrible? After all, the God of the Bible completely destroyed the abominable and sinful cities of Sodom and Gomorrah, along with all of their people without any help from humans.

Likewise, consider the time when the children of Israel were wandering in the desert, and the God of the Bible eliminated a group of people from their midst—that time, it was relatives of Moses who were rebelling against his authority. They had become so intolerable that God destroyed them without any human intervention:

> Then Moses said, "This is how you will know that the LORD has sent me to do all these things and that it was not my idea: If these men die a natural death and suffer the fate of all mankind, then the LORD has not sent me. But if the LORD brings about something totally new, and the earth opens its mouth and swallows them,

151

with everything that belongs to them, and they go down alive into the realm of the dead, then you will know that these men have treated the LORD with contempt."

As soon as he finished saying all this, the ground under them split apart, and the earth opened its mouth and swallowed them and their households, and all those associated with Korah, together with their possessions. They went down alive into the realm of the dead, with everything they owned; the earth closed over them, and they perished and were gone from the community (Numbers 16:28-33, NIV).

In this brief review of open-ended, never-ending warfare found in the Koran—as opposed to the warfare found in the Bible, which allows for a positive conclusion—we can see how God sometimes uses nations to discipline other nations in order to put an end to those who are beyond redemption.

We observe no such occurrence with Allah in the Koran. The God of the Bible does not hold vendettas; instead, He addresses problems, then solves or eliminates them and moves on. Not so with Allah and the Koran, where we see recurring themes such as, "Allah has not taken unto him a son," and his fixation against the Jews right up to and including Judgment Day. The God of the Bible is not a God of war. The God of the Bible is more interested in reconciliation—as we saw with Nineveh—He only uses destruction as a last resort.

_____

NOTES:

1. Ishmael was a young man of at least 19 years old when Abraham sent him and his mother away. While he was with Abraham, he was circumcised at age 13 (Genesis 17:25) and 14 when Isaac was born (Genesis 16:16; 21:25). Ishmael was present when Isaac was weaned five years later, making Ishmael 19 when Abraham sent him away (Genesis 21:8-10).

2. "Hajj," John Bowker, ed., *Oxford Concise Dictionary of World Religions* (Oxford UP, 2000), 227.

3. A.H. or *Anno Hijri*, the year when Muhammad escaped to Medina (622 A.D. or 1 A.H. in Muslim countries). *Anno* is the Latin word for "year."

4. John G. Burke, *Cosmic Debris: Meteorites in History*. (Oakland: University of California Press, 1991), 221–223.

5. Hopfe, Lewis M., Mark R. Woodward. *Religions of the World.* Pearson/Prentice Hall Publ., 2005,) 335.

6. Ibid., 335

7. Ishmael's eldest son was Nabaioth (Genesis 25:13). He had a sister named Mahalath, who became one of Esau's wives (Genesis 28:9; 36:3).

8. Dr. Rafat Amari, Islam: *In Light of History*, 1st ed, n.p. Religion Research Institute, 2004. Also citing Tarikh al-Tabari I, page 524.

9. Amari, Islam: *In Light of History,* 1st ed. Cites A. James, W.F. Sabaean Inscriptions from Mahram Bilqis, Volume III (Baltimore: John Hopkins Press, 1962) 387.

10. Amari citing Al-Azruqi, Akhbar Mecca, 1/6.

11. Amari still citing Al-Azruqi, Akhbar Mecca, 1/6.

CHAPTER 7

PART 1: FUNDAMENTALS OF SUNNI ISLAM FROM THE FIRST PROPHET AND THE FIRST SEVEN CALIPHS

A Caliph Is Like a King, and
A Caliphate Is Like a Kingdom

Because foreign concepts, names, and ideas can be confusing, we have included visual aids that incorporate the relationships of Muhammad's immediate family, as well as the first seven caliphs and their relationships to Muhammad and Islam. Sunnis represent between 85-90% of all Muslims. We hope these aids will make it easier for you to be able to understand the formative stages of the Muslim faith.

Caliphs

A caliph—or as it is spelled in Arabic, *khalīfah*—is the "successor" to the position held by Muhammad as the final authority in Islam. When Muhammad died in 632 A.D., Abū Bakr succeeded him—thereby assuming Muhammad's political and administrative position known as the *khalīfah rasūl Allāh* (i.e., the successor of the "Messenger of Allah"). However, it was probably under Caliph Umar ibn al-Khaṭṭāb (the second caliph) when the title of "caliph" began to be used to describe the head of the religious and political Islamic state.[1] In Islam, the ultimate goal is for a universal caliphate, consisting of a world ruled by a supreme caliph of Islam, where no other religions are allowed, and only Allah is worshiped.

Also, in Islam, there are two main sects: One is known as the Sunni Muslims, which make up 83% to 90% of all Muslims. The second largest sect is the Shi'a (e.g., followers, faction, or party of Ali). They make up about 15.4%. (They are mostly Muslims living in Iran and Iraq.) The split emerged after the assassination of the fourth caliph in 661 A.D. (We will later address the series of Islamic assassinations in this so-called "religion of peace," which—some argue—began with its founder, Muhammad.) The Shi'a sect believes that the succession of caliphs should only come from the bloodline of Muhammad.

Sunnis and Shi'ites are the two largest sects of Islam, and the percentages fluctuate and vary depending on the source. If the percentages of just these two sects are added together, it becomes apparent they would have a combined total—or even over go over—the 100% mark!

The third largest sect consists of the Wahhabis (mostly living in Saudi Arabia), of which Osama bin Laden was a member. Its founder was 'Abd al-Wahhab, born in 1691 A.D., a thousand years after Muhammad. 'Abd-al-Wahhab (or Al-Wahhab) is most noted for his vehement hatred toward Christians. The war cry of the Wahhabis is, "Kill and strangle all infidels that give companions to Allah." There are many other sub sects or spin offs of Islam, including the Kurds, (Whirling) Dervishes, Baha'i Faith, and several other such branches, but these comprise a very small percentage of traditional Islam

Al-Mahdi, the Rider of the White Horse in Revelation 6:2; Not to Be Confused with the Rider in Revelation 19:16

Muslims have their own messiah, known as the "Mahdi" (pronounced **ma**-dee and means divine guidance), who they say will return with

Jesus and claim that the rider on the white horse of the Four Horsemen of the Apocalypse is the one mentioned in Revelation 6.[2]

There is a general acknowledgement in Islam regarding the first seven caliphs, but that is as far as it goes. Despite the early positioning for who would be the caliph—between relatives of Muhammad and powerful Muslims in the community—after the seventh caliph, the split between the Shi'as and Sunnis was complete. Generally speaking, the Shi'ites parted ways with the caliphate and established a system of imams who were preferably comprised from the house of the Prophet Muhammad, including the Quraish (one of seven spellings) Tribe, all of whom were close or distant relatives of Muhammad at the time.

Because of this, the first twelve Shi'a imams (the twelfth being their Mahdi) are somewhat different from the Sunni's list of caliphs, although two of the first seven caliphs (the fourth Caliph, Ali, and the fifth Caliph, Hasan, along with his brother al-Husayn—who was the next heir apparent to the Caliphate), are recognized as Shi'a imams. A caliph is—to the Sunnis—like the pope is to the Roman Catholic Church, which is based upon election, not kinship. Shi'as were more disposed toward imams who were from Muhammad's family, although that was not always realistic.

It is interesting to note that besides Muhammad's untimely death, out of the first five caliphs, four died unnaturally, and out of the first eleven Shi'a imams, all died unnatural deaths as well. The exception is the twelfth imam—who is called the "Mahdi" and is believed to still be living in a deep well in Iran awaiting the Last Days (so much for the "religion of peace" myth).[3] Because identifying a direct descendant of Muhammad would be very difficult to establish, a Shi'a imam became a religious leader whose importance may be the equivalent to that of—or in some instances the same as—a caliph, but they have a much broader reach and might also include religious leaders of local mosques similar to the way the Catholic Church draws from priests and cardinals.

BACKGROUND: Muhammad al-Mahdi (869 A.D.—) was the twelfth Shi'a imam in succession going all the way back to Islam's founder, the Prophet Muhammad. He is believed to have never died but instead went into hiding. The twelfth and last of the exalted imams disappeared mysteriously during the ninth century A.D. (generally believed to be around 874 A.D.). The Mahdi—like the Christian messiah—is expected to return at the End of the Age.

> The term "messianism" in the Islamic context is frequently used to translate the important concept of an eschatological [End Times] figure. The Mahdi, who, as the foreordained leader, "will rise" to launch a great social transformation in order to restore and adjust all things under divine guidance [bracketed clarification mine].[4]

We also referred to the Mahdi at the beginning of this section as the rider of the first horse of the Apocalypse. This belief is further documented by the Egyptian scholars, 'Izzat and Arif, who quote Ka'b al Ahbar, a Jewish Rabbi who allegedly converted to Islam[5] and a contemporary of Caliphs Umar and Uthman:

> I find the Mahdi recorded in the books of the Prophets … For instance, the Book of Revelation says: "And I saw and behold a white horse. He that sat on him … went forth conquering and to conquer …. It is clear that this man is the Mahdi who will ride the white horse and judge by the Qur'an (with justice) and with whom will be men with marks of prostration on their foreheads."[6]

Two things we find interesting in this seventh-century observation: (1) The Mahdi is the rider on the white horse in Revelation 6:2 and (2) everyone who serves him had "marks of prostration on their foreheads." This is alarmingly reminiscent of the Mark of the Beast in Revelation 13:17, where those who serve the Antichrist will, "… receive a mark in their right, hand, or on their foreheads" (Revelation 13:16b)! All Muslim sects believe that the Mahdi will reappear during the End Times and rule a worldwide caliphate. The Shi'ites have a slightly different view and believe that the Mahdi is alive and hiding deep inside the Jamkaran well, which has become a Shi'a pilgrimage spot located in Iran. The Twelvers, Shi'ites who believe in the Mahdi (i.e., sometimes referred to the "hidden twelfth imam") believe that Jesus was converted to Islam in Heaven. That is curious because the Koran claims *Isa* (Jesus) was already an Islamic prophet (Sûrah 5:75; 19:30-35). They also believe that the Mahdi will return with *Isa* (Jesus) to intervene in an apocalyptic war that would otherwise destroy the world (Matthew 24:27-31; Revelation 19:11-15); thus, it is the Mahdi who will usher in world peace under a worldwide caliphate. Additionally, they believe that Jesus will come against churches by breaking their crosses, and if Christians do not repent from believing the "lie" that Jesus is the Son of God and died on the cross, He will destroy them, as well as all the Christians who will not repent and accept Islam as their religion.[7]

[Hadith] Sahih Bukhari, Volume 3, Book 34, Number 425

Narrated [by] Abu Huraira:

Allah's Apostle said, "By Him in Whose Hands my soul is, son of Mary (Jesus) will shortly descend amongst you people (Muslims) as a just ruler and will break the Cross and kill the pig and abolish the Jizya (a tax taken from the non-Muslims, who are in the protection, of the Muslim government). Then there will be an abundance of money, and no-body will accept charitable gifts."

In another Hadith we read:

[Hadith] Sahih Bukhari, Volume 3, Book 43, Number 656

Narrated [by] Abu Huraira:

Allah's Apostle said, "The Hour will not be established until the son of Mary (i.e., Jesus) descends amongst you as a just ruler, he will break the cross, kill the pigs, and abolish the Jizya tax. Money will be in abundance so that nobody will accept it (as charitable gifts)."

In Figure 3, the rider of the white horse in Revelation 6 is wearing a crown. He is the Antichrist and should not be confused with the rider of the white horse in Revelation 19. The rider in Revelation 19 is Jesus, the Christian Messiah, "And He has on His vesture and on His thigh a name written, King of Kings, and Lord of Lords" (Revelation 19:16). Muslims claim the rider in Revelation 6 is the Mahdi, their messiah, which the Bible claims is the Antichrist, as we can see below.

Fig. 3. Four Horsemen of the Apocalypse (1877)
by Russian Artist, Viktor Vasnetsov

THE FOUR HORSEMEN of the APOCALYPSE, who will be released from the River Euphrates (Rev. 9:14), will consist of (1) A white horse (on the right side of the painting). He who sits on him will have a bow and arrow and a crown. Christians believe he is the Antichrist while the Muslims believe he is the "Mahdi;" (2) next to him, moving left across the picture is a red horse and riding him is a horseman given a great sword to take peace from the world; (3) next to him, continuing to the left, is the black horse and on him is a horseman holding a pair of scales in his hand. He will devastate the world's finances, and (4) finally, on the far left is the pale horse. His rider's name is "Death"— and Hell follows him! (Revelation 6:2-8.)

The Five Pillars of Islam

1. Declaration of Faith: Shahada
   The proclamation: "There is no god but Allah, and Muhammad is God's Messenger."

2. Prayer: Salah
   A prayer that must be said five times a day at designated Islamic prayer periods (usually announced from a minaret). Muslims are required to stop what they are doing and submit to the call to prayer—even on sidewalks, in schools, and at their place of business, etc.

3. Compulsory Giving: Zakat
   A charitable offering of 2.5% of a Muslim's savings for the poor and needy

4. Fasting During Ramadan: Sawm
   A time of fasting and practicing self-control during the holy month of Ramadan

   The fast is from morning until evening when a Muslim is allowed to feast. (This is akin to what we in the West refer to as our breaking of fast or breakfast because we have not eaten from night to morning. Basically, this is just reversing the so-called fasting period, while still allowing for one meal a day.)

5. Pilgrimage to Mecca: Hajj
   The all-important pilgrimage to Mecca required of every able-bodied Muslim at least once in a lifetime

FATHERS OF THE SO-CALLED "RELIGION OF PEACE" THE MAJORITY OF WHOM HAD QUESTIONABLE DEATHS

Successions, Assassinations and Schisms (Splits)

When we study Islam, it is puzzling how a so-called "religion of peace" has a history of violence from its very beginning (with the possible exception of when Muhammad was just starting out with his new faith in Mecca and was militarily weak). Not only was Islam spread by the violent use of the sword, Islam has a dark history of how its founding caliphs also met their own violent deaths—except one—the caliph who succeeded Muhammad, Abu Bakr.

THE SUCCESSION OF CALIPHS AFTER MUHAMMAD

The First Caliph Beginning after Muhammad

The first caliph to succeed Muhammad after his death was Abu Bakr. Bakr. He was the first convert to Islam outside the prophet Muhammad's family—the same Caliph Abu Bakr who betrothed his own six-year-old daughter, Aisha, to Muhammad. Their wedding was consummated when little Aisha was nine years old, and it was on her lap where Muhammad laid his head when he died in 632 A.D. It is believed that Caliph Abu Bakr died naturally from an illness in 634 A.D. after being caliph for two years.

The Second Caliph

Umar (Omar) followed Bakr as caliph. It was Umar who, on the death of Muhammad, was the one who suggested to Abu Bakr that he should be the one to inherit (establish) the leadership (caliph) of the Muslim community. In 644 A.D., Caliph Umar was assassinated, but not before setting up a Shura Council, an umbrella organization of mosques and Muslim groups, similar to the upper house of the former bicameral (two-tier) Parliament of Egypt (1883-1971)—where Umar had intended to elect his successor before he died.

The Third Caliph

Uthman was the third caliph and is most noted for giving the directive to gather all of the various versions of the Koran and have them brought to him in order to issue one standardized version. Caliph Uthman was assassinated in 656 A.D. when Egyptian rebels broke into his home and killed both him and his wife.

The Fourth Caliph

The last caliph to rule over a united Islamic religion was the fourth caliph, Ali. Caliph Ali was a member of Muhammad's family—the son of Muhammad's Uncle, Abu Talib, and the husband of Muhammad's daughter, Fatimah. This made him a first cousin, as well as a son-in-law, to the Prophet of Islam and—as some would say—the logical person to inherit the caliphate; however, he turned out to be a weak leader (see Table 5). In 661 A.D., Caliph Ali was assassinated by a Kharijite (i.e., "those who went out"). "Kharijite" is a term, which refers to Muslims who originally supported Caliph Ali, but later turned against him having preferred Mu'awiyah who became caliph in 660 A.D. There could not be two caliphs at the same time, so a Kharijite assassinated Caliph Ali in 661 A.D. The Kharijites were a short-lived Islamic sect who began the first Islamic civil war.

The Fifth Caliph

Hasan (Hassan), Ali's son (the maternal grandson of Muhammad) and the brother of al-Hasayn, became the fifth caliph. As with the other preceding four caliphs, all were assassinated except Abu Bakr. Caliph Hasan (Hassan) had two versions of his death after he retired, as we show in Table 6. His death opened the door for the split (i.e., Shi'a schism).

The Sixth Caliph

Enter Mu'awiyah, a Meccan merchant and founder of the Umayyad Dynasty. It was Caliph Mu'awiyah who relocated the seat of the Islamic empire to Damascus. He was more liberal-minded and allowed Christians in his government and army. Caliph Mu'awiyah was known as the "Caesar of the Arabs;" however, all was not good within Islam since many Muslims desired a hereditary ascension to the position of caliph. In order to protect his dynasty, Caliph Mu'awiyah had to act.

The Seventh Caliph

Mu'awiyah designated his son, Yazid, as his successor to lead the caliphate that was done in an attempt to solidify his hold on the caliphate and thereby outwit the many Muslims who hated the Umayyad Dynasty and wanted to return to a caliphate ruled by one of Muhammad's family members. Toward that end, many of those seeking a return to the Muhammadan Dynasty convinced Ali's son, al-Husayn, to lay claim to the caliphate. Remember, Ali was the first cousin and son-in-law of Muhammad, who made al-Hasan the fifth caliph, the second cousin, as well as the grandson of Muhammad. Those who followed his brother, al-Husayn, formed the minority branch of Islam referred to as "Shi'at Ali" or the "Party of Ali," now known as the Shi'ites—so the split was complete. Unfortunately, Al-Hasayn—who could have succeeded his brother if it were a throne instead of an exalted office—was beheaded in the Battle of Karbala on October 13, 680 A.D.

While al-Hasayn never became a caliph, the Shi'a still acknowledged him as the third Sh'ite imam after his brother whom they considered not only a caliph, but the second Shi'ite imam as well. By doing this, the Shi'ites could make the claim of the imam descendancy proceeding directly from Muhammad himself.

Table 6. Review of the Deaths of the Early Caliphs of Islam (Including Muhammad), Their Years in Office, and How They Died.

MUHAMMAD AND FIRST SEVEN CALIPHS	HOW THEY DIED
Muhammad (c. 570-632 A.D.)	Assassinated (poisoned) in 632 A.D. As recorded in the Hadith, Muhammad died unexpectedly in Medina at age 62.
	Several years earlier, Muhammad almost died after a brief illness from poisoning by a Jewish woman. Although he survived that attempted poisoning, he never completely recovered. ([Hadith] Sahih al-Bukhari, Volume 3, Book 47, Number 786.) As Muhammad lay dying, he believed that his imminent death was again due to being poisoned.
	He told his young wife, "O 'Aisha! I still feel the pain caused by the food I ate at Khaibar, and at this time, I feel as if my aorta is being cut from that poison." ([Hadith] Sahih al-Bukhari, narrated by 'Aisha: Volume 5, Book 59, Number 713.)
	Could Muhammad have been poisoned a second time by someone close to him? Muhammad was familiar with what it felt like to be poisoned (expressed in the above passage) and felt those same effects.

First Caliph: Abu Bakr (June 8, 632-August 22, 634 A.D.)	Bakr was the only caliph of the first seven not to be assassinated.
Second Caliph: Umar (e.g., Omar) (August 23, 634-November 3, 644 A.D.)	Assassinated/bludgeoned to death by rebels.[8]
Third Caliph: Uthman (November 11, 644-656 A.D.) He was also the first Caliph of the Umayyad Caliphate ➤ This symbol refers to the Umayyad Dynasty.	Assassinated by Egyptian rebels on June 20, 656 A.D. [9]
Fourth Caliph: Ali (June 656-January 25/26-661 A.D.) First Shi'a Imam ❖ This symbol refers to the Shi'a line of caliphs.	Assassinated by a Kharijite. He had to deal with internal fighting among various Islamic factions seeking the caliphate, concluding with his assassination. [10]
Fifth Caliph: Hasan ibn Ali (625-670 A.D.) ❖ Second Shi'a Imam	Assassinated (poisoned) by his wife, Ja'da bint al-Ash'at, after he abdicated the caliphate in 670 A.D. it is believed she acted on orders of Caliph Mu'awiya.[11] Ali was the grandson of Muhammad through the Prophet's daughter, Fāṭimah. The fifth caliph stepped down after seven months in office in preference of Caliph Mu'awiya. It should also be pointed out that the fifth caliph's brother, al-Hasayn, while not a caliph, was a contender for the caliphate since he was a direct

	descendant (grandson) of the prophet, Muhammad. Unfortunately, al-Hasayn was executed by beheading after losing an internecine battle to Caliph Yazid, the successor to Caliph Mu'awiyah[12] (see Summary of assassinated caliphs below).
Sixth Caliph: Mu'awiyah I (August/September 661-680 A.D. he re-established Umayyad Dynasty) ➤ Second caliph of the Umayyad Caliphate	Died from natural causes, although some fragmented writings of al-Nisba (800-845 A.D.) suggest that some Shi'as believed he was poisoned—possibly by Zubayr. This has not been substantiated.
Seventh Caliph: Yazid (680 toward the end of 683 A.D.) ➤ Third caliph of the Umayyad Caliphate (and the first one through inheritance)	Possibly assassinated. The story alleges that his horse accidently killed him; however, the remains of the body were never actually confirmed as being his. It is believed that he was buried in Damascus, although no grave exists today. [13]

Summary of the Caliph's Deaths

Muhammad: Assassinated/died through complications from poisoning 632 A.D.

Abu Bakr: Died of natural causes (illness) 634 A.D.

Umar: Assassinated, bludgeoned to death by rebels in 644 A.D.

Uthman: Assassinated by Egyptian rebels in 656 A.D.

Ali: Assassinated by Abd-al-Rahman ibn Muljam al-Muradi in 661 A.D.

Hasan ibn Ali:	Assassinated by wife's (Ja'da bint al-Ash'at) poisoning in 670 A.D.
Mu'awiyah:	Died of natural causes (although there is some question regarding this) in 680 A.D.
Yazid:	Assassinated or allegedly killed by his horse, but there are several explanations of his death, including a mysterious illness or died from the plague in 683 A.D.

Assassinated Heir Apparent to the Caliphate

As we mentioned in the table above, the fifth caliph was Hasan ibn Ali whose brother, Al-Husayn, was an heir apparent to the caliphate as well as a grandson of the prophet, Muhammad. Al-Husayn was assassinated (beheaded) in 680 A.D.

In summary, we have seen that five of the first seven caliphs of Islam (including Muhammad), as well as two questionable caliph's deaths, along with the death of an heir apparent—and eleven of the first Shi'ite imams (possibly the twelfth Imam as well)—in this so-called "religion of peace"—were murdered or met an untimely death. We also discussed that three of the first seven caliphs (including Ali, the first acknowledged Shi'a caliph) were descended from or related by marriage to Muhammad.

When dealing with the history of Islam, there are many problems to address. The dating of ancient history is one, as well as the numbering system of the verses in the Koran, mainly due to Pickthall's use of the Indian order of numbering the koranic verses. Others used the Arab system, or like Yusuf Ali, they used the Egyptian order; still, most Western translators adapted the numbering system developed by Gustav Flüegel in Germany the century before Pickthall, while most Muslim translators use the Egyptian numbering system. The inconsistency of the numbering process is very noticeable if you have several older editions of the Koran. We also have controversies regarding births and deaths of various important figures preceding

Muhammad's time, although nothing serious enough to present a critical problem.

As for the lineage of caliphs, there is a lot of discrepancy among the Sunnis. For instance, the Sunnis acknowledge Abu Bakr, Muhammad's father-in-law, as the first caliph after the death of Muhammad, while the Shiites (known as the followers/faction or "party" of Muhammad) claim that they are the legal heirs to the throne—beginning with Ali—who was both Muhammad's son-in-law and first cousin.

THE SUCCESSION OF ISLAMIC RELIGIOUS RULERS FROM THE PROPHET MUHAMMAD, THROUGH THE FIRST SEVEN CALIPHS— CONSISTING OF RELATIVES AND LOYALISTS

While the succession of caliphs is generally accepted, the cause of death is not. Beginning with Muhammad, the controversy surrounding their deaths is highly debated. While not all caliphs died in office, the mystery surrounding the end of their lives is very suspect, as the visual aid on the next page will show.

Icon Legend:

- Caliphs: Muhammad's line - light turban

- Caliphs: Independent - darker turban

- Caliphs: Umayyad dynasty - dark turban with a "U"

- Non-religious figures

- Assassinated by Poison or Violence

Abd Allah (Abdullah): Father of Muhammad who died before Muhammad was born.

Abu Talib: Brother of Muhammad's father, who raised Muhammad after age 8 when Muhammad's mother, Amina, died. *Abu Talib* was also the father of Ali, the 4th caliph.

Muhammad, *the Prophet of Islam* (610-632): Died from poisoning or complications from a previous poisoning.

1st caliph, Abu Bakr (632-634): While not a blood relative, he was the father of Aisha—Muhammad's child bride—who he espoused to Muhammad when she was age six (consummated at age 9). Abu Bakr was the first convert to Islam outside of Muhammad's family.

2nd caliph, Umar (634-644): Known for his hot temper, he controlled the Muslim warriors through a systematic program of Islamic expansion by the sword. Assassinated/beaten to death by rebels.

3rd caliph, Uthman (644-656): A member of the prestigious *Umayyad Clan in Mecca*. He was responsible for collecting all the various versions of the Korans and making them uniform. Egyptian rebels assassinated him.

4th caliph, Ali (656-661): The 1st cousin and son-in-law of Muhammad (see the previous page). Assassinated in a mosque while praying.

5th caliph, Hasan (al-Hasan): Ali's son and brother of al-Hasayn (661). After approximately 7 months, he relinquished his Caliphate to Mu'awiya. His wife assassinated him by poison believed to be on orders from Caliph Muawiya.

6th caliph, Mu'awiya: (661-680): A Meccan merchant who moved the seat of the Caliphate to Damascus—founded the *Umayyad Dynasty*—known as the "Caesar of the Arabs."

7th caliph, Yazid: (640-683) *Umayyad Dynasty*—He was killed accidentally by his horse and was succeeded by his son, Mu'awiya II. It is believed by some historians that Mu'awiya II was abducted within 40 days and died shortly after from undetermined causes. [14]

THE CALIPHATE AND THE DIFFERENCE BETWEEN SHI'ITES AND SUNNIS

Division of Islam under the First Seven Caliphs

As we can see in Chart 2, Ali was the natural son of Muhammad's uncle, Abu Talib, which would make him Muhammad's first cousin as well as his grandson through Muhammad's daughter—Ali's mother—Fāṭimah. They had a son named, al-Hasan, who in addition to being the second cousin of Muhammad, is also Muhammad's grandson as we can see in the following chart:

Chart 2: Muhammad's Complex Family Tree

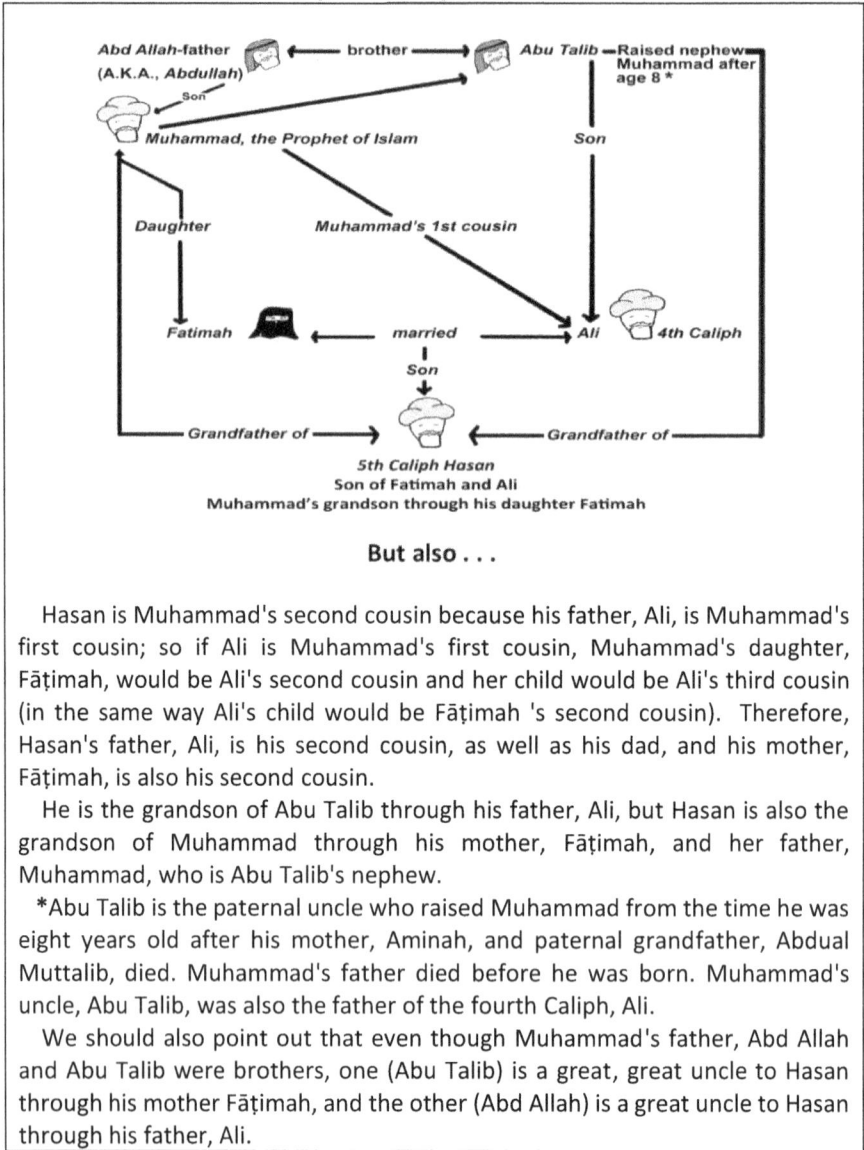

Abd Allah-father
(A.K.A., *Abdullah*)

← brother →

Abu Talib —Raised nephew Muhammad after age 8 *

Son

Muhammad, the Prophet of Islam

Son

Daughter

Muhammad's 1st cousin

Fatimah ← married → Ali 4th Caliph

Son

Grandfather of → ← Grandfather of

5th Caliph Hasan
Son of Fatimah and Ali
Muhammad's grandson through his daughter Fatimah

But also . . .

Hasan is Muhammad's second cousin because his father, Ali, is Muhammad's first cousin; so if Ali is Muhammad's first cousin, Muhammad's daughter, Fāṭimah, would be Ali's second cousin and her child would be Ali's third cousin (in the same way Ali's child would be Fāṭimah 's second cousin). Therefore, Hasan's father, Ali, is his second cousin, as well as his dad, and his mother, Fāṭimah, is also his second cousin.

He is the grandson of Abu Talib through his father, Ali, but Hasan is also the grandson of Muhammad through his mother, Fāṭimah, and her father, Muhammad, who is Abu Talib's nephew.

*Abu Talib is the paternal uncle who raised Muhammad from the time he was eight years old after his mother, Aminah, and paternal grandfather, Abdual Muttalib, died. Muhammad's father died before he was born. Muhammad's uncle, Abu Talib, was also the father of the fourth Caliph, Ali.

We should also point out that even though Muhammad's father, Abd Allah and Abu Talib were brothers, one (Abu Talib) is a great, great uncle to Hasan through his mother Fāṭimah, and the other (Abd Allah) is a great uncle to Hasan through his father, Ali.

We also saw in the list of caliphs when the fifth caliph—and founder of the Umayyad Dynasty—Caliph Mu'awiya died, he was followed by his handpicked successor who happened to be his son, Yazid. The appointment of Yazid as the next caliph proved to be very controversial.

172

Note that in Figure 4, Yazid was the seventh caliph (680-683). He had to deal with the many Muslims who hated the Umayyad Dynasty and totally eclipsed Muhammad's family line. In 750 A.D., the Abbasid Revolution finally toppled the Umayyad Dynasty. As previously stated, if there had been heredity ascendancy to the caliphate, many Muslims believed it should have been through Muhammad's descendants, not the tribe of Umayyad. To that end, they wanted Ali's other son, al-Husayn, who was also Muhammad's grandson, to be caliph. The followers loyal to Muhammad's family refused to acknowledge Yazid, or any of his descendants, as a caliph.

Supporters of Muhammad and his first cousin, Ali (who was also Muhammad's son-in-law) and Ali's son (Muhammad's grandson), al-Husayn, called themselves "Shi'ite Ali" ("Shi'ite" is Arabic for "party"), or as we have come to know them—the Shi'a or Shi'ites. They make up about 13% to 14% of all Muslims and are found primarily in Persia (Iraq and Iran). Sunnis make up the largest sect at around 83% (depending on what source you use). All other sects are made up of a very small percentage of around three to eight percent.

Because of this hatred toward Yazid and his seizing power away from Muhammad's family, Muhammad's grandson, al-Husayn, and one of his brothers—along with 71 followers—refused to acknowledge the right of Caliph Yazid to ascend to the position of caliph. Al-Husayn and his supporters engaged the Umayyad Dynasty's forces—which consisted of thousands of men at arms—with a predictable outcome. Ali's son, al-Husayn and his followers fought bravely, but not only were they defeated, but al-Husayn was also beheaded in the now familiar tradition of the "religion of peace." His head was taken to Damascus and laid at the feet of Caliph Yazid; thus, the Sunnis were able to secure their hold over the office of caliph.

With the passage of time, the office of caliph became open to all exalted Muslim leaders, similar to the process of the Roman Catholic succession of popes, which caused the Shi'ite ("Party") of Ali to permanently split from the Sunni caliphate as we shall see later.

173

Consequently, the Shi'ites' belief that the only proper right of succession to the caliphate should have been heredity, like a monarchy, meant they were only able to recognize Muhammad and the fourth caliph, Ali—and possibly Ali's son and Muhammad's grandson, al-Hasan—as the legal lineage of the founders of Islam.

PART 2: FUNDAMENTALS OF SHI'A ISLAM
FROM THE FIRST PROPHET AND
THE FIRST TWELVE IMAMS

While the Caliphate held control of Islamic power, the Shi'ites, who make up about 10-15% (depending on the source) of all Muslims, had what might be referred to as an Islamic subculture ruled by imams who are directly descended from Muhammad. In studying the twelve imams of the Shi'a, it becomes obvious that the names are not only similar but also confusing. That is because the Imam's names consisted mainly identifying them by including a son's father's name (note the inclusion of the word "ibn" in many of their names, which means "son of"), grandson of, and so on. This procession began with the Prophet Muhammad and the first recognized imam, who was also the fourth caliph, Ali ibn Abi Talib, Muhammad's first cousin, and son-in-law. It was believed that by having only descendants of Muhammad, Islam would be maintained pure. Again, like the disjointed composition of the Koran, dates and names and the order they fall in are just as inconsistent and confusing; therefore, what one source offers as a caliph or imam's name—as well as spellings—might differ, as well as the dates of events in Islamic history—and at times—might do so within the same article!

It is interesting to note that all the first twelve imams were descended through Muhammad by the marriage of his youngest daughter, Fatima, to his first cousin, Ali. Fatima was not only the closest child to Muhammad, but she was the only child of the Prophet to have any male children who survived beyond childhood, making Fāṭimah and Ali's descendants the only male heirs Muhammad would have. Thus, all the first twelve imams were descended from Muhammad through Fatima and Ali.

Imams

Imams are Islamic religious leaders. Although imams are found in both the Sunni and Shi'a branches of Islam, there is a difference between the Sunni and the Shi'a imams. For the Sunnis, an imam is the one who leads the formal prayers, whether in a mosque or other venues. The imam might lead a whole congregation or just pray with another Muslim. Sunni Muslims might also follow the ritual lead of the imam, copying his gestures as they worship. Imams can be found in all mosques, either as volunteers or part of a paid staff. According to the Hadith, imams are chosen based on their knowledge of the Koran and are men of good character and spiritual maturity, although age is not a requirement. Imams should be well versed in knowing the four disciplines of jurisprudence, also known as the Sunni Madhhabs. Women may also be imams, but only as far as instructing and leading among female only congregations.

Shi'a imams are more formal in a sense they are supposed to be godly men par excellence. The Shi'a imam's character should have the attributes ascribed to Allah with a focus on becoming more holy. They are chosen with the goal of them being exceptional examples to those both in and out of their communities and must project an appearance of *ismah*, which is an impeccable sinless life; in other words, a Shi'a imam must be above reproach because it is believed that they are called to their vocation by Allah.

In studying the twelve imams of the Shi'ites, we explained how the names are not only similar but confusing. The first recognized imam whom the Sunnis also considered the fourth caliph was Ali ibn Abi Talib, who was Muhammad's first cousin and his son-in-law. As mentioned above, it was believed that by having only descendants of Muhammad, Islam would be maintained pure. However, as we previously discussed, when researching the lineage of Shi'a imams, along with the dates, names, and the order they fall in, we find them also to be inconsistent and confusing. Therefore, what one source offers as a Caliph or imam's name, as well as spellings, might differ along with the dates of events in Islamic history, and many times, it does so within the same article!

As we previously explained, all the first twelve imams were descended through Muhammad by the marriage of his youngest daughter, Fatima, to his first cousin, Ali. Fatima was not only the closest child to

Muhammad, but she was the only child of the prophet to have any male children who survived beyond childhood. That resulted in Fatima and Ali's descendants being the only male heirs of Muhammad. Consequently, it is safe to say with assurance, that all the first twelve imams were descended from Muhammad through Fāṭimah and Ali.

The Imams of the Shi'a Twelvers and Their Deadly History

The Shi'a sect of Islam holds the belief that the succession of the leadership over Islam should be from a hereditary descendant of Muhammad's family, not unlike the succession of kings.

On the next few pages, we show the first twelve Imams and their untimely deaths—with the exception of the twelfth imam. The Mahdi, known as the "twelfth imam," is a messianic figure believed to have never died and is thought to be in hiding in a well in Iran, preparing to return on the Last Day.

It seems that poisoning the competition (other Shi'a imams) was a favorite past time of the Sunni Caliphs! Is it any wonder that even today, there is still so much bad blood between these two branches of Islam?

THE SUCCESSION OF IMAMS AFTER MUHAMMAD[15]

The First Imam

After Muhammad's death, his first successor was Ali ibn Abu Talib (601-661 A.D.). Although he was the fourth caliph (656-661 A.D.), he is considered the first hereditary imam and rightful successor to Muhammad due to his blood relationship as first cousin and son-in-law. We cannot find any source which tells us the years Ali served as an acknowledged Shi'a imam. It might simply be that Ali was absorbed into the Shi'a lineage of imams after the split between the Sunni and Shi'as occurred, and the time when Ali served as Caliph could also be considered as the time he served as an imam.

Shi'ites regard Ali as the first imam after Muhammad, not only because of his blood tie, but also due to a speech given by Muhammad at Ghadir Khumm where the Prophet of Islam appointed Ali ibn Abu Talib as his successor, which the Sunnis do not deny. Nevertheless, the Sunnis argue that Muhammad was only urging the people to hold his first cousin and son-in-law in high regard and not his heir apparent. On the other hand, Shi'as take what Muhammad said as evidence that Ali was to be Muhammad's hereditary heir. Based on that, they believe Ali and the other Shi'a imams—who were all close relatives of Muhammad—should be the rightful successors to Muhammad's legacy. That disagreement triggered the schism or split in the Muslim community (Ummah) and resulted in having two major divisions of Islam known as the "Sunnis" and the "Shi'as (Shi'ites)."[16]

The Second Imam

Hasan (not to be confused with Husayn below) ibn Ali (625-670 A.D.), was the oldest grandson of the Prophet of Islam. His mother was Fatima, Muhammad's daughter (see Chart 2), and his father was Ali, the first cousin of Muhammad. Hasan reluctantly became the fifth caliph after his father, but stepped down after seven months in favor of Muawiya I. Although Muawiyah I, was born into the Banū Umayyad sub-clan of the Banū Abd-Shams clan, which in turn was a sub-clan of the Quraysh tribe, he was not considered closely related to

Muhammad who was born into the Banū Hāshim clan, also a sub-clan of the Qurash tribe. Because of Hasan's direct lineage to the Prophet Muhammad, Hasan ibn Ali is considered by the Shi'as to be the second, lawful imam and is listed as having served as imam and caliph. It is believed that his wife poisoned him on orders from Caliph Muawiya (656-661 A.D.).[17]

The Third Imam

Husayn (not to be confused with Hasan above) ibn Ali (625-680 A.D.), was also a grandson of Muhammad and brother of the fifth caliph (670 A.D.) and second Shi'a imam. Hasan was killed and beheaded in 680 A.D. while praying at a mosque at Kufa. According to the Shi'a, Husayn ibn Ali served as imam from 670 till 680 A.D.[18]

The Fourth Imam

Ali ibn Husayn (659-713 A.D.) served as imam from 680 until 712 A.D. Ali ibn Husayn, like King David and Solomon, had a poetic flare and is credited with writing what is known as, "The Psalm of the Household of the Prophet." He was devoted to abstinence and the study of Islam. Ali's grandfather was Ali ibn Abu Talib. He was a great-grandson of Muhammad through his father, Husayn, who in turn was Ali ibn Talib's younger son and grandson of Muhammad.[19]

The Fifth Imam

After the death of Husayn, Muhammad ibn Ali (677-732/3 A.D.) became the fifth imam serving from 712 until his untimely death in 732/3 A.D. He was well respected as both a distinguished legal scholar and teacher of Sharia law by the Sunni and Shi'as alike. Because he was the first imam to be descended through both of Muhammad's grandsons, Hasan ibn Ali and Husayn ibn Ali, his full name is, Muhammad bin (son of) 'Ali bin (son of) al-Husayn bin (son of) Ali ibn Abi Talib.[20]

The Sixth Imam

Ja'far ibn Muhammad al-Sadiq (700/2-765 A.D.) became the sixth imam after the assassination of Muhammad ibn Ali and served from 733 until 765 A.D., where he was believed to have been poisoned in Medina by Mansur ad Dawaneeqi the Abbasid. He is descended through Ali on his father's side and is descended through Muhammad ibn Abu Bakr,' son of Abu Bakr' (first Caliph) and father of Aisha, child bride of Muhammad on his mother's side. It was through Ja'far that the theology of the Twelvers would eventually become. He is the last imam to be accepted by all the Shi'a sects, with the exception of the Zaydiyah sect. Ja'far al-Sadiq immersed himself in the study of Sharia law, Islamic theology, science and alchemy and is honored not only by Shi'ites but also by Sunnis as a transmitter of the Hadith. The traditions recorded by al-Sadiq have been estimated to be more numerous than all other Shi'a imam The Hadith combined.[21]

The Seventh Imam

Musa ibn Ja'far (745-799 A.D.) became the seventh Imam after the assassination of his father, Ja'fr al-Sadiq, serving from 765 through 799 A.D. Musa Ja'far was even recognized by Sunnis as a distinguished scholar. He was imprisoned on more than one occasion and was finally eliminated for good when he was ordered poisoned by Caliph Harun al-Rashid while being held in a Baghdad prison.[22]

The Eighth Imam

Ali ibn Musa (765/6-818/9) followed his father as imam from 799 until 819 A.D. Despite the two fractions of Islam being in constant odds with each other, Caliph al-Ma'mun made him a crown prince, only to assassinate him later, as suggested by some Shi'a sources. This occurred when Caliph al-Ma'mun had Ali imprisoned and poisoned like his father was in 817 A.D. [23]

The Ninth Imam

Muhammad ibn, Ali also called Muhammad al-Jawad or Muhammad ibn 'Ali ibn Musa (810-835 A.D.), not to be confused with the fifth imam of the same name or the tenth imam, Ali ibn Muhammad. Ali was in office during 819-835 A.D., which would make him nine years old when he became the ninth imam; nevertheless, it has been said that despite his youth, he was very mature for his age. Muhammad ibn Ali was not only the youngest imam, but also lived the shortest time of any imam. He was poisoned at age 25 by his wife.[24]

The Tenth Imam

Ali ibn Muhammad, also known as Ali al-Hadi (827/8-868 A.D.), became the tenth imam after the death of his father, Muhammad ibn Ali, also known as Muhammad al-Jawad, the ninth imam. Ali ibn Muhammad was in office from 835 until 868 A.D. Like his father, he ascended to the office of an imam at a very early age, possibly around eight or nine years old, although he was in office until his assassination around age 41. He was known as the "Guide" or the "Pure One." He was able to firm up the Shi'a community and its network which generated good cash flow.[25]

The Eleventh Imam

Hasan ibn Ali (846-874) is not to be confused with Hasan ibn Ali, the second imam. Hasan was also called Hasan ibn Ali ibn Muhammad and Abu Muhammad, as well as Ibn al-Ridha. He became the eleventh imam after the death of his father, Ali ibn Muhammad. He served from 868 to 874 A.D. Because the Sunni population far outnumbered the Shi'a population, the Shi'a imams were subjected to the power wielded by the caliphs. Caliph al-Mu'tamid was no exception, and because the Shi'a population was increasing in numbers and power, he went out of his way to pressure Hasan ibn Ali by placing stricter restrictions on him and suppressing the Shi'a population even more. Hasan ibn Ali was assassinated at the age of 28 on the orders of Caliph al-Mu'tamid.[26]

The Twelfth Imam

We now arrive at the twelfth and final imam, Muhammad ibn al-Hasan (868 A.D. — ?), who is believed to still be alive and hiding in an Iranian well until the time of his return is revealed. It is said that Muhammad ibn al-Hasan, known as the Shiite's messianic figure called the "Mahdi" (not to be confused with the Sunni's Mahdi), went into occultation in 872 A.D. (from the word "occult" which means "hidden"). The Mahdi, who is the infallible, male descendant of Muhammad, will return with Christ Jesus at the Last Day to bring justice and peace to the world. As we explained at the beginning of Chapter 7, one way the Mahdi will accomplish this feat is through his lieutenant, *Isa* (Jesus), who will come down with him and break all the crosses. He will tell His followers that He is a Muslim prophet, and they should not believe the lie that He is the son of Allah (one does not join anyone with Allah). He will instruct all the Christians and Jews that they must convert to Islam or be destroyed.[27]

Table 7. Review of the Deaths of the Early Shi'ite Imams (Including Muhammad), Their Years in Office and How They Died

MUHAMMAD AND THE TWELVE IMAMS	HOW THEY DIED
Muhammad (570-632 A.D.)	Assassinated (poisoned) in 632 A.D. As recorded in the Hadith, Muhammad died unexpectedly in Medina at age 62.[28]
First Imam: Ali ibn Abu Talib (656-661 A.D.)	Assassinated by the Kharijite, Abd al-Rahman ibn Muljam, with a poisoned sword while praying in a mosque 661 A.D.[29]
Second Imam: Hasan ibn Ali (625-670 A.D.)	According to most Shi'a sources, he was slain by a poison-covered sword in Medina on the instruction of Caliph Muawiya who became the first Umayyad Caliph in 670 A.D.[30]
Third Imam: Husayn ibn Ali (670-680 A.D)	Because he would not bow to the authority of Caliph Yazid, the Caliph's army intercepted a caravan Husayn was in at Karbala. A battle pursued where Husayn was killed, after which he was beheaded in 680 A.D.[31]
Fourth Imam: Ali ibn Husayn (680- 712 A.D.)	Most Shi'a scholars say Husayn was poisoned on orders of Caliph Hisham ibn Abd al-Malik of the Umayyad Dynasty in Medina during 712/13 AD.[32]
Fifth Imam: Muhammad ibn Ali (712-732/3 A.D.)	Most Shi'a scholars believe Ali was poisoned by Ibrahim ibn Walid 'Abdullah in Medina on the orders of Caliph Hisham ibn Abd al-Malik.[33]
Sixth Imam: Ja'far ibn Muhammad al-Sadiq (733-765 A.D.)	According to most Shi'a scholars, after being imprisoned in Medina, Ja'far ibn Muhammad al-Sadiq was assassinated by poisoning on orders of Caliph Mansur.[34]
Seventh Imam: Musa ibn Ja'far (765-799 A.D.)	Like his father, Musa ibn Ja'far, he was imprisoned in Baghdad by Caliph Harun al-Rashid and ordered to be poisoned.[35]

Eighth Imam: Ali ibn Musa, also known as, Ali al-Ridha (799-818/9 A.D.)	Ali ibn Musa lived under the unpopular Abbasid Dynasty of caliphs when Shi'ites would regularly riot in the streets. Caliph al-Ma'mun wanted to find a way to put an end to the Shi'ite revolts, so he decided to appoint Musa (a Shi'a) as a successor he could control and thus pacify the Shi'as. However, Musa became too popular, so Caliph al-Ma'mun decided to correct his error in judgment by arranging for the assassination of Musa by poison.[36]
Ninth Imam: Muhammad ibn Ali (819-835 A.D.)	Despite his piety and generosity, Muhammad ibn Ali was poisoned by his wife in the city of Baghdad at the request of Caliph al-Mu'tasim in 835 A.D.[37]
Tenth Imam: Ali ibn Muhammad (835- 868 A.D.)	According to Shi'a sources, Ali ibn Muhammad was poisoned in Samarra, Iraq, on orders of Caliph al-Mu'tazz during 868 A.D.[38]
Eleventh Imam: Hasan ibn Ali (868-874 A.D)	Most Shi'a sources say that Hasan ibn Ali was also poisoned in Samarra, Iraq, on orders of Caliph al-Mu'tamid during 874 A.D.[39]
Twelfth Imam: Muhammad ibn al-Hasan, also known as the "Mahdi" (874 A.D.—)	When the Mahdi was only five years old, he became the twelfth imam at the time his father died. He led the Shi'as in prayer at his father's funeral and then returned to his house and disappeared. Fearing the apparent threat of this incredible youngster, the caliph sent his army to find the Mahdi, but they were unable to find him. The doctrine of "Ghayba" (concealment) is the doctrine explaining that the twelfth imam was taken by Allah and placed into protective hiding. The belief is that the Mahdi is still alive and in hiding today. Tradition says he will return on the white horse of Revelation 6:2 with his lieutenant Jesus, who will break the church crosses and usher in the Last Day.[40]

SUMMARY OF THE IMAMS' DEATHS
BEGINNING WITH THE PROPHET OF ISLAM

Muhammad, the Prophet of Islam (610-632), died from poisoning or complications from a previous poisoning.

1st Imam: Ali ibn Abu Talib (also the fourth Caliph) (656-661 A.D.) Son-in-law and 1st cousin of Muhammad. Considered the first imam and rightful successor of all Shi'a. Known as the "Commander of the Faithful." Assassinated while praying in a mosque.

2nd Imam: Hasan ibn Ali (625-670 A.D.). Muhammad's oldest remaining grandson known as "The Chosen." His wife poisoned him on orders of Caliph Muawiya.

3rd Imam: Husayn ibn Ali (670 A.D.) Grandson of Muhammad and brother of Hasan ibn Ali. He was known as the "Master of the Martyrs." He was captured (Battle of Karbla) then beheaded in 680 A.D.

4th Imam: Ali ibn Husayn (680-712 A.D.) was known for his zealous love of Islam and often referred to as the "One who constantly prostrates (in prayer)" and an "Ornament of Worshippers." Assassinated by poison.

5th Imam: Muhammad ibn Ali (712-733 A.D.). A great teacher of Sharia law and known as the "Revealer of Knowledge." Assassinated by poison.

6th Imam: Ja'far ibn Muhammad al-Sadiq (700/2-765 A.D.) A great teacher of Sharia law and known as the "Revealer of Knowledge." He is responsible for developing the theology of Twelvers. Ja'far was a prominent chemist, alchemist, astrologer, engineer, geographer, philosopher, pharmacist, and physician. Assassinated by poison.

7th Imam: Musa ibn Ja'far (765-799 A.D.). He established the network of agents who collected khums (i.e., military obligation to pay one-fifth tax on all the spoils gained in military conquests). He is known as the "Calm One" or the "one who controls his anger." Assassinated by poison.

8th Imam: Ali ibn Musa (799-819 A.D). Known as the "Pleasing One," he was noted for his dialogue with Muslim and non-Muslim theologians alike. Assassinated by poison.

9th Imam: Muhammad ibn Ali (819-835 A.D.). Known for being both a generous man and his piety in the face of persecution. He was known as the "God-Fearing, the Generous." Assassinated by poison.

10th Imam: Ali ibn Muhammad (835-868 A.D.). Fortified the deputies making up the Shi'a community network, he was referred to as the "Guide" or the "Pure One." Assassinated by poison.

11th Imam: Hasan ibn Ali (868-874 A.D.). He was called the "Citizen of a Garrison Town" or "al-Askari" (askar meaning "military" in Arabic) because he made his home in Samarra, which was a military garrison—assassinated by poison.

12th Imam: Muhammad ibn al-Hasan or the *"Mahdi"* AKA the vanished and is believed by secular historians to have been killed, but Sunni Muslims believe he is still alive and in hiding, awaiting the Last Day (tradition says he will return on the white horse found in the book of Revelation 6:2). The Mahdi will be accompanied by the Muslim Jesus, who will break all the crosses and confess that he—Jesus—is a Muslim prophet.[41]

Finally, we are able to conclude that Islam is not the "religion of peace" that many politicians, some non-Muslim religious leaders, and Islamic scholars would have us believe.

Islam was founded on violence, and violence is the legacy bestowed on it by Muhammad and its founders.

NOTES:

1. Caliph (Islamic title), *Encyclopædia Britannica*, last updated November 9, 2014. Web. 06 Feb. 2015.
2. The rider on the white horse in Revelation 6 is generally considered to be the Antichrist. We know it is not Jesus because Jesus—the Lamb of God—is the one who opens the seal revealing the Four Horsemen of the Apocalypse in Revelation 6:1. Jesus then continues to open even more seals (Revelation 6:12; 8:1). Much later in Revelation 19:1, 19:14, Jesus is also mounted on a white horse and descends out of Heaven.
3. Wikipedia contributors, "The Twelve Imams," *Wikipedia, The Free Encyclopedia,* 22 Aug. 2015. Web. 6 Feb. 2015.
4. Abdulaziz Abdulhussein Sachedina, *Islamic Messianism: The Idea of the Mahdi in Twelver Shi'ism* (Albany, State University of New York, 1981), 2.
5. Al-Ahbar, Ka'ab (2015 May 26), *Wikipedia, The Free Encyclopedia.* Web. 06 Feb. 2015. Al-Asqalani, Ibn Hajar (also known as Shaykh al Islam), a 14th-century Shafiite Sunni scholar, believed Ka'ab to be a trustworthy scholar, as opposed to Muhammad al-Tijani, a 20th-century Shi'a scholar who believed "He was a Jew from Yemen who pretended to have embraced Islam, then went to Medina during the reign of Umar ibn al-Khattab."
6. Muhammad Ibn 'Izzat and Muhammad 'Arief *al-Mahdi and the End of Time* (London: Dar Al Taqwa Ltd., 1997), 15.
7. "Narrated [by] Abu Huraira: the Prophet (PBUH) said, 'There is no prophet between me and him, that is, Jesus (PBUH). He will descend (to the earth) ... He will fight the people for the cause of Islam. He will break the cross, kill swine, and abolish jizya. Allah will perish all religions except Islam. He will destroy the Antichrist and will live on the earth for forty years, and then he

will die. The Muslims will pray over him' " [Hadith] Sunan Abu Dawud Book 37, Number 4310; also [Hadith] Sahih al-Bukhari, Volume 3, Book 34, Number 425; Sahih al-Bukhari, Volume 3, Book 43, Number 656; Volume 4, Book 55, Number 657, etc. PBUH is sometimes written P.B.U.H. It is an acronym for "peace be upon him."

8. Mazheruddin Siddiqi, *Modern Reformist Thought in the Muslim World* (Islamabad: Adam Publishers & Distributors, 1982), 147.
9. Richard R. Losch, *The Many Faces of Faith: A Guide to World Religions and Christian Traditions* (Wm. B. Eerdmans Publ. Co., 2001).
10. Seyyed Hossein Nasr, "Ali: Muslim Caliph," *Encyclopedia Britannica Online*. Encyclopædia Britannica, n.d. Web. 06 Feb. 2015.
11. Wilferd Madelung, *The Succession to Muhammad: A Study of the Early Caliphate* (Cambridge: Cambridge University Press. 1997), 3331–3332.
12. The Editors of Encyclopædia Britannica, "Al-Husayn Ibn 'Ali: Biography—Muslim Leader and Martyr," *Encyclopedia Britannica Online*. Encyclopædia Britannica, n.d. Web. 06 Feb. 2015.
13. One of the things we have noticed when researching Islam on line is that facts change and are replaced constantly. Because of that, Yazid's death is hard to document, which gives us more reason to consider foul play. There are many conflicting reports on how he died, with many who completely avoided acknowledging his death entirely. Several say he was killed by his horse or that he fell to death off of his horse (Balādhurī, *Ansāb al-Ashraf,* vol. 5, p.287), while several say he died of an unknown/mysterious illness (poison?). New World Encyclopedia.org says Yazid besieged Mecca, but "the siege ended when Yazid died suddenly in 683" without telling us the cause of his death. The place of his death varies from Bagdad to Mecca to Huwwarin, Syra.

14. Reinhard Federmann, *THE ROYAL ART OF ALCHEMY* (Bala Cynwyd: Chilton Book Co., 1968), 40.
15. The Twelve Imams. (2016, January 30). *In Wikipedia, The Free Encyclopedia*. Retrieved 04:45, March 15, 2016,
16. Highlights: "Wilferd Madelung." *Encyclopaedia Iranica*. n.d. Web. 18 Mar. 2016.
17. Madelung. *"ḤOSAN B. ʿALI B. ABI ṬĀLEB."*
18. Al-Tabataba'i, Muhammad H. *Shi'ite Islam*. Trans. Seyyed Hossein Nasr (Albany: State U of New York Press, 1979), 202.
19. Al-Tabataba'i. *Shi'ite Islam*, 203.
20. Al-Tabataba'i. *Shi'ite Islam*, 201-204.
21. Abdulaziz Abdulhussein Sachedina. *The Just Ruler (al-sultān Al-ʿādil) in Shīʿite Islam: The Comprehensive Authority of the Jurist in Imamite Jurisprudence* (New York: Oxford University Press., 1988), 53-54.
22. Al-Tabataba'i. *Shi'ite Islam*, 205-207.
23. Al-Tabataba'i. *Shi'ite Islam*, 207.
24. Wilferd Madelung, *"ʿALĪ AL-HĀDĪ."*
25. Al-Tabataba'i. *Shi'ite Islam*, 209-210.
26. Al-Tabataba'i. *Shi'ite Islam*, 210-211.
27. (Hadith) *Sahih al-Bukhari*, narrated by 'Aisha: Volume 5, Book 59, Number 713.
28. Seyyed Hossein Nasr. "Ali." (Alternative title: ʿAlī ibn Abū Ṭālib) *Encyclopædia Britannica Online*. Encyclopædia Britannica, n.d. Web. 18 Mar. 2016.
29. Al-Tabataba'i. *Shi'ite Islam*, 195.
30. Madelung. *Hosyayn B. Ali*
31. Al-Tabataba'i. *Shi'ite Islam*, 202
32. Al-Tabataba'i. *Shi'ite Islam*, 203.
33. Al-Tabataba'i. *Shi'ite Islam*, 203-204.
34. Sachedina. *The Just Ruler (al-sultān Al-ʿādil) in Shīʿite Islam*: 53-54.
35. Al-Tabataba'i. *Shi'ite Islam,* 205-207.
36. Al-Tabataba'i. *Shi'ite Islam*, 207.
37. Al-Tabataba'i. *Shi'ite Islam*, 208-209.
38. Al-Tabataba'i. *Shi'ite Islam*, 209-210.
39. Al-Tabataba'i. *Shi'ite Islam*, 210-211.

40. Sahih Bukhari Volume 3, Book 34, Number 425
41. Tamara Sonn. *A Brief History of Islam* (Malden: Blackwell Publ., 2004), 209

CHAPTER 8

ISLAM IS MORE THAN A RELIGION: IT IS A PROTRACTED, WORLDWIDE SOCIOECONOMIC—LEGAL—GEOPOLITICAL MILITARISTIC—RELIGIOUS SYSTEM

Islam is more than a religion. When America's Founding Fathers, with their collective wisdom, enshrined the First Amendment to the Constitution of the United States of America, which guarantees the free practice of religion and forbids the Congress of the United States of America from establishing any formal religion, they did so with the Western understanding of what religion meant. Regarding the wording of the Establishment Clause, we must understand that "denomination" and "religion" were interchangeable when the Constitution was written. Even today—if you were to ask someone what their religion is—you might hear, "I'm a Catholic," "I'm a Lutheran," or "I'm non-denominational," etc.

Many signers of the First Amendment were from England, where the state religion was the Anglican religion or denomination. The Puritans were also English, but they could not freely practice their religion (even though they were Christians) in England. Because the mindset of the Founding Fathers of America associated denomination with religion, Islam was not of primary concern or consideration until around 1785 when the Islamic Barbary pirates began attacking

American shipping vessels near the Middle East. It was not until May of 1801 A.D. when the pasha of Tripoli, Yusuf Karamanli, declared war on the United States, that some Americans began to take notice. Up until then, our ancestors only had a vague idea about Islam. When Thomas Jefferson was the ambassador to France, he had the opportunity to ask the Muslim ambassador from Tripoli why Muslims were attacking American ships.   Jefferson later detailed the ambassador's response:

> It was written in their Koran that all nations which had not acknowledged the Prophet were sinners, whom it was the right and duty of the faithful to plunder and enslave; and that every mussulman [Muslim-man] who was slain in this warfare was sure to go to Paradise ("American Peace Commissioners to John Jay," 28 March 1786, bracketed clarification mine).[1]

Thomas Jefferson continued to be troubled by the ambassador's remarks and the unfounded attacks by the Tripoli pirates on American shipping vessels. He was also disturbed with the enslavement and ransoming of American sailors and passengers, some of whom were women; therefore, Jefferson wanted to learn more about the mindset of the Muslim adversaries. Because the fledgling United States had no Secret Service, CIA, or any spy agency at that time, he turned to a source that contained all he needed to know about America's new enemy—a Koran. He began studying what motivated Muslims, how they thought, and what their religion expected of them. Jefferson learned that the religion of Islam is more than just a religion with rituals and adoration toward its deity—Islam is also a geopolitical and militaristic force. By understanding the mindset of his enemy (unlike most of today's American and European government officials), Jefferson was able to defeat the Barbary pirates in what was America's first foreign war and enshrined in the first line of the Marine's hymn, "From the halls of Montezuma to the shores of Tripoli."

The Arab researcher, Brahim Sene, provides us with some more insight into the perplexing Islamic philosophy as to whether it is simply just a religion or something even more sinister:

Philip Hitti, the late Lebanese-American scholar who taught at Princeton University for nearly fifty years, was a leading expert on the history of Arabs and Islam. One of his books has three parts: Islam as Religion, Islam as State, and Islam as Culture. Whether Muslims are aware of it or no, orthodox Islam is a threefold system—a religious-political-cultural ideology—with the goal to subjugate the world to itself.[2]

The Muslims' worldview is that Sharia law came directly from Allah. When Muslims find themselves living in a non-Muslim country, they are allowed to "go along to get along." In other words, they might publicly live a moderate life in order not to draw attention to themselves, or bring suspicion or being singled out; nevertheless, Muslims do not consider themselves to be subjected to the laws of non-Muslim countries or constitutions because man created those documents. Muslims believe that if laws do not come from the Koran or from Allah, such as countries with a constitution like the United States, Sharia law supersedes those laws because men wrote the documents. A Muslim's loyalty must be applied accordingly.

When a Muslim politician or witness in a court of law takes an oath on the Koran (or any other method of proclaiming what they say is the truth), they are allowed to lie. (Allah himself is the best of schemers, Sûrah 3:54.) For a Muslim, Sharia law is the final authority and tiebreaker. It would be wise for us to be cautious when referring to the religion of Islam as just "another belief system" and whether or not it passes the test of being classified as just "another religion" under the United States Constitution's Freedom of Religion and Establishment clause.

ATTAINING WORLD DOMINATION OF ISLAM
THROUGH THE ELIMINATION OF ALL OTHER FAITHS

Those Who Refuse to Convert to Islam Will Either Be Killed or Punished with a Severe Tax (Jizya)

> And *fight them until persecution is no more,* and religion is all for Allah. But if they cease, then lo! Allah is Seer of what they do (Sûrah 8:39, emphasis added).

> *Fight those who believe not in Allah* nor the Last Day, nor hold that forbidden which has been forbidden by Allah and His Messenger, nor acknowledge the religion of Truth, (even if they are) of the People of the Book, until they pay the Jizya with willing submission, and feel themselves subdued (Sûrah 9:29, Abdullah Yusuf Ali, emphasis added).

> He [Allah] it is Who has sent His messenger with the guidance and the religion of truth, that He may make it *conqueror of all religion[s]* however much idolaters may be averse (Sûrah 61:9, bracketed clarifications mine, emphasis added).

In his book, *Slavery, Terrorism and Islam*, Dr. Peter Hammond explains that once Muslims begin infiltrating a country, they begin to implement a socio-economic-political takeover by the Islamic faithful. Dr. Hammond explains, "The primary aim of Islam is not spiritual but political." To that end, Dr. Hammond explains that once Muslims enter a country as ordinary immigrants or refugees, they are quick to adapt to their host country. Once they begin to grow in numbers (Muslims have a very high birth rate compared to non-Muslims), they start implementing the Islamization of their host country (see Figure 6). We can see how this plays out today by observing Muslims, not only in the European Union (EU), but also in Australia and America.

According to Dr. Hammond:

- At 1% of any given country, they will be regarded as a peace-loving minority and not as a threat to anyone.
- At 2% and 3%, they begin to proselytize from other ethnic minorities and disaffected groups with major recruiting from jails and among street gangs.
- From 5% on the exercise an inordinate influence in the population in proportion to their percentage of the population.
- They will work to get the ruling government to allow them to rule themselves under Sharia (law).
- When Muslims reach 10% of the population, they will increase lawlessness as a means of complaint about their conditions. Any non-Muslim action that offends Islam will result in uprisings and threats ...after reaching 20% expect hair-trigger rioting, jihad military formations, sporadic killings and church and synagogue burnings .... At 40% you will find widespread massacres, chronic terror attacks and ongoing militia warfare.
- From 60% you may expect unfettered persecution of non-believers and other religions, sporadic ethnic cleansing, use of Sharia law as a weapon and Jizya, the tax placed on infidels .... After 80% expect State run ethnic cleansing and genocide.[3]

Does any of this seem familiar, like something you might have recently seen on the news? It appears what Dr. Hammond outlined here is very similar to what we—as Americans—witness daily in our own country. Some may say that Muslims overcoming a nation by growing their numbers is just a conspiracy theory. Conspiracy theory? In England, when this book was first published, the name given to most baby boys was Noah. Beginning in 2003, it was Muhammad. This phenomenon is called the "Jihad of the Womb."

We do know that free speech, freedom of expression (drawing pictures of Muhammad), and the freedom to dress as you like (especially women) are incompatible with Islam. We also know that Islam is bent on world domination and not integration, which makes it incompatible with democracies. Sadly, we are unable to find any

Islamic country that is or has ever remained a true democracy.

Now the Muslim use of our First Amendment, allowing for Freedom of Speech, has proceeded to the next step. In Minneapolis, as well as in other cities, you can now hear Muslim prayers being broadcast five times a day, everyday morning noon and night![4] As if that weren't enough a proposed police patch, which has temporarily been put on hold by Dearborn city Mayor combined the words "Dearborn Hights Police" using Arabic and English![5]

Figure 6. Dearborn Heights Police Badge in Arabic & English

As we are seeing, in America Dr. Hammond's predictions are already being implemented true to form. Another example was on July 24, 2024, when Israel's Prime Minister, Benjamin Netanyahu spoke to a joint meeting of Congress at the US Capitol noticeably missing—showing poor Statesmanship—was the Democrat Vice President who is also the President of the Senate, Kamala Harris. Also absent was Congress woman and former Speaker of the House, Nancy Pelosi (D) and President Joe Bidden (D) who, incidentally, did not greet the Prime Minister's plane when he landed in the United States. Why? Because of Muslim demonstrators who burned the American flag, replacing it with the Palestinian flag and destroying monuments along with threats of not supporting them at the ballot box![6] Make no mistake what we are seeing is exactly the type of take over predicted by Dr. Hammond. Another of many examples is the redesign of

While it is true both Christianity and Islam believe that they must blanket the world with their faith before the End Days (Judgment Day) can come, Christianity seeks to reach the entire world through witnessing and love. Christians were told by Jesus to preach the gospel but not force it on anyone (Matthew 10:14). On the other hand, the religion of Islam seeks to bring about the Last Days through the sword, as we can see in the following comparisons.

✟ Christianity: "And this gospel of the kingdom shall be preached in all the world for a witness unto all nations; and then shall the end come" (Matthew 24:14).

☪ Islam: "The last hour will not come until the Muslims fight the Jews and kill them" (Hadith Sahih Muslim 41:6985a).

End Times Islamic World Dominance
Assisted by a "Vindictive" Muslim Prophet called "Jesus" (Isa)

Fig. 7. Propaganda Billboard Number 1 Sponsored by the Islamic Circle of North America

Islam claims that Jesus will return at the End of the Age as the Mahdi's lieutenant (we read about the Mahdi in Chapter 7), declaring that He never died on the cross and that He is not the son of Allah, but has converted to Islam and is now a Muslim. Jesus will break all the crosses on the churches. If the Jews and Christians do not convert to Islam, He will destroy them all:

[Hadith] Sahih al-Bukhari, Volume 4, Book 55, Number 657

Narrated [by] Abu Huraira:

Allah's Apostle said:

"By Him in Whose Hands my soul is, *surely (Jesus,) the son of Mary will soon descend amongst you and will judge mankind justly (as a Just Ruler); he will break the cross and kill the pigs* [i.e., Jews Sûrah 5:60) and there will be no Jizya (i.e., taxation taken from non-Muslims). Money will be in abundance so that nobody will

197

accept it, and a single prostration to Allah (in prayer) will be better than the whole world and whatever is in it." Abu Huraira added, "If you wish, you can recite (this verse of the Holy Book):—And there is none of the people of the Scriptures (Jews and Christians) but must believe in Him (i.e., *Jesus as an Apostle of Allah and a human being). Before His death. And on the Day of Judgment He will be a witness against them*" (4.159). (See Fateh Al Bari, Page 302, Vol. 7.) [Commentary in parentheses theirs, bracketed clarification mine—bolded emphases added.]

Destruction of Jews during the End of the Age is not only at the hands of Muslims and their Islamic Jesus, but even the stones and trees will assist in their demise:

Abu Huraira reported Allah's Messenger (may peace be upon him) as saying: The last hour would not come unless the Muslims will fight against the Jews and the Muslims would kill them until the Jews would hide themselves behind a stone or a tree and a stone or a tree would say, "Muslim, or the servant of Allah, there is a Jew behind me; come and kill him;" but the tree Gharqad would not say, "for it is the tree of the Jews" (Sahih Muslim Book 41 verse 6985).

NOTES:
1. "American Peace Commissioners to John Jay," 28 March 1786. "Thomas Jefferson Papers," Series 1. General Correspondence, 1651-1827. Library of Congress, 28 March 1786 (handwritten).
2. Brahim Sene, "Islam: More than a Religion," *Answering Islam*, n.d. Web. 20 August 2014.
3. Dr. Peter Hammond. *Slavery, Terrorism and Islam: The Historical Roots and Contemporary Threat* (Cape Town, South Africa: Frontline Fellowship/Xulon, 2010). Dr. Peter Hammond is a prolific author and frontline missionary who has pioneered evangelistic outreaches in the war zones of Mozambique, Angola, and Sudan. Reverend Hammond is the Founder and Director of Frontline Fellowship, the Founder and Chairman of Africa Christian Action, the Director of the Christian Action Network, and the Chairman of The Reformation Society. Dr. Hammond was born in Cape Town (in 1960) and brought

up in Bulawayo (in what was then war-torn Rhodesia—now Zimbabwe). He became a Christian in 1977. Dr. Hammond served in the South African Defense Force and studied at Baptist Theological College in Cape Town. He also earned a Doctorate in Missiology and has an honorary Doctorate of Divinity. Dr. Hammond has witnessed the atrocities of the Islamic influence on the nations of Africa, while also having personally been beaten by Muslim mobs, arrested and imprisoned because of his Christian faith and missionary work among the Muslims. He has been on the receiving end of jihadi stabbings and shootings. Many consider Dr. Hammond an expert on Islam.

4. Tarakji, Leila. "Islam's Call to Prayer Is Ringing out in More US Cities – Affirming a Long and Growing Presence of Muslims in America." *MinnPost*, Minneapolis Post, 6 Feb. 2024, www.minnpost.com/community-voices/2023/06/islams-call-to-prayer-is-ringing-out-in-more-us-cities-affirming-a-long-and-growing-presence-of-muslims-in-america.

5. McFall, Marni Rose. "Dearborn Heights Police Arabic Badge Sparks Fury." *Newsweek*, Newsweek, 5 Sept. 2025, www.newsweek.com/dearborn-heights-arabic-badge-backlash-maga-2125238.

6. "Netanyahu Seeks Support for Gaza War in Address to Congress." *Newsmax*, Newsmax Media, Inc. Newsmax Media, Inc., 24 July 2024, www.newsmax.com/us/netanyahu-speech-congress/2024/07/24/id/1173804/.

CHAPTER 9

SHARIA LAW

Regarding Islamic or Sharia law, the Encyclopædia Britannica states:

> ... Islam has a broader application than any Western secular law since it claims to regulate all aspects of life—duty to God, to one's neighbor, to one's self. It is really a system of duties, ethical, legal, religious, and governs not only the private life of the pious Muslim, but also criminal law. Its historical development began with Muhammad sitting as a judge in Medina; his decisions followed, at one time, the usage of the Arab and Jewish tribes of Medina; at another, his own personal judgment. At his death, he left behind the legislative enactments embodied in the Qur'an and the memory of his legal decisions. These were collected among the traditions (hadith), which recorded his sayings and doings, manners and customs, and his answers to questions on religious life and faith, and his decisions in legal disputes.[1]

The word "Sharia" means "the path" and is also known as "Islamic law." Some references to Sharia law also refer to the word "sunnah" (pronounced **sue**-nuh) (i.e., "a path that is direct, smooth, and an easy flow") as revealed through Muhammad's example of dealings with others. Because Sharia and Sunnah refer to a "path," the two words seem to be synonymous; however, some Muslim scholars insist that Sharia is not a formally written down set of laws and, therefore, cannot be numbered, unlike the formal 614 Hebrew laws. For that reason, Sharia law presented a challenge to codify and organize into a law book containing its hundreds and even thousands of individual existing Sharia laws.[2] It wasn't until the 14th century that a book dealing with Sharia law titled, *Reliance of the Traveller,* was composed by Ahmad Ibn Lulu ibn al-Naqib—a book still in use today.[3] Sharia law remains the motivating force behind the daily life of all Muslims to meditate on and follow.[4]

The foundation of Sharia law basically consists of the opinions from the Islamic community and commentaries, which have been written based on teachings found in the Koran and The Hadith. By no means is Sharia law simply a matter to compile or understand;[5] still, not all Muslims accept the two primary sources of Sharia law: the Koran and the Hadith. The *Quranists*, a small modernist group of Muslims, choose to reject the Hadith as a legitimate source of Sharia law. In some instances, there are many more verses covering the same subject, so because of the overwhelming volume of Sharia law, we have selected just a few examples the reader might find interesting under the subtitle, "Examples of Sharia" later in this chapter.

Sharia: The Shadow Government

The incorporation of Sharia law into any non-Muslim country is very dangerous because Koran believing Muslims will never totally subject themselves to any government's constitution. When push comes to shove, Sharia will always take precedence. Muslims have a duty to diligently work to incorporate Sharia law into their host country's legal system, usually by deception (beginning at first with seemingly inoffensive laws, such as financial transactions and family courts).

Building on this, something curious is happening in America at our Ivy League schools. Up until recently, law schools concerned themselves primarily with Constitutional Law. Harvard Law School (with support from the Saudi King) and Yale University (with the help of a millionaire Saudi businessman) have established schools of Sharia law.[6] In addition to this, Sharia law and Halal prepared food are also filtering down into our public schools. This is cause for concern because once Sharia law is allowed into the secular legal system, it becomes difficult to remove, and as the population becomes accustomed to having Sharia law, it becomes even more likely that it will eventually dominate the legal system. Sooner or later, it will usher in Islam as the overriding religion—which is the goal of Islam (Sûrah 8:39). As we shared previously, Muslim reasoning is because countries governed by constitutions are subjecting themselves to man-made documents, while Sharia law, according to Muslims, was created by Allah and given by Muhammad; therefore, Sharia law, by its very nature, is above all man-made governments and laws—including the Constitution of the United States of America. For Muslims to think otherwise is blasphemous—a condition worthy of death.

As we previously pointed out, Islam is more than just a religion. From a Muslim's point of view, Sharia law encompasses not only the governing of every Islamic nation but every aspect of a Muslim's life, including finances, religious obligations, treatment of women and enslaved people, hygiene, sex, legal obligations, diet, jurisprudence (which supersede the laws of any non-Muslim country), etc.

Since Muhammad began his life as a successful merchant, Muslims use it as an example to conduct various business transactions, write contracts, and do banking. He was the one chosen by Allah to receive the Koran—which also contains Sharia law—making him the final prophet whose authority must be followed. According to the Koran, his marriages and treatment of women and prepubescent girls are an example for all Muslims to follow. In Medina, Muhammad became a respected judge as well as a political and military commander. He founded and developed the formation of the Islamic society that every Muslim must submit to—known as Islam (i.e., "submission"). Again, Islam is more than a religion—it is an ideology on which every aspect of a Muslim's life is based. It is what Muhammad taught, how he fought and lived.

The following verse is an example of how—over time—a simple passage not only becomes a foundational source for Sharia law, but also brings more complicated judicial renderings which develop into a belief that allows the death penalty for anyone who criticizes Islam, the Koran, or its Prophet Muhammad:

Say: "Obey God, and the Messenger. But if they turn their backs [showing rejection], God loves not the unbelievers" (Sûrah 3:32, A.J. Arberry, bracketed clarification mine).

A Muslim could also conclude from this passage that it is permissible to kill a person because Allah rejects infidels. The beginning of this verse clearly states for them to obey Allah and the messenger, but if they turn their backs, reject, or criticize them, then by extension, Allah would not love them. Is it really such a stretch to conclude that incurring Allah's displeasure is reason enough for the death penalty? After all, in other passages of the Koran, we are told that they are to kill the infidels (Sûrahs 2:9; 9:5).

Using a seemingly simple verse of scripture from the Koran to create a complex set of laws, like the one above, is not unique to Islam. Just like Jewish Kosher Laws, cooking utensils cannot be shared to prepare meats or dairy products, based on a passage of Scripture, that does not allow the boiling of a calf in its mother's milk (Exodus 22:19b, repeated in Exodus 34:26 and Deuteronomy 14:21). Jews are not allowed to eat foods that combine meat and dairy because the dairy portion might accidentally be produced from the actual beef's mother. An example of a food that is not kosher is pizza with cheese and pepperoni. Islam also has a similar type of law for the preparation of food called "halal." We will cite this passage again under the heading of *Food Preparation*.

The codified book for Sharia law can be found in the *Reliance of the Traveller: A Classic Manual of Islamic Sacred Law.* The first part of the title, *Reliance of the Traveller,* is based on a verse from the Koran:

Say you: "This is my way [this is the way I travel]: I do invite unto Allah,—on evidence clear as seeing with one's eyes,—I and whoever follows me. Glory to Allah! And never will I join gods [Jesus] with Allah!" (Sûrah 12:108, Abdullah Yusuf Ali, bracketed clarifications mine).

EXAMPLES OF SHARIA

SHARIA LAW

Apostates

An apostate usually means someone who has fallen away from their faith; however, it must be pointed out that those who hold differing denominational viewpoints could be following a wrong (i.e., heretical) path and thus guilty of apostasy. In Islam, there is a debate regarding the level of degrees concerning apostasy and, consequently, the level of punishment to be delivered. A complete rejection of Islam by a former believer usually rises to the level of the death penalty.

Note: If child's father was a Muslim who died or left the family while the child was very young, which resulted in them being raised in another faith—perhaps the Christian faith, they would then be considered an apostate, even though they were never exposed to their father's Muslim faith (Hadith) Sahih al-Bukhari, Volume 9, Book 83, Number 17.

> (Allah's Messenger said), "The blood of a Muslim who confesses that none has the right to be worshipped but Allah and that I am His Apostle, cannot be shed except in three cases: In Qiṣāṣ [retaliation] for murder, a married person who commits illegal sexual intercourse and the one who reverts from Islam [apostate] and leaves the Muslims" (bracketed clarification mine).

We are also informed that a Muslim is required to have a basic knowledge of Islamic fundamentals. This enables jihadists to determine if a person claiming to be a Muslim is pretending in order to save his life by simply asking the intended victim some basic questions regarding the religion of Islam. If they answer correctly, they are allowed to live—if not, they die! This is explained in the following passage found in *Reliance of the Traveller*:

Someone raised among Muslims who denies the obligatoriness of the prayer, zakat, fasting, Ramadan, the pilgrimage, or the unlawfulness of wine and adultery, or denies something else upon which there is scholarly consensus (ijma', def: b7) and which is necessarily known as being of the religion (N: necessarily known meaning things that any Muslim would know about if asked) thereby becomes an unbeliever (kafir) and is executed for his unbelief (O: if he does not admit he is mistaken and acknowledge the obligatoriness or unlawfulness of that which there is scholarly consensus upon. As for if he denies the obligatoriness of something, there is no consensus upon, then he is not adjudged an unbeliever) f1.3. [7]

[Hadith] Bukhari, Volume 52, Book 4, Number 260

Narrated [by] Ikrima:

Ali burnt some people and this news reached Ibn 'Abbas, who said, "Had I been in his place, I would not have burnt them, as the Prophet said, 'Don't punish (anybody) with Allah's Punishment.' No doubt, I would have killed them, for the Prophet said, 'if somebody (a Muslim) discards his religion, kill him.' "

[Hadith] Bukhari, Volume 9, Book 89, Number 271

Narrated [by] Abu Musa:

A man embraced Islam and then reverted back to Judaism. Mu'adh bin Jabal came and saw the man with Abu Musa. Mu'ada asked, "What is wrong with this (man)?" Abu Musa replied, "He embraced Islam and then reverted back to Judaism." Mu'adh said, "I will not sit down unless you kill him (as it is) the verdict of Allah and His Apostle."

Banking

Those who devour usury [consume/charge interest on money loaned] will not stand except as stand one whom the Evil one by his touch Hath driven to madness. That is because they say: "Trade is like usury," but Allah has permitted trade and forbidden usury. Those who after receiving direction from their Lord, desist, shall be pardoned for the past; their case is for Allah (to judge); but those who repeat (the offence) are companions of the Fire: They will abide therein (forever) (Sûrah 2:275, Abdullah Yusuf Ali, bracketed clarification mine).

And if you do not, then be warned of war (against you) from Allah and His messenger. And if you repent, then you have your principal (without interest) [money]. Wrong not, and you shall not be wronged (Sûrah 2:279, bracketed clarification mine).

Blasphemy
(See **Defaming the Prophet Muhammad or Allah and by Extension, the Koran**)

Brushing Teeth

Because Sharia law covers every aspect of a person's life (including toilet habits), we offer this example of the Sharia law regarding the cleaning of teeth as established by Muhammad:

In the 7th century, Muhammad made rules for oral hygiene, and so it became a religious obligation. To this day, a siwak [also known as a miswak], a teeth-cleaning twig composed of aromatic types of wood, is still used. Chewing sticks not only helped to physically clean teeth, but also because they contain antibacterial oils and tannins, may help to prevent plaque.[8]

SHARIA LAW

Continued . . .

Capital Punishment

- ✓ The only reward of those who make war upon Allah and His messenger and strive after corruption in the land will be that they will be killed or crucified, or have their hands and feet on alternate sides cut off, or will be expelled out of the land. Such will be their degradation in the world, and in the Hereafter theirs will be an awful doom (Sûrah 5:33).

- ✓ Those who leave the religion of Islam, or those who will not accept the religion of Islam:

  > ...The Prophet said, "If somebody (a Muslim) discards his religion, kill him" (Bukhari Vol. 4, Book 52, Number 260).

- ✓ Murder, infidelity in marriage, fighting against Allah or Muhammad:

  > Allah's Apostle never killed anyone except in one of the following three situations: (1) A person who killed somebody unjustly was killed (in Qisas[9]); (2) a married person who committed illegal sexual intercourse, and (3) a man who fought against Allah and His Apostle and deserted Islam, thus an apostate (Sûrah 83:27).

- ✓ Jews who convert to Islam, then change their mind after doing so, must be killed:

  > ...A man who embraces Islam, then reverts to Judaism, is to be killed according to "the verdict of Allah and his apostle" (Bukhari Vol. 9, Book 89, Number 271).

- ✓ Homosexuals: "The Prophet (peace be upon him) said: If you find anyone doing as Lot's people did [Genesis 19:4], kill the one who does it, and the one to whom it is done" (Abu-dawud, Book 38, Number 4447, bracketed clarification mine).[10]

Methods of execution are usually a public event, including digging a hole, placing a person in the hole, and then filling the hole up to their neck, followed by throwing stones at the person's head until they are dead. Other methods of execution are lobbing off the head at the neck, cutting off limbs, and then crucifying them until dead. Those practices are still being conducted today. In Saudi Arabia, a maid was sentenced to death by stoning for adultery, but the man she slept with escaped with 100 lashes.[11] Again, we read how the so-called terrorists (in actuality, fundamentalists) group, ISIS, is simply following the teachings of Sharia as found in Sûrah 5:33 and other verses:

> ISIS savages cut off a Christian boy's fingertips in front of his preacher father before crucifying the pair of them, it has been reported. The terror group was trying to force Syrian Christians in a village near Aleppo to convert to their *twisted* interpretation of Islam. The boy, 12, was the son of a Syrian ministry team leader who set up nine churches in the war-ravaged country. (Emphasis added)[12]

Notice how the word "twisted" is injected into the article, yet this is the same Islamic Sharia law being practiced throughout the Muslim world today, including Saudi Arabia, where a man accused of rape and murder was beheaded, and then his body was crucified in public.

Censorship against Those Who Insult Allah and Muhammad

Sharia laws have been passed in many former Christian countries against anyone who speaks out against Muhammad and Islam. In the United Kingdom and Scandinavia, people who have spoken out against Islam and its prophet have been arrested and jailed! It has happened in America too.

In 2012, Nakoula Basseley Nakoula, a Coptic Christian and the producer of the film *Innocence of Muslims*, a crudely made movie spoofing Muhammad, was arrested, sentenced, and jailed after a 14-minute trailer of his film was released on the Internet. Under the Obama Administration, he became the first person in the United States to be jailed for violating Islamic anti-blasphemy laws and conceivably America's first political prisoner.[13]

This should not be surprising, however, in light of what former President Barack Hussein Obama said regarding his feelings toward Islam's prophet when he stated in 2012, before the United Nations, "The future must not belong to those who slander the Prophet of Islam."[14]

Obama said the movie was not listed as the cause of arrest; instead, the United States federal government arrested him for violating his probation from a previous crime. The violation was twofold: (1) He produced the film and posted its trailer on the Internet (supposedly resulting in deaths at Benghazi), and (2) he did this under a nom de plume also known as a "pen name," fearing for his life should his true identity become known (technically a violation of his probation) for which he received one year in prison.[15]

Possibly, some of our readers will remember what happened to the filmmaker, Theo Van Gogh (the great-grandnephew of artist Vincent Van Gogh), who was killed for making a movie exposing the mistreatment of women in Muslim countries. Perhaps the filmmaker, Mr. Nakoula, should have been forgiven for his understandable use of a *nom de plume* (while under probation for something else), which is also a common practice in the film industry—especially in light of what happened to Van Gogh—making it a misdemeanor at best—or maybe this was meant to be an example to those who might be considering making a negative film about the Prophet of Islam.

In America, under the Obama Administration, military training manuals with all references to Islamist terrorists, jihadists, and radical (fundamental) Islam were purged when Barack Obama was president. The Pentagon initiated special exceptions exclusively for Muslim men and women serving in the military.[16] Michele Bachmann, a former member of the United States House of Representatives who was also a member of the House Intelligence Committee under Obama, warned back then:

> And so now the White House has scrubbed all Islamic terms from the national counterterrorism strategy. The White House has removed all Islamic terms from the Pentagon's report on the

210

Fort Hood shooting. And now, Obama is allowing terror suspect groups to write the FBI's terror training manual.[17]

In all Islamic, Sharia-compliant countries, an insult or blasphemy against Islam carries a potential death penalty. The blasphemy laws that are punishable by death are based in part by exaggerating Sûrah 3:32, the first passage we looked at in this section, and is based on the following verse:

Those who annoy Allah and His Messenger—Allah has cursed them in this World and in the Hereafter, and has prepared for them a humiliating Punishment (Sûrah 33:57, Abdullah Yusuf Ali).

What would be a "humiliating punishment?"

Again, just three more verses later in Sûrah 33 we also read:

Truly, if the Hypocrites [professing Muslims who question the faith] and those in whose hearts is a disease, and those who stir up sedition [others who speak out against Muhammad and Islam] in the City, desist not, We shall certainly stir you up against them: Then will they not be able to stay in it as thy neighbors for any length of time:

They shall have a curse on them: whenever they are found, they shall be seized and slain (without mercy) (Sûrah 33:60-61, Abdullah Yusuf Ali, bracketed clarifications mine).

Charity

They ask you what they should spend (In charity). Say: "Whatever you spend that is good, is for parents and kindred and orphans and those in want and for wayfarers. And whatever you do that is good,"—Allah knows it well (Sûrah 2:215, Abdullah Yusuf Ali).

O you who believe! cancel not your charity by reminders of your generosity or by injury,—like those who spend their substance to be seen of men, but believe neither in Allah nor in the Last Day. They are in parable like a hard, barren rock, on which is a little soil: on it falls heavy rain, which leaves it (Just) a bare stone. They will be able to do nothing with aught they have earned. And Allah guides not those who reject faith (Sûrah 2:264, Abdullah Yusuf Ali).

If you disclose (acts of) charity, even so it is well, but if you conceal them, and make them reach those (really) in need, that is best for you: It will remove from you some of your (stains of) evil. And Allah is well acquainted with what you do (Sûrah 2:271, Abdullah Yusuf Ali).

Christians and Jews Who Refuse Islamic Conversion

The Koran says that non-Muslims living in non-Muslims countries are to be conquered for Islam and the growing world caliphate. Christians and Jews must be humiliated and forced to pay a tax if they refuse to accept Allah as god:

> Fight against such of those who have been given the Scripture as believe not in Allah nor the Last Day, and forbid not that which Allah hath forbidden by His messenger, and follow not the Religion of Truth, until they pay the tribute readily, being brought low (Sûrah 9:29).

Circumcision
(Including Female Genital Mutilation)

Under Sharia law, "Circumcision is obligatory (for both men and women)," which frequently results with the amputation of the woman's clitoris and mutilation of the female sex organs.[18]

e4.3 وَيَجِبُ (على كل من الـــذكر والأنثى) الخِتَانُ (وهـو قطع الجلدة التي على حشفـة الـذكـر وأما ختان الأنثى فهو قطع البظر [ويسمى خفاضاً]) .

To the left is a facsimile of the wording in the original 1368 A.D. text for verse e4.3, which addressed circumcision in the Arabic language as written by Ahmad ibn Naqib al-Misri in his book, *Reliance of the Traveller: A Classic Manual of Islamic Sacred Law.* Below is the original passage by Ahmad al-Misri, which reads:

e4.3 Circumcision is obligatory (for every male *and* female) by cutting off the piece of skin on the glans of the penis of the male, but circumcision of the female is by **cutting out the clitoris** (bolded and italicized emphasis added).

The original meaning of this passage is much different from the more acceptable English edited translation published by Nuh Hah Mim Keller in 1991 and revised in 1994. Typically, Muslims in Western countries engage in taqiyya to deny that this controversial and barbaric practice of *female genital mutilation* (FGM) is not sanctioned under Sharia law. They insist it is only an old tribal custom. Giving misinformation such as this is a technique known as *kitmān,* which exploits half-truths and suppresses information by saying it is an "old tribal custom." To some extent, this is true. Keller uses this revisionist spin in a parenthetical note, which he inserted into his translation, which reads in part:

e4.3 Circumcision is obligatory (O: for both men *and* women. For men it consists of removing the prepuce *from the penis*, and for women, removing the prepuce (Ar. bazr) of the clitoris (n: **not the clitoris itself,** as some mistakenly assert). (Itallics and brackets his, bolded and italicized emphasis added).[19]

Curiously, unlike the Bible, the importance of circumcision is never mentioned in the Koran, but circumcision for women (and men) is found in both the Hadith and Sharia Law.[20] Regardless of which translation above is more accurate, the female's sex organs are still mutilated in a horrifying and painful way.

Conquered People (see Dhimmi)

Covering of Women

And say to the believing women that they should lower their gaze and guard their modesty; that they should not display their beauty and ornaments except what (must ordinarily) appear thereof; that they should draw their veils over their bosoms and not display their beauty except to their husbands, their fathers, their husband's fathers, their sons, their husbands' sons, their brothers or their brothers' sons, or their sisters' sons, or their women, or the slaves whom their right hands possess, or male servants free of physical needs, or small children who have no sense of the shame of sex; and that they should not strike their feet in order to draw attention to their hidden ornaments. And O you Believers! turn you all together towards Allah, that you may attain Bliss (Sûrah 24:31, Abdullah Yusuf Ali).

Deception or Holy Deception, Also Known as Taqiyya (Lying)

It is forbidden for a Muslim to be deceptive or lie with four possible exceptions, one of which is—taqiyya (alternate spellings: taqiyeh, taqiya, taqiyah, tuqyah).

It is forbidden for a Muslim to be deceptive or lie, with few exceptions, one of which is taqiyya (alternative spellings: taqiyeh, taqiya, taqiyah, tuqyah). Taqiyya is a legal dispensation given by Allah, which authorizes Muslims who are being threatened because of their faith, to lie, or deceive others into believing they are not Muslims. The reason—for the sake of survival or to trick nonbelievers into accepting Islam as being something it is not (e.g., the appearance of being tolerant toward other religions. It allows for Muslims who live in a foreign country to assure those particular country's citizens there is no fear of a takeover by them. Yet, the Koran says all other faiths are subject to Islam, including laws and governments). Any means of lying is acceptable as a strategy as long as the end is justified by the means (e.g., the establishment of Islam over all religions, laws, and governments—a world caliphate. This concept is based on Allah himself is the greatest of deceivers, as conveyed in Sûrah 3:54 (see **Treaties**).

Any means of lying is acceptable as a strategy as long as the end is justified by the means (e.g., the establishment of Islam over all religions, laws, and governments—a world caliphate. This concept is based on Allah himself is the greatest of deceivers, as conveyed in Sûrah 3:54 (see *Treaties*).

And they (the disbelievers) schemed, and Allah schemed (against them): and Allah is the best of schemers (Sûrah 3:54).

Defaming the Prophet Muhammad or Allah and by Extension, the Koran

If someone defames the Prophet Muhammad, he will be killed:

> And of them are those who vex [blaspheme] the Prophet and say: "He is only a hearer." Say: "A hearer of good for you, who believes in Allah and is true to the believers, and a mercy for such as you as believe." Those who vex the messenger of Allah, for them there is a painful doom (Sûrah 9:61, bracketed clarification mine).

> The Hypocrites are afraid lest a Sûrah should be sent down about them, showing them what is (really passing) in their hearts. Say, "Mock you! But verily Allah will bring to light all that you fear (should be revealed)."

> If you dost [do] question them, they declare (with emphasis): "We were only talking idly and in play." Say, "Was it at Allah, and His Signs, and His Messenger that you were mocking?"

> Make you no excuses: you have rejected Faith after you had accepted it. If we pardon some of you, We will punish others amongst you, for that they are in sin (Sûrah 9:64-66, Abdullah Yusuf Ali, Bracketed clarification mine).

If the mother of a man's children—even if she is pregnant with his child—profanes the prophet, Muhammad—she should be killed:

(Hadith) Sunan Abu Dawood, Book 38, Number 4348

Narrated [by] Abdullah Ibn Abbas:

A blind man had a slave-mother who used to abuse the Prophet (peace be upon him) and disparage him. He forbade her but she did not stop. He rebuked her but she did not give up her habit. One night she began to slander the Prophet peace be upon him) and abuse him. So he took a dagger, placed it on her belly, pressed it,

215

and killed her. A child who came between her legs was smeared with the blood that was there. When the morning came, the Prophet (peace be upon him) was informed about it. He assembled the people and said: I adjure by Allah the man who has done this action and I adjure him by my right to him that he should stand up. Jumping over the necks of the people and trembling the man stood up.

He sat before the Prophet (peace be upon him) and said: Apostle of Allah! I am her master; she used to abuse you and disparage you. I forbade her, but she did not stop, and I rebuked her, but she did not abandon her habit. I have two sons like pearls from her, and she was my companion. Last night she began to abuse and disparage you. So I took a dagger, and put it on her belly and pressed it till I killed her.

Thereupon the Prophet (peace be upon him) said: Oh be witness, no retaliation is payable for her blood.

Dhimmi (Protected Non-Muslims)

In a Muslim country, *dhimmis* are a tolerated group of conquered non-Muslim people who are allowed to remain in their conquered country with the status of a non-citizen (slightly above a slave status), but are forced to pay the jizya (harsh tax).

BACKGROUND: When Muslims conquer an infidel nation (*dhimmis*), two things can occur. First, if they refuse to convert to Islam, they can be killed:

When thy Lord inspired the angels, (saying): I am with you. So make those who believe stand firm. I will throw fear into the hearts of those who disbelieve. Then smite the necks and smite of them each finger (Sûrah 9:12).

Second, they may be permitted to live as non-citizens (almost slaves) and pay a harsh tax called the jizya:

Fight against such of those who have been given the Scripture as believe not in Allah nor the Last Day, and forbid not that which Allah has forbidden by His messenger, and follow not the Religion of Truth, until they pay the tribute [dhimmi] readily, being brought low (Sûrah 9:29, bracketed clarification mine).

Direction of Prayer

We see the turning of your face (for guidance) to the Heavens: now Shall we turn you to a Qibla [indicator in a mosque showing the direction of Mecca] that shall please you. Turn then your face in the direction of the sacred Mosque: Wherever you are, turn your faces in that direction. The People of the Book know well that that is the truth from their Lord. Nor is Allah mindful of what they do (Sûrah 2:144, Abdullah Yusuf Ali, bracketed clarification mine).

Disciplining Children

When a Muslim child reaches the age of discernment (around seven years old), he or she should be able to eat, drink, and clean themselves after using the toilet unassisted. At this age, the child is ordered to perform the prayer, and when that child is ten, they can be beaten for neglecting their duty. The punishment should not be severe, but enough to discipline the child and not more than three "blows."[21]

Divorce

Women who are divorced shall wait, keeping themselves apart, three (monthly) courses. And it is not lawful for them that they should conceal that which Allah hath created in their wombs if they are believers in Allah and the Last Day. And their husbands would do better to take them back in that case if they desire reconciliation. And they (women) have rights similar to those (of men) over them in kindness, and men are a degree above them. Allah is Mighty, Wise (Sûrah 2:228).

A divorce is only permissible twice: after that, the parties should either hold Together on equitable terms, or separate with

217

kindness. It is not lawful for you, (Men) to take back any of your gifts (from your wives), except when both parties fear that they would be unable to keep the limits ordained by Allah. If you (judges) do indeed fear that they would be unable to keep the limits ordained by Allah, there is no blame on either of them if she gives something for her freedom. These are the limits ordained by Allah; so do not transgress them if any do transgress the limits ordained by Allah, such persons wrong (Themselves as well as others) (Sûrah 2:229, Abdullah Yusuf Ali).

And if he has divorced her (the third time), then she is not lawful unto him thereafter until she has wedded another husband. Then if he (the other husband) divorces her it is no sin for both of them that they come together again if they consider that they are able to observe the limits of Allah. These are the limits of Allah. He manifests them for people who have knowledge (Sûrah 2:230).

Food Preparation

According to Sharia law, preparation of food is similar in many ways to the Hebrew Kosher (*Kashrut* in Hebrew) laws we previously discussed. For example, look at the passages from the Koran compared with the Torah about eating an animal that has died by natural means compared with the Kosher Law below it:

He [Allah] has only forbidden you what dies of itself, and blood, and flesh of swine, and that over which any other (name) than (that of) Allah has been invoked; but whoever is driven to necessity, not desiring, nor exceeding the limit, no sin shall be upon him; surely Allah is Forgiving, Merciful (Sûrah 2:173, Muhammad Habib Shakir, bracketed clarification mine).

Do not eat anything you find already dead. You may give it to the foreigner residing in any of your towns, and they may eat it, or you may sell it to any other foreigner. But you are a people holy to the LORD your God. Do not cook a young goat in its mother's milk (Deuteronomy 14:21, NIV).

Of course, as with the Hebrew Kosher Laws, the Koran and Hadith contain many more verses referring to the Halal guidelines for food preparation.

Finances

> O you who believe! When you contract a debt for a fixed term, record it in writing. Let a scribe record it in writing between you in (terms of) equity. No scribe should refuse to write as Allah has taught him, so let him write, and let him who incurs the debt dictate, and let him observe his duty to Allah his Lord, and diminish naught [nothing] thereof. But if he who owes the debt is of low understanding, or weak, or unable himself to dictate, then let the guardian of his interests dictate in (terms of) equity. And call to witness, from among your men, two witnesses. And if two men be not (at hand) then a man and two women, of such as you approve as witnesses, so that if the one errs (through forgetfulness) the other will remember. And the witnesses must not refuse when they are summoned. Be not averse to writing down (the contract) whether it be small or great, with (record of) the term thereof. That is more equitable in the sight of Allah and more sure for testimony, and the best way of avoiding doubt between you; save only in the case when it is actual merchandise which you transfer among yourselves from hand to hand. In that case it is no sin for you if you write it not. And have witnesses when you sell one to another, and let no harm be done to scribe or witness. If you do (harm to them) see! it is a sin in you. Observe your duty to Allah. Allah is teaching you. And Allah is knower of all things (Sûrah 2:282, bracketed clarification mine).

In 2002, Osama bin Laden, after his attack on the U.S. Trade Center in New York, posted a letter accusing the United States of first attacking the Muslim so-called Palestinians. In November 2023, that letter was again exposed and went viral on the Chinese Communist Party's social media platform TikTok. One of the examples of the evils of America was, as he put it, the usury (interest) banks charged their customers. However, he was wrong as "Shariah Finance Watch," a project of the CENTER FOR SECURITY POLICY (Web. 16 July 2017), informs us that many American banking institutions *are* Sharia compliant (no interest on Muslim loans), including Bank of America, Bank of New York, Dow Jones, Barclay's Bank, J.P. Morgan Chase, Goldman Sacks, NASDAQ, CitiBank, etc.

Friends

O you who believe! Take not the Jews and the Christians for friends. They are friends one to another. He among you who taketh them for friends is (one) of them. Lo! Allah guides not wrongdoing folk (Sûrah 5:51).

O You who believe! Choose not for guardians such of those who received the Scripture before you, and of the disbelievers, as make a jest and sport of your religion. But keep your duty to Allah if ye are true believers (Sûrah 5:57).

Let not the believers take the unbelievers for friends rather than believers; and whoever does this, he shall have nothing of (the guardianship of) Allah, but you should guard yourselves against them, guarding carefully; and Allah makes you cautious of (retribution from) Himself; and to Allah is the eventual coming (Sûrah 3:28, Muhammad Habib Shakir).

Genital Mutilation—also known as "Female Genital Mutilation" (FGM). (See **Circumcision**)

Hajj: The Required Pilgrimage to Mecca

Perform the pilgrimage and the visit (to Makkah) [Mecca] for Allah. And if you are prevented, then send such gifts as can be obtained with ease, and shave not your heads until the gifts have reached their destination. And whoever among you is sick or has an ailment of the head must pay a ransom of fasting or almsgiving or offering. And if you are in safety, then whosoever contents himself with the visit for the pilgrimage (shall give) such gifts as can be had with ease. And whosoever cannot find (such gifts), then a fast of three days while on the pilgrimage, and of seven when you have returned; that is, ten in all. That is for him whoso folk are not present at the Inviolable [sacred] Place of Worship. Observe your duty to Allah, and know that Allah is severe in punishment (Sûrah 2:196, bracketed clarifications mine).

Holy War Is Necessary to Spread Islam—
Whether a Muslim Likes It or Not

> Warfare is ordained for you, though it is hateful unto you; but it may happen that you hate a thing which is good for you, and it may happen that you love a thing [avoiding war] which is bad for you. Allah knows, you know not (Sûrah 2:216, bracketed clarification mine).

> Then, when the sacred months have passed, then slay the idolaters wherever you find them, and take them (captive), and besiege them, and prepare for them each ambush. But if they repent and establish worship and pay the poor due, then leave their way. See! Allah is Forgiving, Merciful (Sûrah 9:5).

Honor Killings

Recently, in Western culture, we have been introduced to a new, unwelcome Muslim phenomenon—honor killings. One example is the 2011 murder of Noor Almaleki by her father, Faleh Hassan Almaleki, who ran over her in a mall parking lot in Peoria, Arizona.

> What exactly was Noor's crime? She refused to remain engaged to her fiancé, a prearranged marriage that was to take place in Iraq. She wanted to live in America, not in Iraq, and insisted on dressing like a well-dressed American girl, but even worse in her father's eyes, she dared to choose her own boyfriend, another Iraqi-American. Her father thought she had become too westernized, and in her family's eyes she was a "whore" and a disobedient daughter who deserved to die. Her father's honor depended on her death.

> He made his escape to Mexico with the help of his wife, Seham, Noor's mother and his son, Ali, then made his way to London's Heathrow Airport where he was extradited back to the United States to stand trial. He was convicted of the crime and given 34 1/2 years in prison.[22]

The Koran and the Hadith tell us who qualifies for honor killings:

A. Children Who Disgrace Their Family Should Be Killed

In Sûrah 18, a servant from Allah and Moses were on a trip together:

> They proceeded: along the journey until, when they met a young man and the servant from Allah slew him. Moses said: "Have you slain an innocent person who had slain none? Truly a foul (unheard of) thing have you done!" (Sûrah 18:74, Abdullah Yusuf Ali).

Moses was told to keep quiet and not to ask the servant from Allah why he killed the youth. Later on their journey, the servant from Allah broke the silence and explained to Moses:

> As for the youth, his parents were people of Faith [Muslims], and we feared that he would grieve them by obstinate rebellion and ingratitude (to Allah and man) so we desired that their Lord would give them in exchange (a son) better in purity (of conduct) and closer in affection (Sûrah 18:80-81, Abdullah Yusuf Ali, bracketed clarification mine).

B. Women Who Cheat on Their Husbands Should Be Killed

(Hadith) Sahih al-Bukhari, Vol. 2, Book 23, No. 413

Narrated [by] 'Abdullah bin 'Umar:

The Jew brought to the Prophet a man and a woman from amongst them who have committed (adultery) illegal sexual intercourse. He ordered both of them to be stoned (to death), near the place of offering the funeral prayers beside the mosque.

C. Death to Those Who Say Anything against the Prophet, Muhammad

(Hadith) Sunan Abu Dawud, Book 38, Number 4349
Narrated [by] Ali ibn Abu Talib:

A Jewess used to abuse the Prophet (peace be upon him) and disparage him. A man strangled her till she died. The Apostle of Allah (peace be upon him) declared that no recompense was payable for her blood.

D. Jews, Christians, Daughters, Sons, or Any Person Who Does Harm Against a Muslim Should Be Killed [23]

In *Reliance of the Traveller: A Classic Manual of Islamic Sacred Law*, we find that the following [honor killings] are not subject to retaliation:

A Jewish or Christian subject of the Islamic state for killing an apostate from Islam (O: because of a subject of the state is under its protection while killing an apostate from Islam is without consequences)

When a person who has reached puberty and [who] is sane voluntarily apostatizes from Islam, he deserves to be killed. 08.1

In such a case, it is obligatory for the caliphs (or his representative) to ask him to repent and return to Islam. I he does, it is accepted from him, but if he refuses, he is immediately killed. 08.2.[23]

E Those Who Leave Islam Should Be Killed.

Bukhari: Vol. 9, Book 89, No. 271

Narrated Abu Musa:

A man embraced Islam and then reverted back to Judaism. Mu'adh bin Jabal came and saw the man with Abu Musa.

223

Mu'adh asked, "What is wrong with this (man)?" Abu Musa replied, "He embraced Islam and then reverted back to Judaism." Mu'adh said, "I will not sit down unless you kill him (as it is) the verdict of Allah and His Apostle."

(See also Sahih Bukhari Volume 9, Book 84, Number 58.)

Inheritance

A woman can only inherit half the amount of a man, and in some instances, a wife is only allowed one-third to one-sixth:

It is prescribed for you, when death approaches one of you, if he leaves wealth, that he bequeath unto parents and near relatives in kindness (This is) a duty for all those who ward off (evil) (Sûrah 2:180).

Allah (thus) directs you as regards your Children's (Inheritance): to the male, a portion equal to that of two females: if only daughters, two or more, their share is two-thirds of the inheritance; if only one, her share is a half. For parents, a sixth share of the inheritance to each, if the deceased left children; if no children, and the parents are the (only) heirs, the mother has a third; if the deceased Left brothers (or sisters) the mother has a sixth. (The distribution in all cases is) after the payment of legacies and debts. You know not whether your parents or your children are nearest to you in benefit. These are settled portions ordained by Allah; and Allah is All-Knowing, All-Wise (Sûrah 4:11, Abdullah Yusuf Ali).

They ask you for a legal decision. Say: "Allah directs (thus) about those who leave no descendants or ascendants as heirs. If it is a man that dies, leaving a sister but no child, she shall have half the inheritance: If (such a deceased was) a woman, who left no child, Her brother takes her inheritance: If there are two sisters, they shall have two-thirds of the inheritance (between them): if there are brothers and sisters, (they share), the male having twice the share of the female." Thus does Allah make clear to you (His law), lest you err. And Allah hath knowledge of all things (Sûrah 4:176, Abdullah Yusuf Ali).

Jihad: Martyrdom Is the Guaranteed Path to Heaven

We cannot state it enough—the only assurance a Muslim has of going to Heaven is jihad. While jihad means "to struggle," out of the 164 jihad verses in the Koran, the majority of them—as seen in the last Hadith of this category—deal with some aspect of militaristic struggles, the distribution of the spoils of war both here on earth and in Heaven, including the use of women who are captured. Probably the most important issue to the observant Muslim is the assurance of attaining Heaven, which is guaranteed through dying for the cause of Islam. It is important to note that suicide is an unforgivable sin in Islam. ([Hadith] Sahih al-Bukhari, Volume 2, Book 2, Number 445.) But if Muslims blow themselves up and cause the death of infidels, they are not committing suicide—they believe they are dying as martyrs for the cause of Islam.

> Think not of those who are slain in Allah's way as dead. Nay, they live, finding their sustenance in the presence of their Lord ….

> They rejoice in the bounty provided by Allah: And with regard to those left behind, who have not joined them (in their bliss), the (Martyrs) glory in the fact that on them is no fear, nor have they (cause to) grieve (Sûrah 3:169-170, Abdullah Yusuf Ali).

From the Hadith, we also read:

[Hadith] Sahih Bukhari, Volume 4, Book 52, Number 73

The Prophet said, *"Paradise lies under the shades of the sword"* *(emphasis added)*.

[Hadith] Sahih Muslim, Volume 20, Number 4631

It has been narrated on the authority of Abu Huraira who said...," By the Being in Whose Hand is my life, I love that I should be killed in the way of Allah; then I should be brought back to life and be killed again in His way ..." [also see Sûrah 4:74].

[Hadith] Sahih Muslim, Volume 20, Number 4634

It has been narrated on the authority of Anas b. Malik that "The Prophet said, 'Nobody who enters Paradise will ever like to return to this world even if he were offered everything, except the martyr who will desire to return to this world and be killed 10 times for the sake of the great honor that has been bestowed upon him the Merit of Jihad and the Merit of Martyrdom.' "

Marriage

Do not marry unbelieving women (idolaters), until they believe: A slave woman who believes is better than an unbelieving woman, even though she allures you. Nor marry (your girls) to unbelievers until they believe: A man slave who believes is better than an unbeliever, even though he allures you. Unbelievers do (but) beckon you to the Fire. But Allah beckons by His Grace to the Garden (of bliss) and forgiveness, and makes His Signs clear to mankind: That they may celebrate His praise (Sûrah 2:221, Abdullah Yusuf Ali).

A. Acquiring Wives

Acquiring wives is permissible through war conquests, from close relatives or purchases. Regardless of how a wife is obtained, a Muslim man may only have four wives:

And if you fear that you will not deal fairly by the orphans, marry of the women, who seem good to you, two or three or four; and if you fear that you cannot do justice (to so many) then one (only) or (the captives) that your right hands possess. Thus it is more likely that you will not do injustice (Sûrah 4:3).

As for the first part dealing with orphan girls that are in a Muslim man's care and for whom he has sexual desires, Muhammad's wife, Aisha, provided an answer.

In the Hadith we read:

Sahih Bukhari Volume 4, Book 51, Number 25

Narrated [by] Az-Zuhri:

Urwa bin Az-Zubair said that he asked 'Aisha about the meaning of the Quranic verse:

"And if you fear that you will not deal fairly with the orphan girls then marry (other) women of your choice" (4.2-3).

'Aisha said, "It is about a female orphan under the guardianship of her guardian who is inclined towards her because of her beauty and wealth, and likes to marry her with a Mahr [dowry] less than what is given to women of her standard. So they [i.e., guardians] were forbidden to marry the orphans unless they paid them a full appropriate Mahr [dowry] (otherwise) they were ordered to marry other women instead of them. Later on the people asked Allah's Apostle about it. So Allah revealed the following verse:

"They ask your instruction (O Muhammad!) regarding women. Say: Allah instructs you regarding them ..." (quoting Sûrah 4.127, bracketed clarification mine).

In this verse, Allah indicates that if the orphan girl was beautiful and wealthy, and her guardian desires to marry her but is unable to give her an appropriate *mahr* (dowry) equal to what her peers would receive, he should not disrespect her, but seek to marry some other woman whose *mahr* [dowry] is more affordable.

Observation: While the most wives a Muslim man may have are four, an exception was made for Muhammad to have as many women as he wanted.

O Prophet! Look! We have made lawful unto you your wives unto whom you have paid their dowries, and those whom your right hand possesses of all whom Allah has given you as spoils of war, and the daughters of your uncle on the father's side and the daughters of your aunts on the father's side, and the daughters of your uncle on the mother's side and the daughters of your aunts on the mother's side who emigrated with you, and a believing woman if she give herself unto the Prophet and the Prophet desire to ask her in marriage—a privilege for you only, not for the (rest of) believers—We are Aware of that which We enjoined upon them concerning their wives [limit of four] and those whom their right hands possess—that you may be free from blame, for Allah is ever Forgiving, Merciful (Sûrah 33:50, bracketed clarification mine).

B. Girls and Women Who Have Been-Captured

And all married women (are forbidden unto you) save those (captives) whom your right hands possess. It is a decree of Allah for you. Lawful unto you are all beyond those mentioned, so that you seek them with your wealth in honest wedlock, not debauchery. And those of whom you seek content (by marrying them), give unto them their portions as a duty. And there is no sin for you in what you do by mutual agreement after the duty (has been done). See! Allah is ever Knower, Wise (Sûrah 4:24).

C. Acquiring Child (Prepubescent) Brides

The Prophet of Islam, considered by Muslim tradition to be "the most excellent example for all humanity," set the accepted standard when he (at age 51) asked Abu Bakr (who became the first caliph after Muhammad's death) for his six-year-old daughter's (Aisha) hand in marriage; nevertheless, Muhammad waited to consummate his marriage with her until she was nine years old.[24]

[Hadith]Sahih al-Bukhari, Volume 7, Book 62, Number 18

Narrated [by] 'Ursa:

The Prophet asked Abu Bakr for 'Aisha's hand in marriage. Abu Bakr said "But I am your brother." The Prophet said, "You are my brother in Allah's religion and His Book, but she (Aisha) is lawful for me to marry."

We should point out that it was a common practice in the Orient When a person was born, they used to count the first year in the womb as their first year of life (i.e., they are one year old when they are born. That is why King Herod—knowing that the Messiah was about to be born—had all children two and under killed (Matthew 2:16-18). By our standards in the West, the child would be five years old—in the Middle-East, she would be six years old—therefore, Aisha was probably five when engaged and eight when her marriage was consummated.

D. Sexual Relations with Wife

Your wives are as a tilth [a place to sow a man's seed] unto you; so approach your tilth when or how you will; but do some good act for your souls beforehand; and fear Allah. And know that you are to meet Him (in the Hereafter), and give (these) good tidings to those who believe (Sûrah 2:223, Abdullah Yusuf Ali, bracketed clarification mine).

Also in the Hadith:

[Hadith] Sahih al-Bukhari, Volume 7, Book 62, Number 81

Narrated [by] 'Uqba:

The Prophet said: "The stipulations most entitled to be abided by are those with which you are given the right to enjoy the (woman's) private parts" (i.e. the stipulations of the marriage contract).

Again, in the Hadith we read:

229

[Hadith] Sahih al-Bukhari, Volume 7, Book 61, Number 121

Narrated [by] 'Uqba:

The Prophet said, "If a man Invites his wife to sleep [have sex] with him and she refuses to come to him, then the angels send their curses on her till morning" (bracketed clarification mine).

E.   Beating a Wife

This is found in Sûrah 4:34 and the word used for "beat" is *daraba*.[25] It is interesting how the various English interpretations translate this word. Muhammad Habib Shakir and A.J. Arberry allow the word "beat" to stand by itself because there is no modifier before the word "beat" to soften its meaning. Abdullah Yusuf Ali also uses the word "beat," but does so with the added modifier "lightly," which makes no sense because the meaning of the word "beat" is the use of excessive force as opposed to just striking or slapping someone. Pickthall translates the word "beat" as "scourge" which, according to the Merriam Webster Dictionary, is "to inflict pain." Either way it appears that this passage does allow excessive violence against women:

> Men are the maintainers of women because Allah has made some of them to excel others [stronger than women] and because they spend out of their property [to support their wives]; the good women are therefore obedient, guarding the unseen as Allah has guarded; and (as to) those on whose part you fear desertion, admonish them, and leave them alone in the sleeping-places **and beat them**; then if they obey you, do not seek a way against them; surely Allah is High, Great (Sûrah 4:34, Muhammad Habib Shakir (bracketed clarification mine, bolded emphasis added).

We should point out that some modern Islamic translators—to put on a more positive face for Western consumption—suggest that what is really meant by "beating" is actually referring to using a toothbrush[26] (there were no toothbrushes in the 7th century). See **Brushing Teeth**), or slapping her with a folded handkerchief;[27] so according to them, we are to believe the warrior of Islam taught that if your wife gets out of line, whack her gently with your toothbrush, tenderly trounce her with a twig or lightly hit her with a hankie. You decide which one it is.

Police, Religious (*Mutaween*)

Aside from the familiar law enforcement officers who help keep the peace in our communities, in Islam, there are religious police who enforce Islamic moral laws, including dress codes. This is based on *Hisbah* (Arabic: حسبة *ḥisb[ah]*, or *hisba*), a historical, Islamic doctrine which means "accountability."[28] These enforcers are government sanctioned "volunteers" (*Mutaween* المطوعين) and as such are not usually found wearing any uniform and to the unwary Muslim citizen, they could be anybody on the street. The purpose of the Mutaween is to monitor the population at large to make sure that the strict Islamic rules are observed. This includes beating women on the spot in public for any infringement of Sharia's dress codes or being out in public without a male family escort. Enforcement of Sharia law is the duty of every Muslim, and it is also their duty to report any violation to the proper authorities. This makes George Orwell's novel, *1984*, look tame.

Questioning the Teachings of Muhammad and by Extension, the Koran

> Would you question your Messenger [Muhammad] as Moses was questioned of old? but whoever changes from Faith to Unbelief, Has strayed without doubt from the even way (Sûrah 2:108, Abdullah Yusuf Ali, bracketed clarification mine).

> If the hypocrites, and those in whose hearts is a disease, and the alarmists [those who question Muhammad and Islam] in the city do not cease, We verily shall urge thee on against them, then they will be your neighbors in it but a little while. Accursed, they will be

seized wherever found and slain with a (fierce) slaughter (Sûrah 33:60-61, bracketed clarification mine).

Religious Obligations

And keep up prayer and pay the poor-rate and bow down with those who bow down (Sûrah 2:43, Muhammad Habib Shakir).

This teaching is reflected in the Five Pillars of Islam (also see page 151) which are:

(1) Profession of Faith (2) Alms (3) Prayer (4) Fasting (5) Hajj

Stealing
(See *Thieves*)

Suicide

[Hadith] Sahih al-Bukhari, Volume 2, Book 23, Number 445

Narrated [by] Thabit bin Ad Dahhak:

The Prophet (PBUH[29]) said, "Whoever intentionally swears falsely by a religion other than Islam, then he is what he has said, (e.g. if he says, 'If such thing is not true then I am a Jew,' he is really a Jew)." And whoever commits suicide with piece of iron will be punished Prophet said, "A man was inflicted with wounds and he committed suicide, and so Allah said: My slave has caused death on himself hurriedly, so I forbid Paradise for him"

[Hadith] Sahih al-Bukhari, Volume 2, Book 23, Number 446

Narrated [by] Abu Huraira:

... The Prophet said, "He who commits suicide by throttling [choking] shall keep on throttling himself in the Hell Fire (forever) and he who commits suicide by stabbing himself shall keep on stabbing himself in the Hell-Fire."

Exception: As previously stated under *Jihad: Martyrdom Is the Guaranteed Path to Heaven*, when a Muslim blows him or herself up—and takes not only his or her life, but the lives of infidels—it is not considered suicide. Likewise, a Muslim who causes his or her own death through some other action at the expense of infidel lives (e.g., crashing a car, van, bus, airplane or sinking a ship) it is not considered suicide, but death by martyrdom in a jihad.

Thieves

> As for the thief, both male and female, cut off their hands. It is the reward of their own deeds, an exemplary punishment from Allah. Allah is Mighty, Wise (Sûrah 5:38).

However, there is an exception allowed in the next verse, although it is not always observed:

> But whoever repents after his iniquity and reforms (himself), then surely Allah will turn to him (mercifully); surely Allah is Forgiving, Merciful (Sûrah 5:39).

As we stated above, even if one repents, his hand will still be severed. There are several more verses that command the severing of the offending hand with no exceptions:

[Hadith] Sahih al-Bukhari, Volume 8, Book 81, Number 791

Narrated [by] Abu Huraira:

Allah's Apostle said, "Allah curses the thief who steals an egg (or a helmet) for which his hand is to be cut off, or steals a rope, for which his hand is to be cut off."

Muhammad's child bride, Aisha, informed us that Muhammad would even cut off the hand of his daughter, Fatima:

[Hadith] Sahih al-Bukhari, Volume 8, Book 81, Number 779

Narrated [by] Abu 'Aisha:

The Quraish people became very worried about the Makhzumi lady who had committed theft. They said, "Nobody can speak (in favor of the lady) to Allah's Apostle and nobody dares do that except Usama who is the favorite of Allah's Apostle." When Usama spoke to Allah's Apostle about that matter, Allah's Apostle said, "Do you intercede (with me) to violate one of the legal punishments of Allah?" Then he got up and addressed the people saying, "O people! The nations before you went astray because if a noble person committed theft, they used to leave him, but if a weak person among them committed theft, they used to inflict the legal punishment on him. By Allah, if Fatima, the daughter of Muhammad committed theft, Muhammad will cut off her hand."

This is quite a statement since Fatima became the youngest Muslim convert at the age of five.

Treaties

One of the rules of Islamic war follows the example of the Prophet Muhammad, who—because he was not initially militaristically strong enough—made a ten-year treaty with the Meccan Quraysh Tribe known as the *Treaty of Hudaybiyyah* and sometimes referred to as the *"Treaty of the Prophet."* Once Muhammad was militaristically strong enough—about two years after the treaty was signed—he used an excuse to break the treaty and attacked and conquered the unsuspecting Quraysh, consequently subjecting them to his new religion of Islam;[30] nevertheless, as we previously explained, in Islam taqiyya (i.e., deception) is allowed if it justifies preserving and/or the establishment of Islam (see Chapter 4, "The Doctrine of Taqiyya, Allah Approved Lying to Advance the Cause of Islam.").

Witnesses

When dealing with witnesses regarding legal (Sharia law) matters, a man's testimony is worth double that of a woman.

... And call two witnesses, from among your men, two witnesses. And if two men be not (at hand) then a man and two women, of such as you approve as witnesses, so that if the one errs (through forgetfulness) the other will remember ... (Sûrah 2:282, mid-way through the verse).

Women

IN ISLAM, WOMEN ARE SECOND-CLASS CITIZENS
WHO ARE MENTALLY DEFICIENT AND LEAD MEN ASTRAY;
MOST OF WHOM WILL TO GO TO HELL

Muslims believe a woman's mind is deficient; in other words, she is less intelligent than a man. Muslims also think that women are responsible for leading men astray (we cannot find in the Koran or Hadith where men lead women astray); therefore, the majority of those in Hell are women.

[Hadith] Sahih al-Bukhari, Volume 3, Book 48, Number 826

Narrated [by] Abu Sa'id al-Khudri:

The Prophet said, "Isn't the witness of a woman equal to half of that of a man?" The women said, "Yes." He said, *"This is because of the deficiency of a woman's mind"* (emphasis added).

(Hadith) Sahih al-Bukhari, Volume 1, Book 6, Number 301

Narrated [by] Abu Sa'id Al-Khudri:

Once Allah's Apostle went out to the Musalla (to offer the prayer) o 'Id-al-Adha or Al-Fitr prayer. Then he passed by the women and said, "O women! Give alms, as I have seen that **the majority of the dwellers of Hell-fire were you (women).**" They asked,

235

"Why is it so, O Allah's Apostle." He replied, "You curse frequently and are ungrateful to your husbands. I have not seen anymore more **deficient in intelligence and religion** than you. **A cautious sensible man could be led astray by some of you.**" The women asked, "O Allah's Apostle! What is deficient in our intelligence and religion?" He said, "Is it not the evidence of two women equal to the witness of one man?" They replied in the affirmative. He said, "This is the deficiency in her intelligence. Isn't it true that a woman can neither pray nor fast during her menses?" The women replied in the affirmative. He said, "This is the deficiency in her religion" (bolded emphases added).

THE WORLD UNDER SHARIA:
INSTITUTING SHARIA LAW IN NON-MUSLIM COUNTRIES

On September 16, 2010, the following article appeared in the *Dandenong Leader* [an Australian newspaper]:

DANDENONG'S mayor has called on residents to embrace a Muslim event at which people will be forced to cover up. The event, to be held after hours at the public Dandenong Oasis pool on August 21, 2001, will require all participants older than 10 to follow a dress code of knee-length shorts and t-shirts. Women and men attending the event, aimed at diverse backgrounds, will be required to cover their torsos, extending to the upper arms and from waist to knee.

The Victorian Civil and Administrative Tribunal granted an exemption from the Equal Opportunity Act after an application was logged by Victorian YMCA on behalf of itself and the City of Greater Dandenong. A women's only swim session has operated at Dandenong Oasis from 6:15 pm to 8:15 pm on Sundays for the past two years. Greater Dandenong Mayor Jim Memeti, said the women's only program had requested the council's support to hold a "one-off community event for two hours to celebrate Ramadan ... in a culturally respectful manner."[31]

In England's *The Telegraph*, an article dated August 19, 2009, by Patrick Sawer states, "Swimmers are told to wear burkinis (i.e., full-body coverage with a Burka-type bathing suit)."

> British swimming pools are imposing Muslim dress codes in a move described as divisive by Labor MPs (Members of Parliament).

> Under the rules, swimmers—including non-Muslims—are barred from entering the pool in normal swimming attire.

> Instead they are told that they must comply with the "modest" code of dress required by Islamic custom, with women covered from the neck to the ankles and men, who swim separately, covered from the navel to the knees.

> The practice runs counter to developments in France, where last week a woman was evicted from a public pool for wearing a burkini—the headscarf, tunic and trouser outfit which allows Muslim women to preserve their modesty in the water.

> The 35-year-old, named only as Carole, is threatening legal action after she was told by pool officials in Emerainville, east of Paris, that she could not wear the outfit on hygiene grounds.

> But across the UK municipal pools are holding swimming sessions specifically aimed at Muslims, in some case imposing strict dress codes.[32]

The United States has also been coming under Sharia law according to an article in *USA Today* by Oren Dorell, which reveals:

> Some public schools and universities are granting Muslim requests for call to prayers over a loudspeaker, prayer times, prayer rooms and ritual foot baths, prompting a debate on whether Islam is being given preferential treatment over other religions.

The University of Michigan at Dearborn is planning to build foot baths for Muslim students who wash their feet before prayer. An elementary school in San Diego created an extra recess period for Muslim pupils to pray.

At George Mason University in Fairfax, Virginia, Muslim students using a "meditation space" laid out Muslim prayer rugs and separated men and women in accordance with their Islamic beliefs.

Critics see a double standard and an organized attempt to push public conformance with Islamic law.[33]

In another article we read:

The Kansas City International Airport has added several foot-washing basins in restrooms to accommodate a growing number of Muslim taxicab drivers who requested the facilities to prepare for daily Islamic prayer [required by Sharia law], *WND [World Net Daily]* has learned... "Why are we constructing places of worship for them inside our airports?" said an airport official who requested anonymity. "Why are we catering to their [Sharia required] rituals? We don't do it for any other religion" (bracketed clarifications mine).

The article continues citing other cities dealing with Sharia law:

Other major airports also are dealing with increased demands from Muslim cab drivers. For instance, cabbies at Minneapolis-St. Paul International Airport recently caused a stir when they refused to carry passengers possessing alcoholic beverages or accompanied by seeing-eye dogs. Alcohol is forbidden in Islam [Sharia law], and dogs are considered unclean.

There are approximately 250 taxicab drivers operating at KCI [Kansas City International] Airport in Missouri, one of the largest airports in the U.S., linking some 10 million passengers between mid-America and other U.S. cities. Approximately 70 percent of the drivers are of Middle Eastern heritage and practice the Islamic faith [Sharia law], sources say (bracketed clarifications mine).[34]

This is not the only evidence of America subjecting itself to Sharia compliancy. Consider Walmart:

In what is touted as a definite first in America, a Walmart Supercenter in Michigan has now started to stock Halal meats. The 20,000 square foot facility in Sterling Heights opened this January 16th and is providing a range of services and products geared towards the multi-cultural communities in the neighborhood, C & G newspapers reported.[35]

This is just the beginning. There are also reports that some Subway and Outback Steakhouse franchises,[36] as well as KFC and McDonald's, are caving to Sharia halal compliant foods in the United States.[37]

As for banking institutions becoming financially Sharia-compliant, the government of the United States of America has already entered into Sharia-governed banking services:

On November 6, 2008, the Bush Administration held a seminar titled "Islamic Finance 101." The seminar attendees were welcomed by then Assistant Treasury Secretary of the Treasury, Neel Kashkari,[38] and seven years later (2014) he became a gubernatorial candidate for California.

Sharia banking does not allow interest to be charged when Muslims borrow money. According to the Koran, charging interest sets the banker up to be at war with Allah and Muhammad:

O you who believe! Observe your duty to Allah, and give up what remains (due to you) from usury [interest on a loan], if you are (in truth) believers. And if you do not, then be warned of war (against you) from Allah and His messenger. And if you repent, then you have your principal (without interest). Wrong not, and you shall not be wronged (Sûrah 2:278-279, bracketed clarification mine).

We did not think this could happen here in America where all people are equal under the laws of our Constitution and where everyone is subject to paying the same interest charged by the banks, depending on their credit status; however, an ad for Guidance Residential Mortgage Company promotes Sharia financing:

> Guidance Residential's mission is to offer the growing number of Sharia-sensitive households the opportunity to access financial products that are competitive and of the highest quality without having to compromise their values and principles.
>
> With this in mind, Guidance has created the Declining Balance Co-ownership Program, a unique, soundly designed home financing program in the United States that is competitive and, most important, Sharia-compliant. Also, Guidance has gathered a group of professionals committed to delivering this product with only the highest level of service.[39]

Some argue that this Sharia (Islamic Law) only concerns itself with fair business dealings—and does not impose on our laws. Really? Be forewarned: not even our courts are immune from Sharia encroachment.

During a Halloween parade on October 11, 2012, in central Pennsylvania, an atheist dressed as Muhammad and carrying a sign stating "Zombie Muhammad" was brutally attacked by a Muslim immigrant. When charges against the Muslim attacker finally had its day in court, the judge ruled that a physical attack on someone insulting Islam was a justified attack and that the hapless victim deserved what he got.[40]

In America, our Founding Fathers gave us our Constitution, which was intended to be the highest legal authority in the land; however, today's unscrupulous politicians, educators, and Islamic organizations have conspired to allow the ever-so-subtle encroachment of Sharia law to undermine our Western Judeo-Christian heritage as encapsulated in our founding documents and our rule of law!

In various cities around Europe, there are "no-go zones" where non-Muslims, including the police, do not enter. These enclaves begin with the establishment of a mosque. Gradually, the Muslims buy homes, which surround the mosque. Eventually, the area becomes saturated with the faithful. The result? A Muslim neighborhood is then established, and petitions are created and presented to local governing bodies for permission to allow Sharia law for domestic matters. This then becomes a "state within a state."

No-go zones begin with the establishment of Religious Police, but could this happen in the United States of America? It already has. One example is a Muslim community located in Cedar-Riverside, a suburb of Minneapolis, where there is a group calling themselves the "Muslim Defense Force" and "Religious Police" declaring to be "the civil part of the Sharia law." According to the Minneapolis police, they wear intimidating, dark green uniforms with arm patches displaying two flags associated with ISIS and other terrorist groups. At the time of this writing, members of the Muslim community and the Minnesota chapter of the Council on American-Islamic Relations (CAIR) have come out against this group. Once the seeds are planted, they are like weeds—once you turn your back, they will soon take over.[41] As we are witnessing in the UK and some other cities in Europe, non-Muslims have become afraid to enter the Islamic areas that are now "no-go zones" (see **Religious Police**).

Next, political Islam rears its head, and by the sheer weight of numbers (Jihad of the Womb in Chapter 8) these numbers allow Muslims to win various political offices and gain control of the government in Muslim areas. The city of London has become "London-stan" with the election on May 7, 2016, of Sadiq Khan as the first Muslim Mayor—not only of London, but the first Muslim mayor of any major Western city in the history of Europe. When referring to the possibility of the United States putting a temporary freeze on the relocation of Muslim refugees from the ISIS affected areas of the Middle East—in an effort to prevent terrorists from infiltrating the country—"Khan, for his part, says he would not visit the United States, on principle, if the broader ban were in effect."[42] This proclamation from London's mayor has nothing to do with British-American relations; however, no one should be surprised by the predictable threat of retaliation by the London mayor if America fails to accommodate Middle Eastern Muslims.

It is not crucial whether Mayor Khan followed through on his threat. The ultimate goal of these mini-Islamic states is to "hook up" and flex their Islamic political muscle, thereby bending the will of their host country to their Islamic agenda.

This is no longer just a problem in Europe. In the United States Armed forces, Sharia-compliant Muslims can now wear a beard, and Muslim women can wear a hijab (headscarf) while on duty and in uniform.[43] Many States in the U.S.A. now allow a woman not to have her picture on a driver's license for religious reasons. (We could only find the religion of Islam requiring women's faces to be partially covered or, as in the State of Indiana, for example, exempt from being taken[44]). Thus, the seeds of an Islamic takeover through Sharia law have taken solid root.

Now, for the first time in the United States of America, the Muslim Call to prayer is broadcast daily over loudspeakers in Michigan. It began when the former Polish City of Hamtramck (a Detroit suburb) in 2015 experienced a *landslide election* of the first Muslim-majority city council. Interestingly, the headlines do not mention that the majority of the city's population is now primarily Arab or that three of the elected councilmen were Bangladeshi and one Yemeni but instead refer to them by their religion.[45] This reinforces that Islam is more than just a religion; it is a geopolitical force.

Also shocking, in New Jersey, Andre Sayegh, the Muslim Mayor of Paterson, called his city the "capital of Palestine" and "the fourth holiest [Muslim] city in the world!"[46] It would appear that Dr. Hammond was very accurate in his predictions (p.p. 28-29).

Yet Sharia compliance is not limited to just predominately Muslim-controlled areas, as we can see in America's Islamic-friendly public school systems. At the time of this writing we can no longer celebrate holidays by their names. Christmas—an official holiday passed by

Congress on June 28, 1870—or Easter on our school calendars. On the other hand, many American school districts have begun designating Islam's only two holidays—*Eid al-Fitr* and *Eid al-Adha,* as officially sanctioned public school holidays. *Eid al-Fitr* celebrates the end of *Ramadan,* and *Eid al-Adha* is the holier of the two Eid holidays. It honors the time when God tested Abraham in Mecca by asking him to sacrifice his firstborn son, Ishmael, instead of Isaac, as the Bible teaches in Jerusalem.

While the history and traditions of Christianity and Judaism are no longer allowed in public schools, Islam is not only taught but practiced under the guise of "learning about Islam." In some schools, children take Muslim names and use Muslim prayer rugs, which appears to be indoctrination into the Muslim faith.

We know that the erroneous "separation of Church and State" has been successfully invoked against prayer and the celebration of the Judeo-Christian holidays in American public schools. Therefore, it is naïvely believed that the same observation regarding an academic exercise teaching Islam in the public-school systems would likewise be observed. Leo Hohmann, writing for WND, exposes how some schools are indoctrinating students in the seventh grade into the religion of Islam.

This unorthodox method of teaching was brought to the public's attention by parents who objected to the methods of instruction along with a video titled, "What is Islam, Ans: Faith of divine guidance for humanity, based on peace, spirituality and the oneness of God." This covert endorsement of Islam is being taught to their children in a Chatham, New Jersey, middle school. Parents claim the "Seventh graders in this school are taught: 'May God help us all find the true faith, Islam.' Also taught in the video is the Shahada, which is the Muslim prayer of conversion 'There is no god but Allah and Muhammad is his messenger.' "[47] What is missing is a disclaimer before such claims like, for example, "Muslims believe that ...."

This type of indoctrination is not exclusive to this particular school; stories like this occur on a regular basis in America and in the news media as we can see in this quote from an article written by Todd Starnes at FoxNews.com:

> A public high school has been accused of radical Islamic indoctrination by forcing children to profess the Muslim statement of faith, ordering them to memorize the Five Pillars of Islam and teaching that the faith of a Muslim is stronger than the average Christian, according to a federal lawsuit filed Wednesday.
>
> Thomas More Law Center filed the lawsuit on behalf of John and Melissa Wood. They accuse La Plata High School in Maryland of subjecting their teenage daughter to Islamic indoctrination and propaganda. And when Mr. Wood complained – the school banned him from campus.[48]

In another incident, a student attending Rollins College in Florida was suspended for challenging his Muslim professor, who told the class that the crucifixion of Jesus' was only a Christian hoax. The Washington Times reported:

> Marshall Polston, 20, was suspended March 24 [2017] by Rollins College in Winter Park, after an argument with his Middle Eastern Humanities professor over the historical validity of Jesus' death, [for which he received] a failing grade, and a Muslim student's allegedly [claiming of his] violent rhetoric during a discussion on Sharia law. The professor, Areej Zufari, claimed he was harassed, although video surveillance obtained by a local paper suggests otherwise (bracketed clarifications mine).[49]

A new practice in America—*circumcising little girls!*

Not everyone is familiar with the Muslim tradition of forcing young girls to undergo female circumcision, a custom that is kept quiet and practiced in Muslim countries. It has now been introduced into Western societies, although most people are ignorant of this gruesome practice within the Western population. More than 230 million girls and women alive today have undergone female genital mutilations (FGM) throughout the world.[50]

The circumcision of the female sex organs is also referred to as Female Genital Mutilation or FGM. Under Sharia law, this barbaric and extremely painful, religious ritual can involve removing a girl's vulva and clitoris and, in extreme cases, sewing together what is left of the lips, so they will heal as one vaginal barrier of flesh. This completely closes off any access to the vagina and leaves only a small opening for urine and menstrual blood to flow out. This type of procedure is supposed to prove a woman's honor. On her wedding night, the woman's vaginal area is once again slit with a razor or knife, allowing her husband access to her vagina. You might think that such a despicable, inhuman act would not be tolerated in the United States, much less in American hospitals. Still, Sharia tentacles have a very long reach. Although it is not legal in the United States, this brutal, painful, and disgusting act is forced upon small girls—mere children—living in America. One example was reported on an ABC Network affiliate in Detroit:

> (Dr.) Jumana Nagarwala, 44, of Northville, Michigan, is accused of performing female genital mutilation on underage girls.
>
> According to a criminal complaint, (Dr.) Nagarwala performed the procedure on girls ages six to eight years old at a medical clinic in Livonia.
>
> Some of the children were brought from out of state for the illegal procedure. Female Genital Mutilation (FGM) is considered the complete removal or partial removal of the clitoris, known as a clitoridectomy. FGM is internationally recognized as a violation of the human rights of women and girls.
>
> Some consider FGM as a (Muslim) religious and cultural practice. The purpose of this illegal practice is to suppress female sexuality in order to reduce sexual pleasure.
>
> In the criminal affidavit, (Dr.) Nagarwala performed FGM on girls who were approximately 7 years old at the time at a clinic in Livonia (bracketed clarification added).[51]

These examples only scratch the surface of the ascent of Islam in America. While it is politically incorrect to say anything negative against Islam, the attacks on Christianity and Judaism are permissible and have already begun to escalate.

Sharia law is like many parts of a camel. The camel has a tail, a hump, four legs, a long neck, eyes, a mouth, and a nose. Perhaps now is the time we should be reminded of an old Arab proverb, which warns about the "camel getting its nose under the tent!" Why is this old saying important? Because once the camel has its nose under the tent, it will not be long before the rest of the camel follows. Islam, by its very definition, is not a democracy but a theocracy—it's all or nothing—and for a Muslim to settle for nothing is not an option.

NOTES:

1. Encyclopædia Britannica, 1946 ed., s.v. "ISLAMIC LAW."
2. Hamilton Alexander Rosskeen Gibb, *Mohammedanism: An Historical Survey* (London: Oxford University Press, 1970), 68.
3. Hunt Janin and André Kahlmeyer, *Islamic Law: The Sharia from Muhammad's Time to the Present* (Jefferson: McFarland & Co. Publ., 2007), 3.
4. Ibn-an-Naqīb Aḥmad; Ibn-Lu'lu', *Reliance of the Traveller: The Classic Manual of Islamic Sacred Law*, 'Umdat al-salik, trans., Nuh Ha Mim. Kefller (Beltsville: Amana Publ., 1997).
5. Bjorn Olav Utvik and Knut S. Vikor, "The Middle East in a Globalized World Papers from the Fourth Nordic Conference on Ahmad Ibn Naqib al-Misri, *Reliance of the Traveller: A Classic Manual of Islamic Sacred Law*. Ed. Trans., Sheik Noah Ha Mim Keller (Evanston: Sunna, 1991), [circa 14th century]. Middle Eastern Studies"
6. Michael Memia. "Saudi Businessman Donates 10 Million To Create Islamic Law Center At Yale." HUFFPOST RELIGION. Huffington Post, 13 Sept. 2015. Web. 20 Sept. 2015. "Yale officials say the Abdallah S. Kamel Center for the Study of Islamic Law and Civilization reflects a growing interest at Yale

and other institutions in Islamic law .... Harvard Law School has had its own Islamic legal studies program, established with support from the Saudi king."

7. Al-Misri, *Reliance of the Traveller* f1.3.
8. S.S. Hiremath, MDS, FICD. *Textbook of Preventative and Community Dentistry.* 2nd ed. (Bangalore: Elsevier, 2011), 403.
9. Qisas (Arabic qiṣāṣ) is the Law of Retaliation, i.e., retribution for harm done, "An eye for an eye."
10. "...For ye practice your lusts on men in preference to women: ye are indeed a people transgressing beyond bounds .... And we rained down on them a shower (of brimstone)" - (Sûrah 7:80-84, Abdullah Yusuf Ali [also see Sûrahs 15:74; 27:58; 29:40]). This is an account borrowed from the biblical story of Sodom. Because it talks about "raining down...brimstone" or rocks/stones in other passages, it is generally believed by Muslim scholars that homosexuals should be stoned to death.
11. Sophie Jane Evans, "Saudi Arabia Sentences Maid to Death by Stoning for Adultery—but the Man She Slept with Will Escape with 100 Lashes." The Daily Mail Online. (UK) Associated Newspapers, 28 Nov. 2015. Web. 09 Apr. 2016. 85
12. Jaymi McCann, "Saudi Arabia Beheads Murderer ... and Then CRUCIFIES His Body." Mail Online. Associated Newspapers (UK), 28 Mar. 2013. Web. 09 Apr. 2016.
13. Jim Hoft, "Fallen SEAL's Father: Hillary Told Me at Funeral, 'We're Going to Arrest and Prosecute the YouTube Director (Video).' " N.p., 26 October 2912. Web. 18 January 2015. Citing FOX NEWS and Megyn Kelly: "Speaking to the 'Lars Larson Show,' father of Seal Tyrone Woods, who died in Benghazi defending the consulate annex, shared his experience of meeting President Obama and Secretary Clinton at the memorial service for the fallen heroes a few days after the attack."

    "Charles Woods said Obama 'couldn't look me in the eye' and 'mumbled' 'and I'm sorry.' " He said Secretary [of State] Clinton assured him that they were going to 'arrest and prosecute' the man who made the scapegoated YouTube.com video critical of Muhammad, which had nothing to do with the 9/11 terror attack in Benghazi."

Megyn Kelly played audio from the "Lars Larson Show" yesterday (article dated October 26, 2012). CONSIDER: Some have argued that at any one time, every American is breaking at least three Federal laws.

14. Daniel Greenfield, "Obama: 'The Future Must Not Belong to Those Who Slander the Prophet of Islam.' " FRONTPAGE MAG.com, n.p., 25 September 2012. Web. 23 May 2015.
15. Brooks Barnes, "Man Behind Anti-Islam Video Gets Prison Term." The New York Times, 7 Nov. 2012. Web. 2 Feb. 2015. LOS ANGELES — A federal judge on Wednesday sentenced the man behind "Innocence of Muslims," the anti-Islam YouTube video that ignited bloody protests in the Muslim world, to one year in prison for violating parole.
16. "Pentagon, McDonald's Capitulate to Sharia law," Investor's Business Daily, n.p. 9 4. Web. 18 January 2015. Islamofascism: Caving to pressure from Muslim groups, the Pentagon has relaxed uniform rules to allow Islamic beards, turbans, and hijabs. It's a major win for political correctness and a big loss for military unit cohesion. Also, the Sharia-compliant regulation threatens to expand the jihadi Fifth Column that counterintelligence already is dealing with ..."
17. Thomas Beaumont and Eileen Sullivan, "Michele Bachmann: 'Obama Is Allowing Terror Suspect Groups to Write the FBI's Terror Training Manual,' "TheHuffingtonPost.com, 28 October 2911. Web. 18 February 2015.
18. On Muslim circumcision: Uh Ha Mim Keller, trans. Reliance of the Traveller, A Classic Manual of Islamic Sacred Law. Revised ed. (Beltsville: Amana Publications, 1994), 59. Keller's revised translation, "For men, it consists of removing the prepuce from the penis, and for women, removing the prepuce (Ar. Bazr) of the clitoris (n: not the clitoris itself, as some mistakenly assert). (A: Hanbalis hold that circumcision of women is not obligatory but Sunna (meaning, the normal custom, or a practice decided by the Mohammad), while Hanafis consider it a mere courtesy to the husband)."

19. WikiIslam contributors, "Qur'an, Hadith and Scholars: Female Genital Mutilation." WikiIslam, the Online Source on Islam, n.d. Web. 15 Apr. 2016. "e4.3. Circumcision is obligatory (for every male and female) by cutting off the piece of skin on the glans of the penis of the male, but circumcision of the female is by cutting out the clitoris (this is called Hufaad)." (*Reliance of the Traveller: A Classic Manual of Islamic Sacred Law*, Ahmad ibn Naqib al-Misri).

20. Female circumcision is also found in the Hadith, as we can see by these excerpts. "... 'The fitrah is five things – or five things are part of the fitrah – circumcision ...'" (Bukhari 5891 Muslim 527).

    "Abu al-Malih ibn `Usama's father relates that the Prophet said: 'Circumcision is a law for men and a preservation of honour for women' " (Ahmad Ibn Hanbal 5:75; Abu Dawud, Adab), 167.

    "...The Prophet (peace_be_upon_him) said to her: 'Do not cut severely as that is better for a woman and more desirable for a husband' " (Sunan Abu Dawood, 41:5251).

21. Al-Misri, *Reliance of the Traveller* f1.2

22. Phyllis Chesler, "Justice Served in an American-Islamic Honor Killing," FRONTPAGE MAG.com, n.p. 15 April 2011. Web. 16 December 2014.

23. Al-Misri, *Reliance of the Traveller: A Classic Manual of Islamic Sacred Law:* o1.1-4

24. John L. Esposito, "A'ishah in the Islamic World: Past and Present," Oxford Islamic Studies Online, n.p, n.d. Web. November 12, 2012 (subscription required).

25. Yuksel, Edip, "True Islam - Beating Women." True Islam - Beating Women. Quran-Islam.org, n.d. Web. 02 June 2016. "A Famous Multi-Meaning Word: The problem comes from the word 'Idribuhunne,' which we used to translate as 'beat them.' The root of this word is 'DaRaBa.' If you look at any Arabic dictionary, you will find a long list of meanings ascribed to this word. That list is one of the longest lists in all the Arabic dictionary. It can be said that 'DaRaBa' is the number-one multi-meaning word in Arabic. It has so many different

meanings, and we can find numerous different meanings ascribed to it in the Quran."

26. Muhammad Asad and Ahmed Moustafa, *The Message of the Qur'ān: The Full Account of the Revealed Arabic Text Accompanied by Parallel Transliteration.* (Bitton: Book Foundation, 2004), citing Tabari, who "quot[es] the views of scholars of the earliest times."

27. Muhammad Asad, *The Message of the Qur'an,* citing <u>Razi</u>.

28. Sami Zubaida. Law and Power in the Islamic World. (London: I.B. Tauris & Co., 2005), 58-60.

29. PBUH is sometimes written P.B.U.H. and is an acronym for "peace be upon him."

30. Ibn-Ǧarīr al-Ṭabarī, Muḥammad, *The History of al-Ṭabarī. The Victory of Islam,* Volume III, Michael Fishbein (Albany, NY: State U of New York, 1997), 86.

31. "DANDENONG'S Mayor Has Called on Residents to Embrace a Muslim Event at Which People Will Be Forced to Cover Up," The Dandenong Leader [Australia], 16 September 2010. Web. 10 October 2013.

32. Patrick Sawer, "Swimmers Are Told to Wear Burkinis," The Telegraph [UK]. 15 August 2009. Under the rules, swimmers— including non-Muslims—are barred from entering the pool in normal swimming attire. Web. 25 December 2014.

33. Oren Dorell, "Some Say Schools Giving Muslims Special Treatment," USA TODAY, 26 July 2007.

34. "Airport Adds Foot Basins for Muslim Cabbies," WND, n.p. 28 April 2007. Web. 17 February 2015.

35. "Now Buy Halal Meats at Walmart Supercentre," Halal.com. 28 January 2008. Web. 17 February 2015.

36. Din Suleman, "Fast-food Chains Tap Halal Market," Houston Chronicle. May-June, 2006 Web. 17 February 2015. " 'We give our franchisees leniency, so they can use local options,' said Subway spokesman Kevin Kane. They know what's in their community."

   We also have references regarding halal food in the following: Syed Rasheeduddin Ahmed. "Halal or Not Halal?" The Muslim Observer, 1 June 2006. Web. 17 February 2015.

Muslim businessmen or women, when trying to obtain a mainstream franchise, always forget the Islamic Shariâ€™ah rules, according to the â€˜ulama at Sharia Board Chicago, IL .... Islam prohibits a Muslim from being involved in haram (meaning forbidden by Sharia Law) like selling wine and pork (not to be confused with a harem, a place for family women).

37. Rachel Zoll, "US Muslims: A New Consumer Niche," Bloomberg Businessweek, n.p. Bloomberg, 2 December 2010. Web. 17 February 2015.

38. J.P. Sloane, Ph.D., "Guest Writer Dr. JP Sloane: 'Neel Kashkari and Islamic Finance 101,' Politichicks.com, n.p. 14 May 2014. Web. 17 Feb. 2015. On November 6, 2008, the Bush Administration held a seminar titled 'Islamic Finance 101.' The seminar attendees were welcomed by then Assistant Treasury Secretary of the Treasury, Neel Kashkari."

39. "Home Ownership, the Sharia Way!" Guidance Residential, n.d., n.p. Web. 17 February 2015. "Whether you want to buy a new home or lower your monthly mortgage payments, getting Sharia-compliant financing is easier than you think thanks to our unique Musharaka [financial partnership/contract] or declining balance co-ownership program. At Guidance Residential, we make Islamic finance easy and affordable. Learn more. 'HOW IT WORKS VIDEO' on Interest-Free Finance" (bracketed clarification mine).

40. "Pennsylvania Judge Dismisses Case of Attack on 'Zombie Muhammad,' " Fox News. FOX News Network, 24 Feb. 2012. Web. 31 Oct. 2014.

41. Faiza Mahamud, "Minneapolis Muslims Protest 'Sharia' Vigilante in Cedar-Riverside Area," Star Tribune. N.p., 13 Apr. 2017. Web. 13 Apr. 2017.

42. Peter Apps, "Commentary: London's New Muslim Mayor, Already Tilting the World's Political Chessboard." Reuters. Thomson Reuters, 12 May 2016. Web. 12 May 2016.

43. Pamela Constable, "Pentagon OKs Beards, Turbans." Washington Post. The Washington Post, 22 Jan. 2014. Web. 09 Apr. 2016. The Defense Department released regulations Wednesday, ensuring the rights of religious minority service

members to display their beliefs outwardly — such as wearing a turban, scarf or beard.

44. In the 2016 Indiana Driver's Manual (Bureau of Motor Vehicles, Indiana), page 16: "Photo Exempt Credentials. Photo exempt identification cards are available for religious reasons only." On page 17, under "Credential Restrictions and Endorsements," the code given for the exemption is listed as "3—Photo Exempt."

45. Henry Gass, "Michigan City Elects First Ever Muslim Majority City Council," The Christian Science Monitor. The Christian Science Monitor, 9 Nov. 2015. Web. 11 Nov. 2015.

46. Propper, David. "Paterson Mayor Calls NJ City 'capital of Palestine' in Ramadan Kickoff Remarks: '4th Holiest City in the World.'" *New York Post*, New York Post, 10 Mar. 2025, nypost.com/2025/03/10/us-news/paterson-mayor-calls-nj-city-capital-of-palestine-in-ramadan-remarks/.

47. Leo Hohmann, "Moms Declare Holy War after School Teaches Islam 'true faith,' " *WND*, n.p. 31 Mar. 2017. Web. 16 Apr. 2017. "Leo Hohmann is a news editor for WND. He has been a reporter and editor at several suburban newspapers in Atlanta and Charlotte, North Carolina. He also served as managing editor of Triangle Business Journal in Raleigh, North Carolina."

48. Todd Starnes, "Lawsuit: Public School Forced My Child to Convert to Islam." Fox News. FOX News Network, 29 Jan. 2016. Web. 16 Apr. 2016.

49. Douglas Ernst, "College Suspends Student Who Challenged Muslim Prof's Claim That Jesus' Crucifixion Is a Hoax." *The Washington Times*. 28 Mar. 2017.

50. "Female Genital Mutilation." *World Health Organization*, World Health Organization, 31 Jan. 2025, www.who.int/news-room/fact-sheets/detail/female-genital-mutilation.

51. "Detroit Emergency Room Doctor Charged with Child Genital Mutilation," *WXYZ*. ABC NEWS WXYZ-TV Channel 7 Detroit, 13 Apr. 2017. Web. 13 Apr. 2017.

CHAPTER 10

AN EXAMPLE OF
HOW APOSTATE CHRISTIANITY AND ISLAM
COULD LEAD TO THE ONE WORLD RELIGION

CHRISLAM: THE END TIMES ONE WORLD RELIGION?

The Bible indicates (especially in the book of Revelation) that there will be a one-world religion in the last days, which will include a false prophet (the second beast of Revelation 13:11-15), who is one of the three persons in a demonic and unholy trinity (Revelation 16:13). Is this just a myth or allegorical fantasy?

Consider a new phenomenon called "Chrislam"—a blending of the two largest religions on the face of the earth—an apostate Christianity combined with Islam—and this is happening right now at an alarming rate!

Recently, at Wheaton College, Billy Graham's alma mater, Dr. Larycia Hawkins, a professor at that evangelical institution, announced to the world know that she supports Chrislam. She posted pictures of herself wearing a hijab on her Facebook page and stated, "I stand in religious solidarity with Muslims because they, like me, a Christian, are people of the book." We would challenge her to cite chapter and verse from the Bible, where it mentions Islam, Allah, or Ishmael being offered by Abraham as a sacrifice. Where does it say that a greater prophet than Jesus will come, and his name will be Muhammad? It doesn't!

Figure 8. Propaganda Billboard Number 2 Sponsored by the Islamic Circle of North America

Historically, the religion of Islam began 700 years after Christ, and the biblical canon was closed. What is apparent is that Hawkins bought into the Muslim propaganda that all biblical prophets—from Adam to Moses—from Abraham to Jesus (who Islam claims is not God's Son nor died on the cross) were Muslims. While it is true that Abraham produced a son, Ishmael, with the Egyptian slave (Hagar), her child (Ishmael) is alleged to have become the ancestor of the Arabian Prophet of Islam, Muhammad.[1] Be that as it may, God's covenant with Abraham was passed down exclusively through the lineage of his second son, Isaac (Genesis 17:19, 21), whose mother was Abraham's legitimate wife, Sarah.

To its credit, Wheaton College fired Dr. Hawkins, but the shocking fact is that many of the school's alumni became outraged at her firing and threatened to withhold their financial support if Dr. Hawkins was not reinstated.   What is worse, "... the college's faculty council has unanimously agreed to ask administrators to change their minds." To give credibility to her view, Dr. Hawkins claimed, "And as Pope Francis stated last week, we worship the same God."[2]

In another incident regarding Chrislam, we will share a document published and circulated by one of the movement's most prestigious and powerful organizations, the Yale Center for Faith and Culture, which is part of the Yale Divinity School located at Yale University.

While Jesus is mentioned in the Koran—as this billboard proclaims—what is not mentioned is that the *Koran presents 396 lies regarding who Jesus is,*[3] many of which we show in this volume and in the two volumes to follow. Activist Muslim organizations are using the Islamic

254

art of taqiyya by laying the groundwork for the Chrislam "Jihad of deception" as this propaganda billboard shows near Dallas, Texas— part of a national campaign paid for by the *Islamic Circle of North America,* a group supported by the *Muslim Brotherhood.*

To help you realize the seriousness of this movement, we have reproduced—with commentary—a copy of the Yale University Covenant,[4] a response by a select group of Christians as an outreach from Muslims. It is known as "A Common Word," an open letter from Muslims dated October 13, 2007, and addressed to Christian leaders. It is signed by 138 prominent Muslim leaders from around the world (over 300 Muslims have since signed the document), as well as many of America's clergy. We have taken the liberty of slightly modifying its layout to adapt it to this book's format without losing the covenant's integrity. In the Preamble to the Covenant, there is an apology for the Crusades and the West's oversensitivity to the war on terror, which we will address in Chapter 9, Volume III, of *Islam Exposed, Islam: Science-Bible-Archaeology and Myths* under the subsection titled, "The Crusades and Islam."

The majority of the denominational signatories of the Yale Covenant believe in Supersessionism (i.e., Replacement Theology, which is the unbiblical belief that the Church has replaced Israel) and, therefore, reject God's covenant with Israel and the Jews; however, they are willing to embrace Islam in what is rapidly becoming a New World Religion known as Chrislam (Revelation 13:1-9). We find it interesting to note that one of the signatories is Rick Warren, the Senior Pastor of Saddleback Church, which has numerous branches throughout the world. The late Reverend Billy Graham (1918-2018) was always known as "America's Pastor," but more recently, Rick Warren has been referred to as "America's Pastor." Warren is best known for his book, *The Purpose Driven Church.*

The names of the Yale Covenant signers are listed in the Appendix in alphabetical order according to their last names, although their given names appear first.

Be ye not unequally yoked together with unbelievers: for what fellowship has righteousness with unrighteousness? and what communion has light with darkness? (2 Corinthians 6:14, NIV).

To distinguish our commentaries and scriptural passages from the Yale document, we have shown the Yale document in italics and a different font. Also, to stay within the flow of this document, it becomes necessary from time to time to be repetitious in order to identify or clarify points that we address as troubling claims contained in the covenant.

YALE CENTER FOR FAITH AND CULTURE
"A Common Word Between Us and You"

Loving God and Neighbor Together—a Christian Response to "A Common Word Between Us and You."

The use of the phrase, *"A Common Word,"* refers to the words of the Bible. Christians do not accept the Koran, but they do accept the Bible. Knowing this, Muslims initially approached the "Yale Center for Faith and Culture," using only the Bible as a common denominator. The reason Muslims have no problem using Scriptures to make their arguments is because Allah claims he wrote the Bible (Sûrah 3:3). In order to establish communications with Christians, Bible verses are used as *proof texts* by the Muslims in *"A Common Word"* as a means to make Islam appear more acceptable to Christians. The response here shows how effective this use of Scriptures is by the Muslims. Note: This approach is at the very heart of Chrislam.

In the name [what/whose name] of the Infinitely Good God whom we should love with all our Being. (Bracketed clarification mine.)

Preamble

As members of the worldwide Christian community, we were deeply encouraged and challenged by the recent historic open letter signed by 138 leading Muslim scholars, clerics, and intellectuals from around the world. A Common Word Between Us and You identifies some core common ground between Christianity and Islam which lies at the heart of our respective faiths as well as at the heart of the most ancient Abrahamic faith, Judaism. Jesus Christ's call to love God and neighbor was rooted in the divine revelation to the people of Israel embodied in the Torah (Deuteronomy 6:5; Leviticus 19:18).

The Preamble is an emphasis on love. While love is very important and not something to be taken lightly, we must ask ourselves to whom this love is directed in the verses cited.

The passage referred to in Deuteronomy states:

And you shall love the LORD you God with all your heart, and with all your soul, and with all your might (Deuteronomy 6:5).

The subject of this passage is God (YAWA) and how we must love Him. The next proof text they cite is Leviticus 19:18:

You shall not avenge, nor bear any grudge against the children of your people [the children of Israel], but you shall love your fellow [Hebrew] neighbor as yourself: I am the LORD (Leviticus 19:18, bracketed clarification mine).

This passage from Leviticus is referring to the descendants of the Abrahamic covenant given by God (YAWA) through Isaac and Jacob, who was called "Israel" (Genesis 17:22). It has nothing to do with Abraham's son through Sarah's Egyptian slave, Hagar; however, the Preamble suggests that somehow Muslims are our spiritual brothers and sisters because Ishmael and Jacob were brothers.

As we have shared before, the Koran states that Allah gave us the Torah (the first five books of the Bible and the Gospel (Sûrah 3:3), so we will refer to the Torah and the Gospel for the answer.

In Deuteronomy, which is the fifth book of the Torah, when God was addressing the Hebrews, He stated:

> You *are* the children of the LORD your God .... For you *are* a holy people to the LORD your God, and the LORD has chosen you to be a people for Himself, a special treasure above all the peoples who *are* on the face of the earth (Deuteronomy 14:1-2, NKJV, bolded emphasis added).

Yet God did make a provision that one day He would allow for others to be adopted into His covenant as His children:

> even us whom He called, not of the Jews only, but also of the Gentiles?

> "I will call them My people, who were not My people, And her beloved, who was not beloved" (Romans 9:24-25, NKJV).

How was that accomplished? By what means did God allow those who were not of the Covenant of Abraham, Isaac, and Jacob (Genesis 17:19, 21) to also become His children? The answer is found in the gospel, which tells us:

> Yet to all who did receive Him [Jesus], to those who believed in His name, He gave the right to become children of God (John 1:12, NIV, bracketed clarification mine).

The second proof text used in the Preamble is from Leviticus 19. It would be prudent for us to read it in context from the beginning, where we find out this passage is directed to the "children of Israel." The second thing we learn is who is addressing Moses. The Book of Leviticus bears great importance because it concerns the Levites (priestly clan) and the Law. When we read the first two verses, we find it is "the children of Israel," or as the New International Version states, "... the entire assembly of Israel" who is being addressed:

> And the LORD spoke unto Moses, saying, Speak unto all the congregation of the children of Israel, and say unto them, You shall be holy: for I the LORD your God am holy (Leviticus 19:1-2).

As we can plainly see, the one speaking is God (YAWA), and He is speaking to Moses. Again, the subject of this passage is "the children of Israel." Nevertheless, we will look directly at Leviticus verse 18 of Chapter 19, which the Christian scholars at Yale use to imply that Muslims are also to be included as our neighbors as well:

> Thou shalt not avenge, nor bear any grudge against the children of thy people, but thou shalt love thy neighbour as thyself: I am the LORD. (Leviticus 19:18)

The neighbor(s) mentioned in Leviticus 19:18, where we read "... love your neighbor as yourself," are clearly—as stated—"the children of thy people (Israel)." Consider, because they were wandering alone way out in the desert with no one around for perhaps a hundred miles, to imply that this passage refers to any other people is to read into Scripture something that is not there (eisegesis); however, the argument could be made that the signatories of this declaration are interpreting the Bible allegorically. This unbiblical teaching allows for the Bible to have more than one meaning when we read it—the first, being obvious, and the second, being a hidden or figurative meaning. This was never God's intention because the Bible makes it clear:

> Knowing this first, that no prophecy of the Scripture is of any private interpretation (2 Peter 1:20).

When we allow for more than one meaning (allegorical), it becomes occult (hidden) reasoning, and we can then make a passage mean anything we want it to mean. This has proven to be very deadly since it has been used to establish the unbiblical doctrine of Supersessionism, also known as Replacement Theology, which

259

teaches that God is through with Israel (refuted in Romans 11:1) because the Jews killed Christ (refuted in John 10:17-18). Therefore, it is argued that the Church becomes the recipient of all the covenants and blessings God made with Israel with Supersession. It is evident that the overwhelming majority of signers of the Yale University Covenant believe in the doctrine of Supersessionism. It does not take a great leap of faith to go from anti-Semitism to embracing Muslims.

We receive the open letter as a Muslim hand of conviviality [agreeable nature] and cooperation extended to Christians worldwide. In this response we extend our own Christian hand in return, so that together with all other human beings we may live in peace and justice as we seek to love God and our neighbors (bracketed clarification mine).

It is interesting to observe here that we know of no formal outreach extended by Muslims to the Jewish people or Israel.

Muslims and Christians have not always shaken hands in friendship; their relations have sometimes been tense, even characterized by outright hostility. Since Jesus Christ says, "First take the log out your own eye, and then you will see clearly to take the speck out of your neighbor's eye" (Matthew 7:5).

This section of the Preamble presents us with some curious problems. When taken out of context, the use of Matthew 7:5 in the Yale Covenant makes the point we must confess our sins (including against Muslims) and forgive others (including Muslims); however, this is not what the passage in Matthew is saying. Matthew 7 is an instruction on judgment and has been misquoted by many people for years claiming that the Bible teaches, "Judge ye not that ye be not judged …" (Matthew 7:1-2). But this is not what Jesus is teaching. He is teaching that before we can justly point out the things we see as biblically wrong with others, we are to correct those areas in our own life first. Now we have the verse from Matthew 7, which is used as a proof text to show how Christians have misjudged our Muslim neighbors:

Since Jesus Christ says, "First take the log out your own eye, and then you will see clearly to take the speck out of your neighbor's eye" (Matthew 7:5).

The above passage—in its biblical context—is not telling us that it is wrong to judge others, but instead, we must first make sure we are not guilty of the same thing ourselves before we can rightfully judge them. Consider a burglar telling a teenager not to shoplift because it is wrong; his reprimand would not be credible. If we are guilty of the same problem but ignore it in our own lives while accusing others of being guilty of doing it, we bring ourselves under the same judgment. It is like a man using a ruler to measure a distance. If he uses the metric system, then God will judge him by the metric system. In other words, God will hold us to the same standard by which we measure others. The verse referred to in John 7 commands us:

Judge not according to the appearance, but judge [with] righteous judgment (John 7:24, bracketed clarification mine).

This kind of judgment is not forbidden, as the YALE CENTER FOR FAITH AND CULTURE would have us believe.

The Preamble then shifts into the following confession of Christian wrongdoing against the Muslims:

We want to begin by acknowledging that in the past [e.g., in the Crusades) and in the present (e.g., in excesses of the "war on terror") many Christians have been guilty of sinning against our Muslim neighbors. Before we "shake your hand" in responding to your letter, we ask forgiveness of the All-Merciful One and of the Muslim community around the world.

It is interesting how many liberal apologists have used the Crusades as an example to prove that Christians were just as bad as the Muslims were by bringing up how the Crusaders sometimes attacked and killed unfortunate Middle Eastern non-combatants. To begin with, the Crusades were a response to the incredibly fast conquests of much of

Europe, Asia Minor, and the Middle East by Muslim hordes. Muslims were fierce in battle because dying in the cause of Allah is their only sure guarantee of going to Heaven (Sûrah 61:10-12); therefore, Muslims conquered and held Spain for over 700 years, Sicily for 300 years and Byzantium (the Eastern Roman Empire) from 1453 A.D until this very day, to name a few countries.

Fearful of the Islamic threat, Pope Leo IV took a page from the Koran in 852 A.D. and promised that those who died fighting the Muslim invaders under the sign of the cross would be guaranteed immediate entrance into Heaven; this idea was picked up later by Pope Urban II for the first Crusade 1096-1099 because of the Muslim conquest against the Christians. Yet in this Yale document, they are apologizing for following the Muslim's lead!

As for the Yale document asserting Christians being *"... in excesses of the 'war on terror,' many Christians have been guilty of sinning against our Muslim neighbors,"*[5] one word comes to mind, "Huh?" We would suggest these learned scholars of theology buy a copy of the Koran and read it!

Religious Peace—World Peace

"Muslims and Christians together make up well over half of the world's population. Without peace and justice between these two religious communities, there can be no meaningful peace in the world." We share the sentiment of the Muslim signatories expressed in these opening lines of their open letter. Peaceful relations between Muslims and Christians stand as one of the central challenges of this century, and perhaps of the whole present epoch. Though tensions, conflicts, and even wars in which Christians and Muslims stand against each other are not primarily religious in character, they possess an undeniable religious dimension. If we can achieve religious peace between these two religious communities, peace in the world will clearly be easier to attain. It is therefore no exaggeration to say, as you

have in A Common Word Between Us and You, that "the future of the world depends on peace between Muslims and Christians."

One part of this section stands out when we read:

Though tensions, conflicts, and even wars in which Christians and Muslims stand against each other are not primarily religious in character, they possess an undeniable religious dimension.

This is a little disingenuous in light of koranic teachings. Nowhere in the Bible did God initiate a never-ending state of war with any group of people, but not so in the Koran where Allah commanded Muslims to be in a perpetual state of war against all non-Muslims. In Islam, there are two houses—the "House of Peace," *Dar al-Islam* and the "House of War," *Dar al-Harb,* which pertains to anyone who is not a Muslim

> Warfare is ordained for you, though it is hateful unto you; but it may happen that you hate a thing which is good for you, and it may happen that you love a thing [avoiding war] which is bad for you. Allah knows, you know not (Sûrah 2:216, bracketed clarification mine).

> So when the sacred months have passed away, then slay the idolaters wherever you find them, and take them captives and besiege them and lie in wait for them in every ambush, then if they repent and keep up prayer and pay the poor-rate, leave their way free to them; surely Allah is Forgiving, Merciful (Sûrah 9:5, Muhammad Habib Shakir).

In the Bible, we are told to preach the gospel throughout the world. Never does the Bible claim Judaism or Christianity must become the only or predominant world religion, but Christians are advised that before Christ returns:

... this gospel of the kingdom shall be preached in all the world for a witness unto all nations; and then shall the end come (Matthew 24:14).

The Bible also talks about the final days when there will be a world religion of the Antichrist (Revelation 13), and if it were possible in the Last Days, even the very elect would be led astray (Matthew 24:24). In the quote from the Yale Covenant, under the heading, *"Religious Peace—World Peace,"* we can see the beginning of a one-world religion through this thinly veiled statement:

> *Muslims and Christians together make up well over half of the world's population ... If we can achieve religious peace between these two religious communities, peace in the world will clearly be easier to attain. It is therefore no exaggeration to say, as you have in A Common Word Between Us and You, that "the future of the world depends on peace between Muslims and Christians."*

There is a running theme in the Koran, which rejects and attacks the deity of Christ and denies that He is the Son of God, despite the fact that Jesus Himself claims to be the Son of God (John 10:36).

Basically, the Yale University Covenant presupposes that we worship and hold to one God in common, but if that God is not God the Son, then we are at a crossroads. The Bible warns not to take lightly another Jesus or gospel:

> But I am afraid that just as Eve was deceived by the serpent's cunning, your minds may somehow be led astray from your sincere and pure devotion to Christ. For if someone comes to you and preaches a Jesus other than the Jesus we preached, or if you receive a different spirit from the Spirit you received, or a different gospel from the one you accepted, you put up with it easily enough (2 Corinthians 11:3-4, NIV).

To accept Jesus simply as a prophet and a good teacher is to deny who Jesus is:

Do not be yoked together with unbelievers. For what do righteousness and wickedness have in common? Or what fellowship can light have with darkness? (2 Corinthians 6:14, NIV).

Therefore, according to the Yale Covenant, the only way Christians and Muslims can forge an alliance of common faith is through the emerging, new pseudo faith of Chrislam.

Common Ground

What is so extraordinary about A Common Word Between Us and You is not that its signatories recognize the critical character of the present moment in relations between Muslims and Christians. It is rather a deep insight and courage with which they have identified the common ground between the Muslim and Christian religious communities. What is common between us lies not in something marginal nor in something merely important to each. It lies, rather, in something absolutely central to both: love of God and love of neighbor. Surprisingly for many Christians, your letter considers the dual command of love to be the foundational principle not just of the Christian faith, but of Islam as well. That so much common ground exists – common ground in some of the fundamentals of faith – gives hope that undeniable differences and even the very real external pressures that bear down upon us cannot overshadow the common ground upon which we stand together. That this common ground consists in love of God and of neighbor gives hope that deep cooperation between us can be a hallmark of the relations between our two communities.

True believers in the Koran cannot possibly fellowship with Christians. On a faith-based level, it would be going against a foundational Islamic doctrine:

O you who believe! do not take the Jews and the Christians for friends; they are friends of each other; and whoever amongst you takes them for a friend, then surely he is one of them; surely Allah does not guide the unjust people (Sûrah 5:51, Muhammad Habib Shakir).

We ask the Yale Covenant signatories what part of Allah's commandment to Muslims they find so difficult to understand when he orders them, "Do not take the Jews and the Christians for friends." Notice that this warning is given in Sûrah 5, which replaces all other passages, which speak kindly toward Christians and Jews, before it (from Sûrah 6 to Sûrah 114).

Love of God

We applaud that A Common Word Between Us and You stress so insistently the unique devotion to one God, indeed the love of God, as the primary duty of every believer. God alone rightly commands our ultimate allegiance. When anyone or anything besides God commands our ultimate allegiance – a ruler, a nation, economic progress, or anything else – we end up serving idols and inevitably get mired in deep and deadly conflicts.

This seems to indicate that both Muslims and Christians believe in the same God, only using different names. *"You stress so insistently the unique devotion to one God, indeed the love of God, as the primary duty of every believer."* It goes on to say, *"When anyone or anything besides God commands our ultimate allegiance—a ruler, a nation, economic progress, or anything else – we end up serving idols;"* so if Allah is a different god than the one Christians believe in, he would be an idol—and this passage gives no indication this is the case. Are we to believe Allah and YAWA are really the same God? This seems to point toward that conclusion. To believe otherwise—we are told—would lead us to be *"… mired in deep and deadly conflicts."*

We find it equally heartening that the God whom we should love above all things is described as being Love. In the Muslim tradition, God, "the Lord of the worlds," is "The Infinitely Good and All-Merciful." And the New Testament states clearly that "God is love" (1 John 4:8). Since God's goodness is infinite and not bound by anything, God "makes his sun rise on the evil and the good, and sends rain on the righteous and the unrighteous,"

266

according to the words of Jesus Christ recorded in the Gospel (Matthew 5:45).

It appears that finding *"things of common faith"* is the equivalent of saying "things of the same faith," and that sets a dangerous precedent. No matter how much some would like to find things in common with our faiths—that would be compromising our beliefs.

What really stands out here is how they use the passage from 1 John 4:8 out of context and even misrepresent the passage they are misusing as a proof text when they state, *"And the New Testament states clearly that "God is love" (1 John 4:8).* Really? Is that what 1 John 4:8 "states clearly?"

Perhaps we should see what the Bible actually states in context:

"He that loves not knows not God; for God is love" (1 John 4:8).

Next, we must also ask ourselves, who is God, and how are we to know Him? Jesus tells us He is God when He states:

He that has seen me has seen the Father (John 14:9b).

If that is not plain enough, Jesus also clearly stated that the reason the Chief Priest and the Sanhedrin wanted to kill Him is because He said that He is God (John 10:33). Now we must consider that if God is love and Jesus is God—while Muslims insist that Jesus is a third rate prophet behind Muhammad and the "al-Mahdi" the Muslim Messiah—then how can we hold 1 John 4:8 "in common" with Muslims if Jesus is who He says He is?

As previously stated, the subject of 1 John 4:8 is for the nonbeliever as opposed to the believer, but in context, it is even more revealing because the topic of 1 John 4 revolves around the spirit of the Antichrist and false prophets. Muhammad taught against the Trinity (Sûrah 4:48; 5:72) and against the divinity of Christ (Sûrah 17:111. 23:91). He taught that Jesus did not die on the Cross (Sûrah 4:157); however, the Bible warns, "... the preaching of the Cross is to them that perish foolishness; but unto us which are saved it is the power of God" (1 Corinthians 1:18). Let's look at this passage once again only in the context in which it was given:

> Beloved, believe not every spirit, but try the spirits whether they are of God: because *many false prophets* are gone out into the world.
>
> Hereby know you the Spirit of God: Every spirit that confesses that Jesus Christ is come in the flesh is of God:
>
> And every spirit that *confesses not that Jesus Christ is come in the flesh is not of God: and this is that spirit of antichrist,* whereof you have heard that it should come; and even now already is it in the world.
>
> You are of God, little children, and have overcome them: because greater is He that is in you, than he that is in the world.
>
> They are of the world: therefore speak they of the world, and the world hears them.
>
> We are of God: he that knows God hears us; he that is not of God hears not us. Hereby know we the spirit of truth, and the spirit of error.
>
> Beloved, let us love one another: for love is of God; and every one that loves is born of God, and knows God.
>
> He that loves not knows not God; for God is love (1 John 4:1-8, emphases added).

If we are honest and apply 1 John 1:8 in its complete context, it becomes a rejection of all things Islamic!

> *For Christians, humanity's love of God and God's love of humanity are intimately linked. As we read in the New Testament: "We love because he [God] first loved us" (1 John 4:19). Our love of God springs from and is nourished by God's love for us. It cannot be*

268

otherwise, since the Creator who has power over all things is infinitely good.

Love of Neighbor

We find deep affinities with our own Christian faith when A Common Word Between Us and You insists that love is the pinnacle of our duties toward our neighbors. "None of you has faith until you love for your neighbor what you love for yourself," the Prophet Muhammad said. In the New Testament we similarly read, "whoever does not love [the neighbor] does not know God" (1 John 4:8) and "whoever does not love his brother whom he has seen cannot love God whom he has not seen" (1 John 4:20). God is love, and our highest calling as human beings is to imitate the One whom we worship.

Once again, we have a proof text—1 John 4:20—that is used to suggest Muslims are our brothers through the love of God. It sounds good, but what does the passage really tell us when it is presented in context?

If anyone acknowledges that Jesus is the Son of God, God lives in them and they in God.

And so we know and rely on the love God has for us.

God is love. Whoever lives in love lives in God, and God in them.

This is how love is made complete among us so that we will have confidence on the Day of Judgment: *In this world we are like Jesus.*

There is no fear in love. But perfect love drives out fear, because fear has to do with punishment. The one who fears is not made perfect in love.

We love because He first loved us.

Whoever claims to love God yet hates a brother or sister is a liar. For whoever does not love their brother and sister, whom they have seen, cannot love God, whom they have not seen (1 John 4:15-20, emphases added).

When we read this passage in context, we can plainly see it is telling us that people need to acknowledge that Jesus is the Son of God before God can live in them and them in God. How does this apply to Muslims who reject the divinity of Christ (Sûrah 17:111; 23:91; 25:02, etc.)? How does this draw Muslims and Christians closer together, as the Yale Covenant implies it will when putting 1 John 4:20 in context?

The Koran is full of Bible speak. There are many stories purported to be from the Bible, yet they all contain some portions of error or anachronisms. Many things the prophet, Muhammad, stated are simply inaccurate paraphrases of the Bible, which we can see in more detail in Volume II of *Islam Exposed, The Koran: Selected Sûrahs, Commentary and Bible Comparisons.*

We applaud when you state that "justice and freedom of religion are a crucial part" of the love of neighbor. When justice is lacking, neither love of God nor love of the neighbor can be present. When freedom to worship God according to one's conscience is curtailed, God is dishonored, the neighbor oppressed, and neither God nor neighbor is loved.

Since Muslims seek to love their Christian neighbors, they are not against them, the document encouragingly states. Instead, Muslims are with them. As Christians we resonate deeply with this sentiment. Our faith teaches that we must be with our neighbors — indeed, that we must act in their favor —even when our neighbors turn out to be our enemies. "But I say unto you," says Jesus Christ, "Love your enemies and pray for those who persecute you, so that you may be children of your Father in heaven; for he makes his sun rise on the evil and on the good" (Matthew 5:44-45). Our love, Jesus Christ says, must imitate the love of the infinitely good

Creator; our love must be as unconditional as is God's—extending to brothers, sisters, neighbors, and even enemies. At the end of his life, Jesus Christ himself prayed for his enemies: "Forgive them; for they do not know what they are doing" (Luke 23:34, NIV).

That is true of Christ, but what did Muhammad pray at the end of his life?

> Allah's Apostle, in his fatal illness said, "Allah cursed the Jews and the Christians, for they built the places of worship at the graves of their prophets." And if that had not been the case, then the Prophet's grave would have been made prominent before the people. So (the Prophet) was afraid, or the people were afraid that his grave might be taken as a place for worship.[6]

This Hadith has had long-reaching ramifications down through history. Recently the Islamic group known as ISIS (Islamic State of Iraq and Syria), also known as ISIL (Islamic State of Iraq and the Levant i.e., Middle East), who literally follow the teachings found in the Koran and the examples set by Muhammad, have not only destroyed irreplaceable and valuable Assyrian and Parthian artifacts, but they have also mindlessly destroyed biblical artifacts. The tomb of Jonah, the Old Testament prophet who was swallowed by the great fish[7] and Iraq's oldest Christian monastery, St. Elijah, which has "stood as a place of worship for 1,400 years, including most recently for U.S. troops,"[8] has now been forever erased from the face of the earth.

Despite the fact Muhammad wielded a sword and was known as the "warrior prophet," the following dialogue makes him almost seem like a hapless victim—a figure of bigoted persecution.

The Prophet Muhammad did similarly when he was violently rejected and stoned by the people of Ta'if. He is known to have said, "The most virtuous behavior is to engage those who sever relations, to give to those who withhold from you, and to forgive those who wrong you." (It is perhaps significant that after the Prophet Muhammad was driven out of Ta'if, it was the Christian

271

slave 'Addas who went out to Muhammad, brought him food, kissed him, and embraced him.)

This reference to a shadowy, Christian slave figure named, "Addas," is extra-koranic (not found in the Koran) and taken out of context from a Hadith narrated by Al-Tabarani; regardless, it might be wise for us to re-read Muhammad's conciliatory message as well as his "endearing" last words toward Christians and Jews.

For the sake of argument, let's assume—as the Yale Covenant suggests—that most of the minority Muslim communities and Mosques in America have only the most sincere motives in desiring to fellowship with Christians through Yale University, but we would be remiss if we did not reiterate that the Koran specifically forbids Muslims from making friends with Christians or Jews; however, the Koran also makes an allowance to the contrary as we explained in Chapter 4, "The Doctrine of Taqiyya: Allah Approved Lying to Advance the Cause of Islam."

A Muslim is allowed to develop a scheme for the benefit of deceiving infidels (in this case, Christians). Allah makes it very clear:

O you who believe! Take not the Jews and the Christians for friends. They are friends one to another. He among you who take them for friends is (one) of them. See [pay attention]! Allah guides not wrongdoing folk (Sûrah 5:51, bracketed clarification mine).

The Koran points out several times how Allah himself is the best of schemers/deceivers.

And they (the disbelievers) schemed, and Allah schemed (against them): and Allah is the best of schemers [deceivers] (Sûrah 3:54, bracketed clarification mine).

Are they then secure from Allah's scheme [deception]? None deemed [considered] himself secure from Allah's scheme

272

[deception] save [except] folk that perish (Sûrah 7:99, bracketed clarifications mine).

Again, we read in the Koran:

So they plotted a plot: and We [Allah] plotted a plot, while they perceived [understood] not (Sûrah 27:50, bracketed clarifications mine).

We can see next how Allah reworked Sûrah 5:51, which does not allow Muslims becoming friends with Christians and Jews, and then abrogated it to allow for the pretense of befriending Christians in Sûrah 3:28:

O ye who believe! Take not the Jews and the Christians for friends. They are friends one to another. He among you who takes them for friends is (one) of them. Lo! Allah guides not wrongdoing folk (Sûrah 5:51).

Let not the believers [Muslims] Take for friends or helpers Unbelievers [Christians and Jews] rather than believers [in Islam]: if any do that, in nothing will there be help from Allah: except by way of precaution [pretending friendship], that you may Guard yourselves from them [the non-Muslims in order to prevent them from harming you. until you are stronger than they are] But Allah cautions you (To remember) Himself; for the final goal is [establishing Islam] to Allah (Sûrah 3:28, Abdullah Yusuf Ali, bracketed clarifications mine).

A skeptic could make the argument that this might be what we see happening here with this unidentified group of Muslims offering to befriend Christians engaged in the Yale dialogue, "A Common Word between Us and You."[9]

The Task Before Us

"Let this common ground" – the dual common ground of love of God and of neighbor—"be the basis of all future interfaith dialogue between us," your courageous letter urges. Indeed, in the generosity with which the letter is written you embody what you call for. We most heartily agree. Abandoning all "hatred and strife," we must engage in interfaith dialogue as those who seek each other's good, for the one God unceasingly seeks our good. Indeed, together with you we believe that we need to move beyond "a polite ecumenical dialogue between selected religious leaders" and work diligently together to reshape relations between our communities and our nations so that they genuinely reflect our common love for God and for one another.

This paragraph begins:

"Let this common ground..." who or what is the "common ground?"

As we read further, we discover that common ground is:

"... the one God [who] unceasingly seeks our good. Indeed, together with you we believe that we need to move beyond 'a polite ecumenical dialogue ..." (bracketed clarification mine).

This is very confusing because to make the argument that Allah and the God of the Christians are one and the same, either Muslims must accept Jesus as God,[10] or Christians must reject Jesus as God. (Allah only reconciles with the Christians if they acknowledge Allah as the God of the Bible[11] who never had a son.[12]) Muhammad—and by extension, all Muslims—are instructed in the Koran as to what they should say when they are dealing with Christians:

Say [to the Christians and Jews Muhammad]: "O People of the Book! Do you disapprove of us for no other reason than that we believe in Allah, and the revelation that has come to us and that which came before (us), and (perhaps) that most of you are rebellious and disobedient?"

Say [to the Christians and Jews, Muhammad]: "Shall I point out to you something much worse than this (as judged) by the treatment it received from Allah? those who incurred the curse of Allah and His wrath, those of whom some He transformed into apes and swine, those who worshipped evil;- these are (many times) worse in rank, and far more astray from the even path" (Sûrah 5:59-60, Adullah Yusuf Ali, bracketed clarification mine).

Contrast Sûrah 5:59-60 with these words from the Yale Covenant:

Given the deep fissures in the relations between Christians and Muslims today, the task before us is daunting. And the stakes are great. The future of the world depends on our ability as Christians and Muslims to live together in peace. If we fail to make every effort to make peace and come together in harmony you correctly remind us that "our eternal souls" are at stake as well.

This is very disturbing at best and is at complete odds with what the Bible teaches when the Yale covenant states, *"If we fail to make every effort to make peace ... our (Christians and Muslims) eternal souls are at stake as well."*

Perhaps the signers of the Yale Covenant think that their souls are at stake, but I have accepted Jesus as my Lord and Savior (John 3:16), and because there is no other way to Heaven (John 14:6), I have the assurance my soul is saved (Ephesians 2:8-9), unlike the Yale Covenant's suggestion, *"If we fail to make every effort to make peace and come together in harmony you correctly remind us that 'our eternal souls' are at stake as well."* Biblically speaking, coming together in love, forgiveness, and fellowship will not save either the Muslims or the signers of this document. We can be confident in saying that because there is no salvation available to us through any other than Christ because there is no other name given under Heaven

275

through whom we may be saved (Acts 4:12), be it Buddha, Krishna, Zoroaster, Muhammad or Allah.

> *We are persuaded that our next step should be for our leaders at every level to meet together and begin the earnest work of determining how God would have us fulfill the requirement that we love God and one another. It is with humility and hope that we receive your generous letter, and we commit ourselves to labor together in heart, soul, mind and strength for the objectives you so appropriately propose.*

In conclusion, it becomes apparent that those involved with this movement make it unashamedly clear that they, along with their Muslim counterparts, believe that Allah and YAWA are really the same God. They maintain that YAWA and Allah were revealed through different languages and cultures, thus making it perfectly all right to work on "... determining how God would have us fulfill the requirement that we love God and one another." Despite these scholarly sounding words, God tells us how we are to deal with those who are unbelievers in God the Son.

> Do not be yoked [joined] together with unbelievers. For what do righteousness and wickedness have in common? Or what fellowship can light have with darkness? What harmony is there between Christ [—the light of the world (John 8:12)]—and Belial [Satan?] Or what does a believer have in common with an unbeliever [Muslim]? (2 Corinthians 6:14-15, NIV, bracketed clarifications mine).

We are dealing with two separate deities here—Allah and YAWA. If we are indeed a Christian—a follower of Christ—then we must take to heart the warning Jesus gave us regarding the serving of two masters; in this case, Allah and YAWA:

> No servant can serve two masters: for either he will hate the one, and love the other; or else he will hold to the one, and despise the other ... (Luke 16: 13a).

Thus, by blurring the lines between the Bible and the Koran, we see the emergence of what has come to be known as the heresy called— Chrislam.

THE CHRISLAM CATHOLIC CONNECTION

The merging of Islam with Christianity is not limited to just the Protestant churches, as we can see with the release of the New Catholic Catechism, which states:

> **841** *The Church's relationship with the Muslims.* "The plan of salvation also includes those who acknowledge the Creator, in the first place amongst whom are the Muslims; these profess to hold the faith of Abraham, and together with us they adore the one, merciful God, mankind's judge on the last day" (footnote 330).[13]

Referring to the opening statement, "The plan of salvation also includes those who acknowledge the Creator, in the first place amongst whom are the Muslims." How can Muslims be first among those who are in the plan of salvation when the Bible clearly teaches that the Jews are the apple of God's eye (Zechariah 2:8), and predate Islam by almost three thousand years? God's Covenant flows through Isaac. The Messiah descended from Isaac, not Ishmael (Genesis 17:19-21), so how is it, according to the New Catholic Catechism, that Ishmael takes precedence over Isaac? How can it be that Jesus (a descendant of Isaac) is not necessarily a part of God's salvation plan, as the Bible clearly teaches (John 14:6; Acts 4:12)? Now we are to believe that merely being a descendant of Abraham, we can be saved too. How cruel that would be for a Father to make His Son suffer such excruciating[14] pain on the cross like Jesus did if there was another means of salvation!

It is important to point out that the claim presented here in the New Catholic Catechism cannot simply apply to all the descendants of Ishmael because he was the father of the Ishmaelites—they were Pagans. Many of his descendants are also from Arabia—they were

Pagans until the time of Muhammad's revelations in 610 A.D. This means that for some 2700 years, the family of Ishmael (descended from Abraham) was not observing the "faith of Abraham" and, therefore, could not be saved as the Catechism suggests; nevertheless, even if they were to be counted saved as sons of Abraham, there is no basis for this in either the Old or New Testaments.

What we do see here is the great falling away of believers in the last days spoken of in the Bible. The Roman Catholic Church has over 1.1 billion members (as of 2010), which is about 50% of all Christians on the planet.[15] Because the pope is so inclined to embrace Islam, as many mainline Protestant churches are doing, it seems that the End Times World Religion spoken of in the Bible could not only be but probably will be, Chrislam! If so, the Antichrist and the False Prophet are both alive today, which brings up an intriguing question: if Chrislam is the One World Religion, who will be the False Prophet who goes against the Jews and demands to be worshiped in the Holy Temple?

NOTES:

1. Ishmael is the father of the Ishmaelites, who are also a Semitic tribe who integrated with the Arab tribes. "Arabian literature has its own version of prehistoric times, but it is entirely legendary" (Encyclopedia Britannica, Vol. 2:176).
2. Jack Minor, "For Shame - Wheaton Alumni Defend Chrislam Professor." Prophecy News Watch, 03 Feb. 2016. Web. 03 Feb. 2016.
3. "Jack Van Impe Presents," Dir., Jerry Rimmer, 29 min., Jack Van Impe Ministries, October 10, 2015.
4. YALE University. " 'A Common Word Between Us and You.' " *The New York Times*, 18 Nov. 2007.
Yale University, "A Common Word," a Christian Response,

Yale University, 2008. Web. 1 Oct. 2014. 2008 Conference Christians and Jews.

5. This apology to Muslims on behalf of all Christians is not unique to Yale University's, "A Common Word." Here is another example (of many), "Christian Leaders Ask for Muslim Forgiveness—Khaleej Times." Christian Leaders Ask for Muslim Forgiveness—Khaleej Times, n.p., 26 Nov. 2000. Web. 09 Oct. 2014. ABU DHABI—Peaceful relations between Muslims and Christians stand as one of the central challenges of this century, according to leading Christian leaders.

6. Hadith Sahih Bukhari, Narrated by Aisha (Muhammad's child bride upon whose lap Muhammad died when she was approximately 18 years old), Volume 2, Book 23, Number 472.

7. Dana Ford and Mohammed Tawfeeq. "Jonah's Tomb Destroyed, Officials Say - CNN.com." CNN Cable News Network, 25 July 2014. Web. 20 Jan. 2016.

8. "ISIS Destroys Iraq's Oldest Christian Monastery, Satellite Photos Confirm | Fox News." Fox News. FOX News Network, 20 Jan. 2016. Web. 20 Jan. 2016.

9. This outreach by Muslim leaders to the Yale Center for Faith and Culture fits the proposal laid out by the Muslim Brotherhood on how to dupe and infiltrate unsuspecting Western organizations.

CONSIDER: According to Swiss journalist, Sylvain Besson of Le Temps, in his book published October 2005 in France, *La conquête de l'Occident: Le projet secret des Islamistes* (The Conquest of the West: The Islamists' Secret Project), on December 1, 1982, during a raid by government authorities in the Swiss village of Nada, a document was found which listed a 12-point strategy outlined to "establish an Islamic government on earth." This document is known as "The Project." The Swiss authorities said some "Islamic researchers" who were allied with the Muslim Brotherhood, the same Brotherhood that has close ties with the United States government and has had advisers to Presidents Bush and Obama, allegedly drew up this unsigned document. "The Project" provides us with a close look at a relatively new

279

assault upon the Western world—an Islamic cultural jihad. Jihad (struggle) and has been associated with Islamic violence for over a millennium against all things that are not Muslim. Among some of the points included are: **Developing a comprehensive 100-year plan to advance Islamist ideology throughout the world; cultivating an Islamist intellectual community, including the establishment of think-tanks and advocacy groups, and publishing "academic" studies to legitimize Islamist positions and to chronicle the history of Islamist movements; instrumentally using existing Western institutions until they can be converted and put into service of Islam; ally-elected institutions on all levels in the West, including government, NGOs, private organizations and labor unions; Instrumentally using existing Western institutions until they can be converted and put into service of Islam;** etc. (bolded emphasis added).

10. Jesus claimed to be God: "Jesus heard that they had cast him out [the blind man He had just healed]; and when He had found him, He said unto him, 'Do you believe on the Son of God [Gk, *Theos*]?' " (John 9:35, bracketed clarification mine). "Say you of Him, 'whom the Father hath sanctified, and sent into the world, You blaspheme; because I said, 'I Am the Son of God?' "(John 10: 36). The earliest recorded event where Jesus claimed that God is His Father was when He was 12 years old. You can find it in the Gospel of Luke (Luke 2:46-48).

11. The Koran makes the claim: "It is He [Allah] Who sent down to thee (step by step), in truth, the Book [Bible], confirming what went before it; and He sent down the Law (of Moses) and the Gospel (of Jesus) before this, as a guide to mankind, and He sent down the criterion (of judgment between right and wrong)" (Sûrah 3:3, Abdullah Yusuf Al, bracketed clarifications mine).

12. And say: "Praise be to Allah, Who has not taken unto Himself a son, and Who hath no partner in the Sovereignty, nor hath He any protecting friend through dependence. And magnify Him with all magnificence" (Sûrah 17:111).

13. CCC (Catechism of the Catholic Church), Paragraph 841 with footnote #330, which refers to Lumen Gentium, the Dogmatic Constitution of the Church, number 16 from the Second Vatican Council, November 21, 1964. Number 16 addresses those who do not know Christ through no fault of their own and, therefore, cannot be blamed for something they do not know but are, nevertheless, g true seekers of God; however, paragraph 841 is narrower in scope and is specifically addressing the Church's relationship with the Muslims, then proceeds to explain "the Muslims;" who are part of the family of Abraham "who acknowledge the Creator" can be saved outside of Christ because they "profess to hold the faith of Abraham."

14. "Excruciating" comes from the Latin word, *Semitic*, from *cruciare*, meaning to crucify. The Latin word *crux*, which means "cross," is incorporated in the word "crucifixion." Crucifixion is considered the most painful and brutal way to die. It was first invented in Persia during 300 B.C. and later perfected by the Romans.

15. Joseph Liu. "The Global Catholic Population." Pew Research Centers Religion Public Life Project RSS, n.p., 13 Feb. 2013. Web. 23 June 2016.

APPENDIX

Christian Notables, Seminarians, Scholars, and Clergy Who Signed the Yale Covenant

For those of you who might want to learn who the supporters of the Yale Covenant are, we have reproduced the document's concluding acknowledgment of the Yale Center's illustrious staff, church leaders, and people of prominence who have signed onto this document.[1]

Harold W. Attridge
Dean and Lillian Claus Professor of
New Testament, Yale Divinity School

Miroslav Volf
Founder and Director of the Yale Center
for Faith and Culture, Henry B. Wright
Professor of Theology, Yale University

Joseph Cumming
Director of the Reconciliation Program,
Yale Center for Faith and Culture

Emilie M. Townes
Andrew Mellon Professor of African
American Religion and Theology
and President-elect of the American
Academy of Religion

A Selection of Prominent Signatories Follows:

These signatories consist of those featured in the November 18th, 2007, *New York Times* publication of "Loving God and Neighbor Together," as well as of a selection of other prominent signatories.

These signatories were all confirmed via email and, in most cases, were reconfirmed by further email exchange [stated the New York Times].

- Capt. Bradford E. Ableson, Chaplain Corps, US Navy and Senior Episcopal Chaplain in the US Navy
- Dr. Martin Accad, Academic Dean, Arab Baptist Theological Seminary (Lebanon), Director, Institute of Middle East Studies (Lebanon), Associate Professor of Islamic Studies, Fuller School of Intercultural Studies
- Scott C. Alexander, Associate Professor of Islam and Director, Catholic-Muslim Studies, Catholic Theological Union
- Dr. Mogamat-Ali Behardien, Minister, African Reformed Church, Paarl, South Africa
- Roger Allen, Professor of Arabic and Comparative Literature and Chair, Department of Near Eastern Languages and Civilizations, University of Pennsylvania, member of Middle East Study Group of the Episcopal Diocese of Pennsylvania
- Jean Amore, CSJ, for the Leadership Team of the Sisters of St. Joseph, Brentwood, New York
- Leith Anderson, President, National Association of Evangelicals
- Rev. Daniel S. Appleyard, Rector, Christ Episcopal Church, Dearborn, Michigan
  William Aramony, Consultant
- Yvette A. Assem, Student, Interdenominational Theological Center, Atlanta, Georgia
- Harold W. Attridge, Dean and Lillian Claus Professor of New Testament, Yale Divinity School
- Dr. Don Argue, Chancellor, Northwest University, Former President, National Association of Evangelicals, Commissioner, United States Commission on International Religious Freedom

284

- David Augsburger, Professor of Pastoral Care and Counseling, Fuller Theological Seminary, Pasadena, California
- Gerald R. Baer, M.D., Minister of Christian Education, Landisville, Pennsylvania
- Dwight P. Baker, Associate Director, Overseas Ministries Study Center
- Dr. Ray Bakke, Convening Chair, Evangelicals for Middle East Understanding:
  An International Coalition, Tempe, Arizona
- His Lordship Bishop Camillo Ballin, MCCI, Vicar Apostolic of Kuwait
- Leonard Bartlotti, Associate Professor of Intercultural Studies, Biola University, LaMirada, California
- Charles L. Bartow, Carl and Helen Egner Professor of Speech Communication in Ministry, Princeton Theological Seminary
- Rt. Rev. Barry Beisner, Bishop, Episcopal Diocese of Northern California
- Federico Bertuzzi, President, PM Internacional, Latin America
- James A. Beverley, Professor of Christian Thought and Ethics, Tyndale Seminary, Toronto, Canada
- J.D. Bindenagel, former U.S. Ambassador and Vice President, DePaul University, Chicago, Illinois
- Rev. Dr. Thomas W. Blair, The Second Presbyterian Church of Baltimore
- Walter R. Bodine, Pastor, International Church at Yale and Research Affiliate, Near Eastern Languages, Yale University
- Rev. Timothy A. Boggs, St. Alban's Episcopal Church, Washington, District of Columbia
- Regina A. Boisclair, Cardinal Newman Chair of Theology, Alaska Pacific University, Anchorage, Alaska
- David Bok, Independent Bible Teacher, Hartford Seminary, Hartford, Connecticut

- Rev. Jim Bonewald, Pastor, Knox Presbyterian Church, Cedar Rapids, Iowa
- Jonathan J. Bonk, Executive Director, Overseas Ministries Study Center and Editor, International Bulletin of Missionary Research
- Rev. Michael S. Bos, Director, Al Amana Centre, Sultanate of Oman
- Steven Bouma-Prediger, Professor of Religion, Hope College, Holland, Michigan
- Gerhard Böwering, Professor of Religious Studies, Yale University
- Mary C. Boys, Skinner and McAlpin Professor of Practical Theology, Union Theological Seminary, New York, New York
- Dan Brannen, International Students, Inc.
- Revs. Scott & Katarina Breslin, Protestant House Church Network, Istanbul Turkey
- Rev. Dr. Stuart Briscoe, Minister at Large, Elmbrook Church, Brookfield Wisconsin, USA; Founder, "Telling the Truth, Inc."
- Rev. Douglas Brown, Pastor, Valley View United Methodist Church Overland Park, Kansas
- Joseph Britton, Dean, Berkeley Divinity School at Yale
- Huib Bruinink, Developer of Marketing, PT. Puteri Mawar Sari, Central Java, Indonesia
- John M. Buchanan, Editor/Publisher, The Christian Century.
- James J. Buckley, Dean, College of Arts and Sciences, Loyola College in Maryland
- Eugene W. Bunkowske, Ph.D., Fiechtner Chair Professor of Christian Outreach, Oswald
- Huffman School of Christian Outreach, Concordia University, St. Paul, Minnesota
- John R. Burkholder, Professor Emeritus, Religion and Peace Studies, Goshen College, Goshen, Indiana

- David Burkum, Pastor, Valley Christian Church, Lakeville, Minnesota
- Rt. Rev. Joe Goodwin Burnett, Bishop, Episcopal Diocese of Nebraska
- Allen Busenitz, International Student Ministry, West Lafayette, Indiana
- Very Rev. Samuel G. Candler, Dean, Cathedral of St. Philip (Anglican), Atlanta, Georgia
- Juan Carlos Cárdenas, Academic Director, Instituto Iberoamericano de Estudios Transculturales, Granada, Spain
- Joseph Castleberry, President, Northwest University
- Rev. Colin Chapman, Former Lecturer in Islamic Studies, Near East School of Theology, Beirut, Lebanon, and author of Whose Promised Land
- Ellen T. Charry, Assoc. Professor of Systematic Theology, Princeton Theological Seminary
- David Yonggi Cho, Founder and Senior Pastor of Yoido Full Gospel Church, Seoul, Korea
- Hyung Kyung Chung, Associate Professor of Ecumenical Studies, Union Theological Seminary in New York
- Rev. Richard Cizik, Vice President of Governmental Affairs, National Association of Evangelicals
- Rev. Dr. Emmanuel Clapsis, Professor of Systematic Theology, Holy Cross Greek Orthodox School of Theology, Brookline, Massachusetts
- William Clarkson IV, President, the Westminster Schools, Atlanta, Georgia
- Emily Click, Lecturer on Ministry and Assistant Dean for Ministry Studies and Field Education, Harvard Divinity School
- Corneliu Constantineanu, Dean and Associate Professor of New Testament, Evangelical Theological Seminary, Osijek, Croatia
- Robert E. Cooley, President Emeritus, Gordon-Conwell Theological Seminary, South Hamilton, Massachusetts

- Rev. Shawn Coons, St. Philip Presbyterian, Houston, Texas
- Harvey Cox, Hollis Professor of Divinity, Harvard Divinity School
- Joseph Cumming, Director of the Reconciliation Program, Yale Center for Faith and Culture, Yale Divinity School
- Daniel A. Cunningham, Executive Pastor, Temple Bible Church, Temple, Texas
- Bryant L. Cureton, President, Elmhurst College, Elmhurst, Illinois
- Fr. John D'Alton, President, Melbourne Institute for Orthodox Christian Studies, Melbourne, Australia
- Fr. Joseph P. Daoust, S.J., President, Jesuit School of Theology at Berkeley, California
- Rev. David R. Davis, Special Projects Coordinator, The Evangelical Alliance Mission, Wheaton, Illinois
- John Deacon, Leader, Branch Out Ministries, The Olive Branch Community Church, Markham, Ontario, Canada
- Rev. Joseph C. Delahunt, Senior Pastor, Silliman Memorial Baptist Church, Bridgeport, Connecticut
- André Delbecq, Thomas J. and Kathleen L. McCarthy University Professor, Center for Spirituality of Organizational Leadership and former Dean of the Leavey School of Business at the University of Santa Clara, Santa Clara, California
- David A. Depew, President, Seed of Abraham Association, Broadcasting radio Bible studies in the Middle East
- Keith DeRose, Allison Foundation Professor of Philosophy, Yale University
- Curtiss Paul DeYoung, Professor of Reconciliation Studies, Bethel University
- Andrew Dimmock, Director, Doulos Community, Nouakchott, Mauritania
- Chip Dobbs-Allsopp, Associate Professor of Old Testament, Princeton Theological Seminary
- Andrés Alonso Duncan, CEO, LatinoAmerica Global, A.C.

- Kent A. Eaton, Professor of Pastoral Ministry and Associate Dean, Bethel Seminary San Diego, California
- Diana L. Eck, Professor of Comparative Religion and Indian Studies in Arts and Sciences and member of the Faculty of Divinity, Harvard University
- Mike Edens, Professor of Theology and Islamic Studies, Associate Dean of Graduate Studies, New Orleans Baptist Theological Seminary, New Orleans, LA
- Mark U. Edwards, Jr., Senior Advisor to the Dean, Harvard Divinity School
- James Ehrman, Director, Global Ministries Office, Evangelical Congregational Church
- Bertil Ekstrom, Executive Director, Mission Commission, World Evangelical Alliance
- Nancie Erhard, Assistant Professor of Comparative Religious Ethics, Saint Mary's University, Halifax, Nova Scotia
- John Esposito, University Professor & Founding Director Prince Alwaleed Bin Talal Center for Muslim-Christian Understanding, Georgetown University
- Chester E. Falby, Priest Associate, St. Catherine's Episcopal Church, Manzanita, Oregon
- Thomas P. Finger, Mennonite Central Committee, Evanston, Illinois
- Rev. Dr. David C. Fisher, Senior Minister, Plymouth Church, Brooklyn, New York
- David Ford, Regius Professor of Divinity, Cambridge University
- Marlene Malahoo Forte, 2007 Yale World Fellow, Fuller Theological Seminary, Pasadena, California
- Rev. Susan L. Gabbard, St. John's United Church of Christ, Mifflinburg, Pennsylvania
- Millard Garrett, Vice President, Eastern Mennonite Missions, Salunga, Pennsylvania
- Siobhan Garrigan, Assistant Professor of Liturgical Studies and Assistant Dean

- Marquand Chapel, Yale Divinity School
- Timothy George, Dean, Beeson Divinity School, Samford University
- William Goettler, Assistant Dean for Assessment and Ministerial Studies, Yale Divinity School
- Michael J. Goggin, Chairperson, North American Interfaith Network (NAIN)
- Robert S. Goizueta, Professor of Theology, Boston College
- Bruce Gordon, Professor of History, University of St. Andrews
- William A. Graham, Murray A. Albertson, Professor of Middle Eastern Studies in Arts and Sciences, Harvard University
- Wesley Granberg-Michaelson, General Secretary, Reformed Church in America
- Rev. Bruce Green, Bridge Building Facilitator, FCM Foundation, Centerville Presbyterian Church, Fremont, California
- Joel B. Green, Professor of New Testament Interpretation, Fuller Theological Seminary, Pasadena, California
- Lynn Green, International Chairman, Youth with A Mission
- Frank Griffel, Associate Professor of Islamic Studies, Yale University
- Rev. Giorgio Grlj, Pastor, Rijeka Baptist Church, Baptist Union of Croatia
- Rev. Kent Claussen Gubrud, Christus Victor Lutheran Church, Apple Valley, Minnesota
- Rt. Rev. Edwin F. Gulick, Jr., Bishop, Episcopal Diocese of Kentucky
- Judith Gundry-Volf, Adjunct Associate Professor of New Testament, Yale Divinity School
- David P. Gushee, Distinguished Professor of Christian Ethics, McAfee School of Theology at Mercer University and President, Evangelicals for Human Rights
- Kim B. Gustafson, President, Common Ground Consultants, Inc.

- Elie Haddad, Provost, Arab Baptist Theological Seminary, Lebanon
- Dr. Anette Hagan, Elder, Mayfield Salisbury Parish Church, Edinburgh, Scotland
- Martin Hailer, Professor of Theology, Leuphana University, Lueneburg, Germany
- Rev. L. Ann Hallisey, Hallisey Consulting and Counseling, Interim Vicar, Good Shepherd Episcopal Church, Berkeley, California
- Gloria K. Hannas, Member, Peacemaking Mission Team of the Presbytery of Chicago, PCUSA, La Grange, Illinois
- Paul D. Hanson, Florence Corliss Lamont Professor of Divinity, Harvard Divinity School
- Pastor Peter Hanson, Director of Studies, Dept. of Theology and Training, Lutheran Church of Senegal
- Heidi Hadsell, President, Hartford Seminary, Hartford, Connecticut
- David Heim, Executive Editor, The Christian Century
- Richard Henderson, Director of Studies, Westbrook Hay, United Kingdom
- Mary E. Hess, Associate Professor of Educational Leadership, Luther Seminary
- Richard Heyduck, Pastor, First United Methodist Church, Pittsburg, Texas
- Rev. Dr. David M. Hindman, United Methodist campus minister, The Wesley Foundation at The College of William and Mary, Williamsburg, Virginia
- Rev. Norman A. Hjelm, Director, Commission on Faith and Order (retired), National Council of the Churches of Christ in the USA
- Carl R. Holladay, Charles Howard Candler Professor of New Testament, Candler School of Theology, Emory University
- Jan Holton, Assistant Professor of Pastoral Care, Yale Divinity School
- Marian E. Hostetler, former worker, Mennonite Mission Network and Eastern Mennonite Mission, Elkhart, Indiana

- Joseph Hough, President and William E. Dodge Professor of Social Ethics, Union Theological Seminary in New York
- Bill Hybels, Founder and Senior Pastor, Willow Creek Community Church, South Barrington, Illinois
- Dale T. Irvin, President and Professor of World Christianity, New York Theological Seminary, New York, New York
- Dr. Nabeel T. Jabbour, Consultant, Professor, Colorado Springs, Colorado
- Todd Jenkins, Pastor, First Presbyterian Church, Fayetteville, Tennessee
- David L. Johnston, Lecturer, Religious Studies Department, University of Pennsylvania
- Robert K. Johnston, Professor of Theology and Culture, Fuller Theological Seminary, Pasadena, California
- Rt. Rev. Shannon Sherwood Johnston, Bishop Coadjutor, Episcopal Diocese of Virginia
- Rt. Rev. David Colin Jones, Bishop Suffragan, Episcopal Diocese of Virginia
- Gary D. Jones, Rector, St. Stephen's Episcopal Church, Richmond, Virginia
- Tony Jones, National Coordinator, Emergent Village
- Stefan Jung, Economist, Germany
- Rev. Dr. Riad A. Kassis, Theologian, Author, and Consultant
- Sister Helen Kearney, Sisters of Saint Joseph, Brentwood, New York
- Sister Janet Kinney, CSJ, Sisters of St. Joseph, Brentwood, New York
- Doris G. Kinney, associate editor (ret.), Time Inc., New York
- Steve Knight, National Coordinating Group Member, Emergent Village, Charlotte, North Carolina
- Paul Knitter, Paul Tillich Professor of Theology, World Religions and Culture, Union Theological Seminary in New York
- Dr. Manfred W. Kohl, Vice President of Overseas Council International, USA

- Very Rev. Dr. James A. Kowalski, Dean, The Cathedral Church of Saint John the Divine, New York New York
- James R. Krabill, Senior Executive for Global Ministries, Mennonite Mission Network, Elkhart, Indiana
- Hank Kraus, Founder and Director, Peace Mark
- Sharon Kugler, University Chaplain, Yale University
- Catherine Kurtz, Landisville Mennonite Church, Landisville, Pennsylvania
- Peter Kuzmic, Eva B. and Paul E. Toms Distinguished Professor of World Missions and European Studies, Gordon-Conwell Theological Seminary and Rektor, Evandjeoski Teoloski Fakultet, Osijek, Croatia
- Jonathan L. Kvanvig, Distinguished Professor of Philosophy, Baylor University
- David Lamarre-Vincent, Executive Director, New Hampshire Council of Churches
- John A. Lapp, Executive Secretary Emeritus, Mennonite Central Committee, Akron, Pennsylvania
- Dr. Warren Larson, Director of the Zwemer Center for Muslim Studies, Columbia International University, South Carolina
- Traugott Lawler, Professor of English emeritus, Yale University
- Dr. Maurice Lee, post-doctoral fellow, Harvard University
- Rt. Rev. Peter J. Lee, Bishop, Episcopal Diocese of Virginia
- Kristen Leslie, Associate Professor of Pastoral Care, Yale Divinity School
- Linda LeSourd Lader, President, Renaissance Institute, Charleston, South Carolina
- Rev. R. Charles Lewis, Jr., Parish Associate, First Presbyterian Vintage Faith Church, Santa Cruz, California
- Julyan Lidstone, OM, Glasgow, Scotland
- Erik Lincoln, Author of Peace Generation tolerance curriculum for Muslim Students, Indonesia
- John Lindner, Director of External Relations, Yale Divinity School

293

- Greg Livingstone, Founder of Frontiers and Historian of Muslim-Christian Encounters
- Albert C. Lobe, Interim Executive Director, Mennonite Central Committee, Akron, Pennsylvania
- Rick Love, International Director, Frontiers and Adjunct Associate Professor of Islamic Studies, Fuller Theological Seminary, author of Peacemaking
- Donald Luidens, Professor of Sociology, Hope College, Holland, Michigan
- Owen Lynch, Associate Pastor, Trent Vineyard, Nottingham, United Kingdom
- Douglas Magnuson, Associate Professor of Intercultural Programs and Director of Muslim Studies, Bethel University
- Peter Maiden, International Coordinator, OM
- Jozef Majewski, Doctor of Theology, Professor of Media Studies at the University of Gdansk, Poland
- Danut Manastireanu, Director for Faith & Development, Middle East & East Europe Region, World Vision International, Iasi, Romania
- Rev. Dr. John T. Mathew, Minister, St. Mark's United Church of Canada, & Department of Religious Studies, Huntington/Laurentian Universities, Sudbury, ON Canada
- Rev. Steven D. Martin, President, Vital Visions Incorporated and Pastor, United Methodist Church, Oak Ridge, Tennessee
- Harold E. Masback, III, Senior Minister, The Congregational Church of New Canaan
- Rt. Rev Gerald N. McAllister, Retired Bishop, Episcopal Diocese of Oklahoma
- The Rev. Donald M. McCoid, Executive for Ecumenical and Inter-Religious Relations, Evangelical Lutheran Church in America
- C. Douglas McConnell, Ph.D., Dean, School of Intercultural Studies, Fuller Seminary, Pasadena, California

- Sister Mary McConnell, CSJ, Sisters of St. Joseph, Brentwood, New York
- Jeanne McGorry, CSJ, Sisters of St. Joseph, Brentwood, New York
- Elsie McKee, Archibald Alexander Professor of Reformation Studies and the History of Worship, Princeton Theological Seminary
- Scot McKnight, Karl A. Olsson Professor in Religious Studies, North Park University, Chicago, Illinois
- Brian D. McLaren, Author, Speaker, Activist
- C. Edward McVaney, Retired Chairman, CEO and President, J.D. Edwards and Company
- Kathleen E. McVey, J. Ross Stevenson Professor of Early and Eastern Church History, Princeton Theological Seminary
- Carl Medearis, President, International Initiatives, Denver, Colorado
- Greg Meland, Director of Formation, Supervised Ministry and Placement, Bethel Seminary, Minnesota
- Mennonite Central Committee, Akron, Pennsylvania
- Harold E. Metzler, Member, Church of the Brethren and heritor of the Amish/Mennonite tradition
- Alan E. Miller, Lead Pastor, Conestoga Church of the Brethren, Leola, Pennsylvania
- David B. Miller, Pastor, University Mennonite Church, State College, Pennsylvania
- Rev. Dr. Sid L. Mohn, President, Heartland Alliance for Human Needs and Human Rights, Chicago, Illinois
- Brother Benilde Montgomery, O.S.F., Franciscan Brother of Brooklyn
- Steve Moore, President & CEO, the Mission Exchange
- Douglas Morgan, Director, Adventist Peace Fellowship
- Richard Mouw, President and Professor of Christian Philosophy, Fuller Theological Seminary, Pasadena, California

- Salim J. Munayer, Academic Dean, Bethlehem Bible College, Jerusalem
- Rich Nathan, Senior Pastor, Vineyard Church of Columbus
- David Neff, Editor in Chief & Vice President, Christianity Today Media Group
- Alexander Negrov, President, Saint Petersburg Christian University, St. Petersburg, Russia
- Arnold Neufeldt-Fast, Associate Dean, Tyndale Seminary, Toronto
- Craig Noll, Assistant Editor, International Bulletin of Missionary Research, Overseas Ministries Study Center
- Rev. Roy Oksnevad, Institute of Strategic Evangelism at Wheaton College
- John Lord O'Brian Professor of Divinity Dean in the Divinity School, Harvard University
- Dennis Olsen, Charles T. Haley Professor of Old Testament Theology, Princeton Theological Seminary
- Richard R. Osmer, Thomas Synnot, Professor of Christian Education, Princeton Theological Seminary
- Rev. Canon Mark Oxbrow, International Mission Director, Church Mission Society, United Kingdom
- Rt. Rev. George E. Packard, Bishop Suffragan for Chaplaincies of the Episcopal Church
- George Parsenios, Assistant Professor of New Testament, Princeton Theological Seminary
- Greg H. Parsons, General Director, USCWM, Pasadena, California
- Stephanie A. Paulsell, Houghton Professor of the Practice of Ministry Studies, Harvard Divinity School
- James R. Payton, Jr., Professor of History, Redeemer University College, Ancaster, Ontario, Canada and President, Christians Associated for Relationships with Eastern Europe
- Emily A. Peacock, Circuit Judge, 13th Judicial Circuit of Florida, Tampa, Florida

- Doug Pennoyer, Dean, School of Intercultural Studies, Biola University, LaMirada California
- Howard Pepper, M.A., M.Div., President, Nurture Press, San Diego, California
- Douglas Petersen, Margaret S. Smith Professor of Intercultural Studies, Vanguard University of Southern California
- Rev. Edward Prevost, Rector, Christ Church, Winnetka, Illinois
- Bruce G. Privratsky, Elder, Holston Conference, United Methodist Church
- Sally M. Promey, Professor of Religion & Visual Culture, Professor of American Studies, Professor Religious Studies and Deputy Director, Institute of Sacred Music, Yale University
- Rev. Earl G. Purnell, Rector, Old Saint Andrew's Episcopal Church, Bloomfield, CT
- Rev. John C. Ramey, President, Aslan Child Rescue Ministries and President, The Olive Branch Institute
- Robert M. Randolph, Chaplain to the Massachusetts Institute of Technology, Cambridge, Massachusetts
- Thomas P. Rausch, S.J., T. Marie Chilton Professor of Catholic Theology, Loyola Marymount University, Los Angeles, California
- James D. Redington, S.J., Associate Professor in the Dwan Family Chair of Interreligious Dialogue
  Dialogue, Jesuit School of Theology at Berkeley/Graduate Theological Union, California
- David A. Reed, Professor Emeritus of Pastoral Theology and Research, Wycliffe College, University of Toronto, Canada
- Neil Rees, International Director, World Horizons
- Rev. Warren Reeve, Lead Pastor, Bandung International Church, Bandung, West Java, Indonesia and Founder and Facilitator of the Missional International Church Network
- Rodney Allen Reeves, Former moderator of the Christian Church (Disciples of Christ) in Oregon and board member,

Greater Portland Institute for Christian-Muslim Understanding and member, Interfaith Council of Greater Portland.

- Dr. Evelyne A. Reisacher, Assistant Professor of Islamic Studies and International Relations, Fuller Theological Seminary, Pasadena, California
- Cornel G. Rempel, Retired pastor, chaplain and supervisor of clinical pastoral education, Winnipeg, Manitoba, Canada
- Steve Robbins, Pastor and Director, Vineyard Leadership Institute
- Cecil M. Robeck, Jr., Professor of Church History and Ecumenics, Fuller Theological Seminary, Pasadena, California, and the Director of the David du Plessis Center for Christian Spirituality
- Leonard Rodgers, Executive Director, Evangelicals for Middle East Understanding: An International Coalition, Tempe, Arizona
- Dudley C. Rose, Lecturer on Ministry and Associate Dean for Ministry Study, Harvard Divinity School
- Rev. Herschel Rosser, Associate Pastor, Vineyard Church of Sugar Land, Stafford, Texas, and Texas Area Church Planting Coordinator, Vineyard, USA
- Glenna N. Roukes, Elder, First Presbyterian Church, Santa Cruz, CA and Secretary, Mission Team
- Philip Ruge-Jones, Associate Professor of Theology, Texas Lutheran University, Seguin, Texas
- William L. Sachs, Director, Center for Reconciliation and Mission, St. Stephen's Episcopal Church, Richmond, Virginia
- Robert A. Sain, Pastor, Messiah Lutheran Church, ELCA, Hildebran, North Carolina
- Lamin Sanneh, D. Willis James Professor of Missions and World Christianity, Yale University
- Andrew D. Saperstein, Associate Director of the Reconciliation Program at the Yale Center for Faith and

Culture Tyler Savage, Missionary with Church Resource Ministries, Germany and South Africa
- Meritt Lohr Sawyer, International Program Director, Langham Partnership International
- Warren C. Sawyer, President and CEO, The Caleb Foundation, Swampscott, Massachusetts
- Rev. Dr. Christian Scharen, Director, Faith as a Way of Life Program, Yale Center for Faith & Culture
- Rev. Dr. Robert Schuller, Founder, Crystal Cathedral and "Hour of Power"
- Elizabeth Schüssler Fiorenza, Krister Stendahl Professor of Divinity, Harvard Divinity School
- Francis Schüssler Fiorenza, Stillman Professor of Roman Catholic Studies, Harvard Divinity School
- William Schweiker, Edward L. Ryerson Distinguished Service Professor of Theological Ethics, University of Chicago
- Waldron Scott, President emeritus, Holistic Ministries International, Paterson, New Jersey
- Andrew J. Sebanc, Senior Pastor, Green Timbers Covenant Church, Surrey, British Columbia, Canada
- Rev. Donald Senior, C.P., President, Catholic Theological Union, Chicago, Illinois
- C. L. Seow, Henry Snyder Gehman Professor of OT Language and Literature, Princeton Theological Seminary
- Rev. Dr. Perry Shaw, Chair, Faculty of Ministerial Studies, Arab Baptist Theological Seminary, Beirut, Lebanon
- Michael T. Shelley, Director, Center of Christian-Muslim Engagement for Peace and Justice, Lutheran School of Theology at Chicago
- David W. and K. Grace Shenk, Global Consultants, Eastern Mennonite Missions, Salunga, Pennsylvania
- Wilbert R. Shenk, Senior Professor of Mission History and Contemporary Culture, Fuller Theological Seminary

- John N. Sheveland, Assistant Professor of Comparative Theology, Gonzaga University, Washington, District of Columbia
- Marguerite Shuster, Harold John Ockenga Professor of Preaching and Theology, Fuller Theological Seminary, Pasadena, California
- Frederick J. Sigworth, Professor, Department of Cellular and Molecular Physiology, Yale University
- Mark Siljander, Member of the U.S. Congress (R) & former U.S. Ambassador to the U.N.
- Walt Simmerman, Pastor, First United Methodist Church, Galax, Virginia
- The Community Council of the Sisters of the Precious Blood, Dayton, Ohio, Sister Florence Seifert, CPPS, President; Sister Jeanette Buehler, CPPS, Vice President; Sister Madonna Ratermann, CPPS, Councilor; Sister Edna Hess, CPPS, Councilor; Sister Marita Beumer, CPPS, Councilor
- C. Donald Smedley, Associate Director, the Rivendell Institute, New Haven, Connecticut
- John D. Spalding, Founder and Editor, SOMAreview.co
- Rev. Andrew Spurr, Vicar of Evesham with Norton and Lenchwick Diocese of Worcester
- John G. Stackhouse, Jr., Sangwoo Youtong Chee Professor of Theology and Culture, Regent College, Vancouver, Canada
- Glen H. Stassen, Lewis B. Smedes Professor of Christian Ethics, Fuller Theological Seminary, Pasadena, California
- Sally Steenland, Senior Policy Advisor, Faith & Progressive Policy Initiative, Center for American Progress, Washington, District of Columbia
- Wilbur P. Stone, Program Director and Lead Faculty, Global and Contextual Studies, Bethel University/Seminary
- Rev. Dr. John Stott, Rector Emeritus, All Souls Church, Langham Place, London, United Kingdom

- Frederick J. Streets, The Carl and Dorothy Bennett Professor in Pastoral Counseling, the Wurzweiler School of Social Work, Yeshiva University, Adjunct Associate Professor of Pastoral Theology, Yale Divinity School, Former Yale University Chaplain
- Diana Swancutt, Associate Professor of New Testament, Yale Divinity School
- Merlin Swartz, Professor of Islamic Studies, Boston University
- Donald K. Swearer, Director, Center for the Study of World Religions, Harvard Divinity School
- Dr. Glen A. Taylor, Cooperative Studies Teaching Fellow, Tajikistan State National University, Dushanbe, Tajikistan
- William Taylor, Global Ambassador, World Evangelical Alliance
- Harvey Thiessen, Executive Director, OM Canada
- Rev. John Thomas, General Minister and President, United Church of Christ
- Stephen Thomas, European Team Leader, Salt & Light Ministries Senior Pastor, Oxford, United Kingdom
- Dr. J. Milburn Thompson, Chair and Professor of Theology, Bellarmine University, Louisville, Kentucky
- Iain Torrance, President, Princeton Theological Seminary
- Emilie M. Townes, Andrew Mellon Professor of African American Religion and Theology, Yale Divinity School, and President-elect of the American Academy of Religion
- Michael W. Treneer, International President, The Navigators, Colorado Springs, Colorado
- Geoff Tunnicliffe, International Director, World Evangelical Alliance
- Fr. Benjamin J. Urmston, S.J., Director Emeritus Peace and Justice Programs, Xavier University, Cincinnati, Ohio
- Birgit Van Hout, Executive Director, MCCJ, Florida
- Harold Vogelaar, Director Emeritus: A Center of Christian-Muslim Engagement for Peace and Justice, Lutheran School of Theology at Chicago

- Miroslav Volf, Founder and Director of the Yale Center for Faith and Culture, Henry B. Wright Professor of Theology, Yale Divinity School
- Fr. H. Eberhard von Waldow, Professor Emeritus, Pittsburgh Theological Seminary
- Rev. Berten A. Waggoner, National Director, Association of Vineyard Churches
- Robin Wainwright, President, Middle East Fellowship, Pasadena, California and Chairman of the Executive Committee, Oxford Centre for Mission Studies
- Dr. Dale F. Walker, Affiliate Professor, Asbury Theological Seminary, Wilmore, Kentucky
- Jim Wallis, President, Sojourners
- Charlotte R. Ward, Associate Professor of Physics, Emerita, Auburn University and Life Deacon, Auburn First Baptist Church
- Charles H. Warnock III, Senior Pastor, Chatham Baptist Church, Chatham, Virginia
- Rick Warren, Founder and Senior Pastor, Saddleback Church, and The Purpose Driven Life, Lake Forest, California
- Very Rev. Debra Warwick-Sabino, Rector, Grace Episcopal Church, Fairfield, California
- Mark R. Wenger, Director of Pastoral Studies, Lancaster Eastern Mennonite Seminary P.O., Lancaster, Pennsylvania
- Dr. Bob Wenz, Renewing Total Worship Ministries, Colorado Springs, Colorado
- Rev. Laura Westby, Pastor, First Congregational Church of Danbury, Connecticut
- Robert R. Wilson, Hoober Professor of Religious Studies, Associate Dean for Academic Affairs, Yale Divinity School
- Rev. Michael D. Wilker, Executive Director, Lutheran Volunteer Corps, Washington, District of Columbia
- Leslie Withers, Coordinator, Interfaith Pilgrimage Project, Friendship Force International, Atlanta, Georgia

- Dr. John Wolfersberger, Retired Executive, Christian Church (Disciples of Christ), Southern California
- Nicholas Wolterstorff, Senior Fellow, Institute for Advanced Studies in Culture, University of Virginia
- J. Dudley Woodberry, Professor of Islamic Studies and Dean Emeritus of the Fuller School of International Studies
- Rev Dr Christopher J H Wright, International Director, Langham Partnership International, London, United Kingdom
- John Wright, Senior Pastor, Trent Vineyard, Nottingham, England
- Godfrey Yogarajah, General Secretary, Evangelical Fellowship of Asia
- Rev. Andrea Zaki Stephanous, Vice President of the Protestant Church in Egypt, Director of Dar El Thaqafa Communications House-CEOSS
- Rev. John D. Zeigler, First Presbyterian Church, PCUSA, Canton, Texas

Additional Signatories

"These signatories primarily include those whose names have been received in writing through this website, and in most cases have not been reconfirmed. We regret, due to the overwhelming response, we have not been able to include all the people who wrote and asked to be added to this list."

- Rob Acheson, Chairman, Toronto Chapter, Canadian Department of Peace Initiative
- Peter Adams, Intercultural Relations Worker, St Mary's Church, Luton, England
- Rev. William J. Adams, Rector, Trinity Episcopal Church, Sutter Creek, California
- Dr. Rev. Tokunboh Adeyemo, Executive Director, Centre for Biblical Transformation (CBT), Nairobi, Kenya

- Justin Anderson, member, First Baptist Church, Washington, District of Columbia
- Fidel Arnecillo, Jr., Lecturer in Philosophy, California State University, San Bernardino, College/Career Pastor, Charisma Life Community Church, Pomona, California
- Rev. Dianne Astle, Pastor, Chemainus/Cedar United Church, BC, Canada
- Chris J Baltzley, Director of MultiCampus Development, Lakeside-Orangevale Camp
- Pastor, Lakeside Church, Folsom, California USA
- Andrew Tower Barnhill, Furman University, Greenville, South Carolina
- Rev. D. Clyde Bartges, Minister, Presbyterian Church USA, Midlothian, Virginia
- Dr. Anthony Bartlett, Assistant Professor of Theology, Bexley Hall Episcopal Seminary, Rochester, New York
- Rev. Ann Barton, Pastor, McKenzie United Methodist Church Honey Grove, Texas
- Marilyn R. Barry, Academic Dean and Professor of English, Alaska Pacific University, Anchorage, Alaska
- Rev. Rosemary D. Baue, Pastor, Union Chapel (UCC), Fishers Island, New York
- Bruce Baumgartner, OSB, Spiritual Director
- Dr. Jolly Beyioku, Associate Professor, Indiana Wesleyan University, Marion, Indiana
- Cheryl Biller, Elder Presbyterian Church USA, Fargo, North Dakota
- Dr. William L. Bingham, Associate Prof. Emeritus, North Carolina State University,
- Raleigh, North Carolina and President of Triangle Interfaith Alliance (North Carolina)
- Luke Birky, Goshen, Indiana
- Barbara Blodgett, Director of Supervised Ministries, Yale Divinity School, New Haven, Connecticut
- Stephen Blum, Professor of Music, CUNY Graduate Center

- Whitney S. Bodman, Assoc. Professor of Comparative Religion, Austin Presbyterian Theological Seminary, Austin, Texas
- Dr. Dean A. Boldon, Professor Emeritus, Maryville College, Maryville, Tennessee
- Prof. Eduard J. Bomhoff, Director, School of Business, University of Nottingham, Malaysia Campus Kuala Lumpur, Malaysia
- Richard Bowser, Sunland Park, New Mexico
- Rev. M Christopher Boyer, Pastor, Good Shepherd Baptist Church, Lynnwood, Washington
- Matt Brandon, Frontier Trek & Tours, Travel Photographer
- Mark Lau Branson, Homer Goddard Associate Professor of Ministry of the Laity, Fuller Theological Seminary, Pasadena, California
- Timothy Brenneman, Harrisonburg, Virginia
- Linda C. Brinkman, Naples, Florida
- Margaret Brookover, Mother, Teacher, CODEPINK leader, Bend, Oregon
- Stephen Brown, Chaplain, St. Joseph's Medical Center, Stockton, California
- Rev. Judy Buck-Glenn, Associate Rector, Christ Church Episcopal, Ridley Park, Pennsylvania
- Rev. Dr. Ned A. Buckner, LMFT, Pastor, New Hope Baptist Church, Gastonia, North Carolina, Marriage & Family Therapist, Piedmont Psychological Associates, Gastonia, North Carolina
- Robert & Betty Lou Buckwalter, Prince of Peace Mennonite Church, Anchorage, Alaska
- George D. Burazer, coordinator of the Justice and Peace Committee of Queen of the Apostles Catholic Church, Belmont, North Carolina
- Dawn Burdick, Nazareth Presbyterian Church, Moore, South Carolina
- Julie Burgess, Omaha, Nebraska
- Rev. J Daniel Burke, Episcopal priest, retired

- John Buttrey, Retired Pastor, United Church of Christ, Holland, Michigan
- Rev. Dr. Josephine C. Cameron, Pastor, Riverdale Presbyterian Church, Bronx, New York
- Vincent M. Cannistraro, Cannistraro Associates, McLean, Virginia
- Mark Carey, Doctor of Physical Therapy Student, Grand Valley State University, Grand Rapids, Michigan
- Joseph P. Carson, PE, President, Affiliation of Christian Engineers, Knoxville, Tennessee
- Dan R. Cates, Assistant Professor, Kutztown University, Kutztown, Pennsylvania
- Liz Cates
- Sister Lynn Caton, CSJ, Sisters of St. Joseph, Brentwood, New York
- Rev. James H. Cavanaugh, UCC pastor retired, Uplands Retirement Village, Tennessee
- Patricia Anne Cavanaugh, Recognized UCC Lay Pastor, Uplands Retirement Village, Tennessee
- Rev. Paul Chaffee, Executive Director, Interfaith Center at the Presidio, San Francisco, California
- Rev. Dr. W. Michael Chittum, Minister
- Susan Civil-Brown, Author
- Scott Claassen, Los Angeles, California
- W. Malcolm Clark, Professor Emeritus of Religion, Butler University, Indianapolis, Indiana
- Michael Clawson, Pastor, Via Christus Community Church, Yorkville Illinois
- Jeffrey C. Clayton, Pastor, Southminster Presbyterian Church, Prairie Village, Kansas
- Adam Walker Cleaveland, M.Div./M.A., Princeton Theological Seminary, Princeton, New Jersey
- Bruce J. Clemenger, President, The Evangelical Fellowship of Canada, Kenneth L. Clum, Rochester, New York
- Tim Cochran, Member, McGregor Baptist Church (Southern Baptist), Fort Myers, Florida

- David Cooper, Picton Uniting Church, Picton, NSW Australia
- Yvonne Cooper, Picton Uniting Church, Picton, NSW Australia
- Victor Copan, ThD, Chair, Dept. of Ministry Leadership Studies Palm Beach Atlantic University, West Palm Beach, Florida
- Rev. Christopher Cottingham, Hospice Chaplain, Member of Emmanuel Baptist Fellowship, Lexington, South Carolina
- Charles Courtney, Professor Emeritus, Drew University, Madison, New Jersey
- Dr. James D. Cramer, Secretary, Atlantic City Mission Board, Episcopal Diocese of New Jersey
- Mrs. Cheryl Crist, Pentecostal, Peru, Indiana
- Jane F. Crosthwaite, Professor, Mount Holyoke College
- Alistair Crow, Transform Network, London, United Kingdom
- Bobbi Crow, Global Outreach Team, Real Life Christian Church Gilbert, Arizona Common Ground Consultation Attendee
- John Matthew Cummins, Chatham, New Jersey
- Mark Czyzewski, SFO
- Kathleen Danaher de Cardenas, Garner, North Carolina
- The Rev Dr. Lillian Daniel, Senior Minister, First Congregational Church, UCC, 535 Forest Ave, Glen Ellyn, Illinois, 60137
- Rev. Dr. Julian A. Davies, Pastor, The University Church, Toledo, Ohio
- John T. DeBevoise, Pastor, Palma Ceia Presbyterian Church, Tampa, Florida
- Dr. Ralph Del Colle, Theology Department, Marquette University, Milwaukee, Wisconsin
- Rev. Colette Volkema DeNooyer, Holland, Michigan
- Robert J. DeNooyer II, Holland, Michigan
- Frannie Derm, Independent Scholar, Waterbury, Connecticut

- Paige DeWees, Student, Luther Seminary, St. Paul, Minnesota
- Rev. Dr. Winfield J. Devonshire, Jr., Senior Pastor, the Evangelical Lutheran Church of the Holy Trinity, Hershey, Pennsylvania
- Eileen McCafferty DiFranco, East Regional Administrator, WomenPriests
- Reverend Johan Dodge, Compass Point Church, Paso Robles, California
- Jane Dugdale, member, Central Baptist Church, Wayne, Pennsylvania
- Rev. Jeffrey S. Dugan, Rector, St. James Episcopal Church, Farmington, Connecticut
- Brenda Manthorne Dyck, spiritual director, pastor, Calgary Inter-Mennonite Church, Calgary, Alberta, Canada
- Omar and Anna Kathryn Eby, Harrisonburg, Virginia
- Jason von Ehrenkrook, Ph.D. Candidate (Near Eastern Studies), University of Michigan, Ann Arbor, Michigan
- Rusty Eidmann-Hicks, Holmdel Community UCC, Holmdel, New Jersey
- Dr. Matthias Eigenbrodt, Praxis am Viktoriapark, Berlin, Germany
- Dr. Stewart L. Elson, Willcox United Methodist Church, Willcox, Arizona
- Rev. Daniel J. Fahs, Pastor, Hayward United Methodist Church, Hayward, Wisconsin
- Audry Falk, Artist
- Richard Falk, former Chair Board of Trustees, The Friendship Force
- Steven Fenwick Ph.D., Counselor in private practice, Olympia, Washington
- Sandra L. Fischer, Esq., Cooperative M. Div. student, Hartford Seminary, Hartford, Connecticut
- Rev. Dr. David C. Fisher, Senior Minister, Plymouth Church, Brooklyn, New York

- Rev. Tim Fitch, Minister of Family Life First Congregational Church of Akron, Akron, Ohio
- Rev. Carey D. Fletcher, Red River Baptist Church, Benton, Louisiana
- Patrick Foley, Educator
- Rev. Dr. F. Peter Ford, Jr., Coordinator of the Program in Christian-Muslim Relations, Mekane Yesus Seminary, Addis Ababa, Ethiopia
- John R. Franke, Professor of Theology, Biblical Seminary, Hatfield, Pennsylvania
- Barbara Freeman, Church Musician, Haslett Community Church (UCC), Haslett, Michigan
- Matthew Friedman, Th.M. Candidate, Asbury Theological Seminary
- Makoto Fujimura, Artist
- Clarice Garvey, Our Lady's Missionaries Fortaleza,Ceará, Brazil
- Gary A. Gaudin, Pastor, South Arm United Church, Richmond, British Columbia, Canada
- Sr. Christine Gebel, Our Lady's Missionaries, Toronto, Canada
- Cheryl German, Knoxville, Tennessee
- Alexander J. G. Gilchrist, Elder, Presbyterian Church USA, Wappingers Falls, New York
- Rev. Douglas W. Giles, MDiv, STS, Retired Evangelical Lutheran Church in Canada (ELCIC), Cold Lake, Alberta, Canada
- Michael Glenn, Cashiers, North Carolina
- Leon & Elaine Good, Lititz, Pennsylvania
- Ave Regina Gould, CSJ, Sisters of St. Joseph, Brentwood, New York
- James Goulding, Professor Emeritus and VP for Academic Affairs, Emeritus, MacMurray College in Jacksonville, IL; currently Instructor in Religious Studies, Edgewood College, Madison, Wisconsin
- Rev. Benjamin Gray, Youth pastor, Griffin, Georgia

- Dr. Victor Greene, Chaplain, Angel Hospice, Franklin, North Carolina
- Jeanette Grenz, Overland Park, KS
- Kenneth K. Grenz, Overland Park, KS, retired clergy, Kansas East Conference, United Methodist Church
- Carol S. Guilbert, Reverend, First Presbyterian Church of Hilton Head Island
- Brian Gumm, Interim Lay Pastor, Ankeny Church of the Brethren, Ankeny, Iowa
- Anne-Marie Gustavson-Claverie, sister of bishop Pierre Claverie of Algeria
- Ellen Halperin, Member, St. John the Baptist Episcopal Church, Hardwick, Vermont
- Elaine S. Hansen, Fairfield, Ohio
- Hendrik Hart, Senior Member (ret'd), Institute for Christian Studies, Toronto, Canada
- Peter C. Hart, President, Data Loggers, Inc., Holland, Michigan
- Rev. Dr. William L. Hathaway, Pastor, First Presbyterian Church, Annapolis, Maryland
- Rev William L. Hawkins, Pastor, First Presbyterian Church, New Bern, North Carolina
- Rob Hazel, High Wycombe, England
- Eike J. Heinze, Hartford, Wisconsin
- Rev. Amanda Hendler-Voss, Faith Communities Coordinator, Women's Action for New Directions (WAND)
- Rev. Abigail A. Henrich, Co-Pastor, Union Congregational Church, East Walpole, Massachusetts
- Scott Hinton, First Congregational Church of Glen Ellyn, Illinois
- Sheryll Hix, Behavior Specialist, Stuart, Florida
- Rev. Mark E. Hoelter, Unitarian Universalist, Coordinator for Grassroots Interfaith Dialogues, The InterFaith Conference of Metropolitan Washington, Washington, District of Columbia

- Shirley Eid Holm, Church Librarian, Grace Lutheran Church, River Forest, Illinois
- Rev. Charles Homeyer, Rector of Holy Cross Episcopal Church, Grand Rapids, Michigan
- Jon Hoover, Assistant Professor of Islamic Studies, Near East School of Theology, Beirut
- Rev. David M. Horst, Minister, First Parish in Malden, Universalist, Malden, Massachusetts
- Imogen Hawthorne Howe, West Redding, Connecticut Lieutenant-Colonel (Retired) Alan Howes, Australian Regular Army, Canberra, Australia
- Robert W. Huntington 3rd, MD, Member, Madison Wisconsin Monthly Meeting, Religious Society of Friends (Quakers)
- Carol Ingells, Spiritual Director, Episcopal lay leader, Lansing, Michigan
- Carlos Iwaszkowiec, Sales Director, MECS, Inc., St. Louis, Missouri
- Dr. Mary Ellen Jacobs, University of Connecticut Health Center, Farmington, Connecticut
- Linda Jame, MS, ACSW, Psychotherapist, New York, New York
- Charles B. Jenkins, Church of the Messiah United Methodist, Westerville, Ohio and member of the Interfaith Association of Central Ohio
- Jeromy Johnson, Pastor, Sacramento, California
- Joseph L. Johnson, Pastor, Evergreen Presbyterian Church, Dothan, Alabama
- R. Boaz Johnson, Ph.D., Director, Division of Christian Life and Thought, North Park University, Chicago, Illinois
- Rev. Dr. Gregory Knox Jones, Westminster Presbyterian Church, Wilmington, Delaware
- Margaret Jayne Jones, Co-contact, United Religions Initiative, San Francisco Peninsula
- Susan Jones, Cary, North Carolina

- Jolyn Joslin, retired teacher, member of United Church of Christ, Waitsfield, Vermont
- Rev. Daniel Junkuntz, D. Min., (ELCA), LMFT, LPC, Retired Director, Peninsula Pastoral Counseling Center, Newport News, Virginia
- Sister Karen Kaelin, Sisters of St. Joseph, Brentwood, New York
- Abdul Kasim, Vice President, Critical-Links, New Jersey
- Robert Mace Kass, M.D., Trustee, Berkeley Divinity School at Yale
- Mona Kelly, Our Lady's Missionaries, Fortaleza, Ceará, Brazil
- Rev. D. Andrew Kille, Interfaith Space, San Jose, CA
- Rev. Mike King, President, Youth Front; Pastor, Jacob's Well Church, Kansas City, Missouri
- Ann King-Grosh, Lancaster, Pennsylvania
- Rev. Kurt Kirchhoff, Haslett, Michigan
- Ann Kirkland, Toronto, Canada
- Michael Kirtley, President, The Friendship Caravan, Arlington, Virginia
- Dr. Robin J. Klay, Professor of Economics, Hope College, Michigan
- Charles Klingler, Professor Emeritus of English, Manchester College, North Manchester, Indiana
- Susie Klingler, Member of Manchester Church of the Brethren, North Manchester, Indiana
- Rev. Alfred C. Krass, VP, The Interfaith Gathering of Lower Buck County, Pennsylvania, retired United Church of Christ pastor, United Christian Church, Levittown, Pennsylvania
- Mark Kurtz, Director of Business Development, BioOne, Washington, District of Columbia
- Vincent La Marca, Webmaster, New Utrecht Reformed Church, Assistant Secretary, Friends of Historic New Utrecht, Brooklyn, New York
- Perry Landes, Lighting and Sound Designer, Hope College, Holland Michigan

- Andrew E. Larsen, Department of World Mission, The Evangelical Covenant Church of North America, Chicago, Illinois
- Rev. Rebecca Larson, Pastor, Monadnock Congregational Church, UCC, Colebrook, New Hampshire
- Thiel L. Larson, Educator, Bend LaPine School District in Bend, Oregon
- Michael Lauchlan, Dearborn, Michigan
- Stephen Lawson, Joplin, Missouri
- Paul Leggett, Pastor, Grace Presbyterian Church, Montclair, New Jersey
- "Let There Be Peace" Prayer and Reflection Group, St. Noel Catholic Church, Willoughby Hills, Ohio
- Norman Lindholm, Ohio
- Dr. Scott Little, Lay Leader, First United Methodist Church, Smithville, Tennessee
- Jerry Ludeke
- Matthew D. Lundberg, Assistant Professor of Theology, Calvin College, Grand Rapids, Michigan
- Dr. Elaine Z. Madison, Associate Professor of Literature, Hawaii Pacific University, Honolulu, Hawaii
- Brent D. Maher, Upland, Indiana
- Velandy Manohar, MD, FAPA, Distinguished Life Fellow, Am. Psychiatric Association, Haddam, Connecticut
- Natalia Marandiuc, Ph.D. Student, Theology, Yale University
- Dr. Henry B. Marksberry, Minister of Health and Wholeness, St. John's United Church of Christ, Newport, Kentucky
- Rev. Ben C. Martin, Honorably Retired, Presbytery of Giddings-Lovejoy, Presbyterian Church (U.S.A.), St. Louis, Missouri
- Caleb J.D. Maskell, PhD student, Department of Religion, Princeton University

- Martha B Matuska, "Let There Be Peace" Prayer and Reflection Group, St. Noel Catholic Church, Willoughby Hills, Ohio
- Shaun Mazurek, Denver, Colorado
- Sister Regina McAuley CSJ, Brentwood New York
- Pastor Sandy McCormack, Soma Christou International, Houston, Texas
- Deborah McEvoy, Dearborn, Michigan
- Rev. Loren McGrail, Chaplain at Abbott Northwestern Hospital Minneapolis, Minnesota
- Dr. James F. McGrath, Assistant Professor of Religion, Butler University, Indianapolis, Indianapolis
- Maryann McHugh, CSJ, sister of St. Joseph, Brentwood, New York
- Mickey J. Mercer, Teacher, Flagstaff High School, Flagstaff, Arizona
- Nathan Messarra, Ecclesia Clear Lake, Friendswood, Texas
- Roel Meeuws, M.Sc. Delft University of Technology, Delft, member of the Reformed Church of the Netherlands as present in the Pilgrim Fathers Church, Rotterdam, the Netherlands
- Rev. Michael Merkel, Pastor, Bethesda Lutheran Church, New Haven, Connecticut
- Elizabeth Moody, Our Lady of Mt. Carmel Catholic Church, Mill Valley, California., and member, World Religions Building Bridges Program Committee with Marin Interfaith Council, International Assoc. of Sufism, and Dominican University in Marin County, California
- Re. David L. Mosher, Co-Minister, Unity of Loudoun County, Leesburg, Virginia
- Daniel H. Miller, Chaplain, Houston Hospice and Palliative Care System, Houston, Texas
- Luke Miller, National Coordinating Group Member, Emergent Village, Dallas, Texas
- Rosa Lynne Miller, Asbury United Methodist Church, Lafayette, Louisiana

- The Rev. Dr. W. Douglas Mills, Associate General Secretary for Dialogue and Interfaith Relations, General Commission on Christian Unity and Interreligious Concerns, The United Methodist Church, New York, New York
- Timothy D. Moore, Teacher, Milwaukee, Wisconsin
- Barbara Mueller, teacher emerita, Holy Cross Lutheran Church, Ft. Wayne, Indiana
- John Mueller, Minister of Music, Holy Cross Lutheran Church, Ft. Wayne, Indiana
- John Mulholland, University of Chicago Law Library staff, Chicago Illinois
- Rev. Dr. Stephen Butler Murray, College Chaplain, Director of Religious and Spiritual Life, and Lecturer in Religion, Skidmore College, Saratoga Springs, New York
- Stephanie Nash, Pastor for Education and Outreach, Second Baptist Church, Lubbock Texas
- Bradley Nassif, Professor of Biblical and Theological Studies, North Park University, Chicago, Illinois
- Norm Nelson, President, Compassion Radio, Lake Forest, California
- Carole Nuckon, Bend, Oregon
- Rev. Gus Nussdorfer, Interim, First Presbyterian Church, Bryan, Ohio
- Clarke K. Oler, Associate Pastor, All Saints Episcopal Church, Pasadena, California
- Steven J Ondersma, Assistant Professor, Wayne State University School of Medicine & Deacon, PCUSA
- Robert C & Roberta G Ouderkirk, Normandy Park, Washington
- John D. Painter, Pastor, Centenary United Methodist Church, Metuchen, New Jersey
- Dr. Stephen Pavey, Research Associate, Institute for Community Research, Hartford, Connecticut
- Rev. Dr. Protopresbyter Professor George C. Papademetriou

- Rev. Jeanne C. Parker, clergywoman, ABC/RGR, Rochester, New York
- Rev. Urbane Peachey, retired Pastor, formerly in Middle East, Lititz, Pennsylvania
- Michael Peacock, seminarian, chaplain, attorney; Palma Ceia Presbyterian Church, Tampa, Florida
- Jonathan Pedrone, Youth Pastor, New Testament Baptist Church, Miami, Florida
- Dan Peters, Thousand Oaks, California
- Reverend Clare L. Petersberger, Minister, The Towson Unitarian, Universalist Church Lutherville, Maryland
- Gene Peterson, Board Member, Churches Together, Minneapolis, Minnesota
- Prof. Joseph M. Pirone, Ph.D, Sam Draper Honors Program, SUNY and Advisor, Awareness in Motion, Interfaith Club Enneapsychodramatics
- Rev. Vincent Pizzuto, Ph.D., University of San Francisco, California, New Skellig Contemplative Christian Community
- Keith Plate, MD, International Student Ministry, Iowa City, Iowa
- Kenneth Polsley Jr., Pastor, All Nations Baptist Church, Iowa City, Iowa
- Eve Pope, Trustee Emeritus, United Religions Initiative
- Viola Deavours Powers, Cincinnati, Ohio
- Alfred C. Price, Philadelphia, Pennsylvania
- Stan Purdum, Pastor, Centenary United Methodist Church, Waynesburg, Ohio
- Georgia Quailey, Pittsburgh, Pennsylvania
- Rev. Charles W. Rawlings, Presbytery of Newark Middle East Work Group, New Jersey
- David Redfield, Episcopalian, Grosse Pointe, Michigan
- Dr. Donald H. and Mary M. Reimer, Charleswood Mennonite Church, Winnipeg, Manitoba
- Dr. Andreas Renz, Lecturer, LMU Munich, Germany
- David Reynolds, Australia

- Robert E. Riddle, First Presbyterian Church, Asheville, North Carolina
- Jack Ridl, Professor Emeritus of English, Hope College, Holland, Michigan
- Rev. Marchiene Rienstra, Minister, Unity Church on the Lakeshore, Douglas, Michigan
- Dr. Kevin Riggs, Senior Pastor, Franklin Community Church, Franklin, Tennessee and Sociology Professor, State Community College, Nashville, Tennessee
- Dr. M. K. Rigsby, Professor of Philosophy and Religion, Eastern New Mexico University, Portales New Mexico
- Mark Andrew Ritchie, Author, Commodities Trader
- Heath and Courtney Robinson, Temple, Texas
- Rev. Dr. Errol G Rohr, Chaplain, King College, Bristol, Tennessee
- Rev. Betsy Payne Rosen, Deacon, Our Saviour Episcopal Church, Mill Valley, California
- Rosetta E. Ross, Associate Professor of Religion, Spelman College, Atlanta, Georgia
- Rev. Dr. Greg Roth, Senior Pastor, Centerville Presbyterian Church, Fremont, California
- Chaplain Reggie B. Rowell, Medical University of Charleston, Charleston, South Carolina
- Dr. Mark Rutledge, United Church of Christ Campus Minister at Duke University, Durham, North Carolina
- Fleming Rutledge, Episcopal Diocese of New York
- Phil Saksa, International Student Specialist, Detroit, Michigan
- Tim Samoff, Blogger, Kansas City, Missouri
- Alan P & Maria G Sandner, First Presbyterian Church, Bend, Oregon
- Clara Santoro, CSJ
- David G. Delos Santos, ICT Specialist, PACTEC International, Kabul, Afghanistan
- Edwin G. Saphar, Jr, Elder, Downtown United Presbyterian Church, Rochester, New York

- Brother Satyananda, Minister, Self-Realization Fellowship, Los Angeles, California
- Theresa Scanlon, Principal, St. Francis of Assisi School, Brooklyn, New York
- Rev. Dr. Jill Schaeffer, United Presbyterian Church of Cincinnatus, New York and Adjunct Professor, New York Theological Seminary, New York, New York
- Andrew Schill, Oil and Gas Attorney, Durango, Colorado
- Rev. Mark Schindler, Unity of Auburn, Auburn, California
- Perry Schmidt-Leukel, Professor of Systematic Theology and Religious Studies, University of Glasgow, Chair of World Religions for Peace
- Carolyn Schneider, Associate Professor of Theology, Texas Lutheran University, Seguin, Texas
- Edward H. Schreur, Senior Pastor, Protestant Church in Oman, Muscat, Sultanate of Oman
- Glen G. Scorgie, Ph.D., Bethel Seminary, San Diego, California
- Jonathan H. Scruggs, Associate Pastor, First Assembly of God, Gastonia, North Carolina
- Pastor Timothy Seitz-Brown, Paradise Lutheran Church (ELCA), Thomasville, Pennsylvania
- Robert P. Sellers, Connally Professor of Missions, Logsdon School of Theology, Hardin-Simmons University, Abilene, Texas
- Samir Selmanovic, Program Director, Faith House Manhattan, New York, New York
- Emily Shaffer, US Department of State, Kigali, Rwanda Donna Shank, LCSW, Lancaster, Pennsylvania
- Joey Shaw, Masters candidate at Center for Middle East Studies and LBJ School of Public Affairs, the University of Texas at Austin
- N. Gerald Shenk, Professor of Church & Society Eastern Mennonite Seminary, Harrisonburg, Virginia
- Rev. Dr. Stephen J. Sidorak, Jr., Executive Director, Christian Conference of Connecticut

- Frederick A. Smith, MD, Consultant in Palliative Medicine, North Shore-Long Island Jewish Health System, Assistant Professor of Medicine, NYU School of Medicine, Communicant, Christ Episcopal Church, Garden City
- Paul. V. Sorrentino, Director of Religious Life, Amherst College, Amherst, Massachusetts
- Rebecca L. Syme, MATL student - Bethel Seminary, St. Paul, Minnesota
- Rev. Andrea Zaki Stephanous, Ph. D., Vice President of the Protestant Church in Egypt, Director of Dar El Thaqafa Communications House-CEOSS
- Rev. John Paul Sydnor, Assistant Professor of World Religions, Emmanuel College (Boston) and Co-Pastor, Union Congregational Church, East Walpole, Massachusetts
- Jim Somerville, Pastor, The First Baptist Church of the City of Washington, District of Columbia
- Dr. Barbara Spitzer, Clinical Psychologist, Stamford, Connecticut
- Rev. Susan F. Sprowls, Campus Pastor, Lord of Light Lutheran Campus Ministry (ELCA), University of Michigan, Ann Arbor, Michigan
- Rev. Lauren R. Stanley, Episcopal Missionary in Sudan
- Rev. Harvey Stob, Pastor of Congregational Life, Ann Arbor Christian Reformed Church, Ann Arbor, Michigan
- Arthur J. Stock, member Wellesley Village Church, and former Chair Board of Directors, Massachusetts Conference, United Church of Christ
- John K. Stoner, Consultant, Every Church A Peace Church, Akron, Pennsylvania
- Rev. Jim Strader, Episcopal Chaplain/Priest, University of Arizona, Tucson, Arizona
- James A. Strnal, Secular Franciscan Order
- Dan Sullivan, Saint Augustine's Episcopal Church,Wilmette, Illinois
- Helen Katharine Swearingen

- Christine Talbott, Licensed Clinical Professional Counselor, Castine, Maine
- Dennis Teall-Fleming, Director of Faith Formation, Queen of the Apostles Catholic Church, Belmont, NC and Facilitator, Gaston Trialogue (Jews, Christians, and Muslims), Gaston County, NC and Instructor in Religion, Gaston College, Dallas, North Carolina
- Rev. Dr. Mari Thorkelson, Pastor Bethel Lutheran Church, Willmar Minnesota
- Rev. Dr. James A Todd, Honorably Retired, Presbyterian Church (U.S.A.), Member of the Presbytery of Southern New England
- John L. Tipton, CEO, Telephone Jack's Communications, Adrian, Michigan
- Judy and Woody Trautman, Founding Co-Chairs of the MultiFaith Council of Northwest Ohio, Toledo, Ohio
- Barbara H. Trought, Elder, Presbyterian Church (USA), Burlington, New Jersey
- Monte D. Tucker
- Rev. Philip H. Troutman, M.Div., Ordained Elder, Church of the Nazarene, Doctoral Student, Asbury Theological Seminary, Wilmore, Kentucky
- James and Susan Vagnier, Columbus, Ohio
- Rev. Dr. Timo Vasko, The Evangelical Lutheran Church of Finland, Espoo
- Sister Nancy Vendura, CSJ, Sisters of Saint Joseph, Brentwood, New York
- Dr. David H. Vila, Associate Professor of Religion and Philosophy, John Brown University, Siloam Springs, Arkansas
- Marlene M. von Friederichs-Fitzwater, Assistant Adjunct Professor, Division of Hematology/Oncology, UC Davis School of Medicine and Director of Outreach Research and Education, UC Davis Cancer Center
- Case Wagenvoord, Chair, Adult Education Committee, Holmdel Community UCC, Holmdel, New Jersey

- Rev. Dr. Francis K. Wagschal, Retired Lutheran Pastor, Waynesville, North Carolina
- Barbara Wall, Certified speech and language pathologist Bandhagen, Sweden
- Sammy Wanyonyi, World Evangelist, Sammy Wanyonyi International Ministries (SWIM), Minneapolis, Minnesota
- Michael J. Watts, Instructor in Religion, Johnston Community College, Smithfield, North Carolina
- Derek Ivan Webster, Beth Emunah Messianic Synagogue, Agoura Hills, California
- Rev. Gordon V. Webster, Co-Pastor, Downtown United Presbyterian Church, Rochester, NY
- Rev. Dr. Dave Weidlich, Pastor, First Presbyterian Church of Petaluma, Petaluma, California
- Susan Weissert, Ossining, New York
- Rev. Terry Weller, Interfaith Minister and Editor, Interfaith Unity Newsletter, Toronto, ON, Canada
- Charlie West, Pastor, Grace/Skandia United Methodist Churches, Marquette, Michigan
- Roger G. Whetsel, Engineering Consultant, Winchester, Tennessee
- Jerald Whitehouse, Director, Global Center for Adventist Muslim Relations, General Conference of Seventh Day Adventists, Loma Linda, California
- Rev. Dr. Gary A. Wilburn, Senior Pastor, First Presbyterian Church, New Canaan, Connecticut
- Prof. Stefan Wild, University of Bonn, Germany
- Bett and Talbert Williams, St Anne's Episcopal Church, Atlanta, Georgia
- Boyd H. Wilson, Ph.D., Professor of Religion, Hope College, Holland, Michigan
- Don Wilson, Temple of Understanding Advisory Board
- Rev. Dr. Emmanuel M. Wilson, Spiritual Care Coordinator, Heartland Home Health Care & Hospice, Jacksonville, Florida

- Dr. Norman G. Wilson, Coordinator of Intercultural Studies Department, Indiana Wesleyan University, Marion, Indiana
- Hester F. Witchey, AMI Montessori Teacher
- Pecki Sherman Witonsky, Author, the Cave of Reconciliation, An Abrahamic/Ibrahimic Tale
- Wayne R. Wohler, Pasadena, California
- Rev. Dean A. Woodward (retired), Park Hill United Methodist Church, Denver, Colorado
- Rev. Daniel Wolpert, Pastor, First Presbyterian Church, Crookston, Minnesota
- Carol M. Woods
- Harry Woods, Edmond, Oklahoma
- Anna Woodiwiss, Kabul, Afghanistan
- Prof. Ashley Woodiwiss, Director of the Drummond Center for Statesmanship, Erskine College, South Carolina
- Robyn Yates, Children's Pastor, Fellowship Bible Church, Arapaho, Dallas, Texas
- Byard & Judy Yoder, Landisville Mennonite Church, Pennsylvania
- Liz Yoho, Director of Children & Youth Ministries, Congregational Church of New Fairfield (UCC), Connecticut
- Larry E. Yonker, Business Owner, The Elevation Group, Colorado Springs, Colorado
- Rick Zachar, Phoenix, Arizona
- Daniel Zelesko, M.A., Instructor of Philosophy and Comparative of Religion, Harrisburg Area Community College
- Rev. Curtis L. Zieske, Pastor, Trinity Lutheran Church (ELCA), Albert Lea, Minnesota
- John & Velma Zook, Lititz Mennonite Church, Lititz, Pennsylvania

---

NOTES:

1   Yale University, "A Common Word" Christian Response. Yale

University, 2008: n.pag. Web. 01 October 2014.
This is a partial list of the Christian signatories. There are also many imams and Muslim academia who have signed this document

More signatures are being added all the time.

GLOSSARY OF KORANIC ARABIC

Adhān   A call to prayer

Adl   Justice (i.e, political, social, economic and environmental)

Aḥad   This can be taken literally to mean "one." Religiously, Aḥad means "only one" (e.g., something exclusive). God is unique.

Aḥkām   Laws and guidelines which are found in the Qu'ran and Sunnah (The Hadith): There are five types of these guidelines: (1) *Wajib* (e.g., mandatory); (2) *Mustahab* (e.g., righteous); (3) *Muharram*, the beginning month of the Muslim year; (4) *Makruh* (e.g., offensive), and (4) *Halal*, foods prepared according to Sharia law.

Ahl al-Bayt   Immediate members of Muhammad's family

Ahl al-Fatrah Those who are unaware of the doctrine concerning any formal religion but have a fitra (e.g., basic internal knowledge of nature's embedded religious awareness), a concept borrowed from Romans 1:

"Because that which may be known of God is manifest in them; for God has showed it unto them. For the invisible things of Him from the creation of the world are clearly seen, being understood by the things that are made, even His eternal power and Godhead; so that they are without excuse" (Romans 1:19-20).

Ahl al-Kitāb Usually refers to the "People of the Book," but can also refer to some of the other pre-Islamic believers in monotheism who had some type of writings thought to be from god, such as the Sabians and Magians. The Magians were an early form of Zoroastrianism. These religions are mentioned in the Koran (Sûrah 22:17).

Ālamīn Not to be confused with *al-Amin,* which means "trustworthy" and is one of the nicknames bestowed upon Muhammad. *Ālamīn* means worlds or cosmos which includes humans, jinns (i.e.., demons), angels and everything which exists in this world for things that need a physical existence or the world of non-physical matter—the spirit world

Alayhi-as-salām

"Peace be upon him;" sometimes expressed in the Koran as the acronym (P.B.U.H.). An expression of respect used after a person utters the name of Muhammad or other prophets of Islam; however, this expression of respect is not limited to just Muslim prophets. It also includes angelic beings such as Gabriel (Jibreel) and Michael (Mikaeel) (see **As-Salāmu ʾAlaykum**).

Allāh This is considered a synonym as well as the personal name of God in Arabic; however, Allah is not Arabic for god (see *Ilāh*), but merely a theophoric name. In Greek, theophoric (θεόφορος) means a name containing (or bears the name of) a god, such as the Greek name, Apollonia (Acts 17:1); also "Martin" which means "of (the god) Mars," "Godalupe" or "Guadalupe" of Spanish origin, referring to the Virgin Mary (not a goddess, but mother of God) and used as a girl's name.

Allāhu ʾAkbar

A proclamation declaring "Allah is the Greatest"

AH/A.H. Latin phrase *Anno Hegirae* or "In the year of the Hijra," which was the journey Mohammad made when he escaped from Mecca to Yathrib (Medina) in 622 A.D. or AH 1, the first year in the Muslim calendar.

Ālim A knowledgeable person, scholar (in any formal discipline of study), theologian or scientist (see **Ulamā**)

Āmīn The same as "amen" in the English language meaning an affirmation such as "truly spoken," "verily," "so be it"

Āminah   Muhammad's mother, who died in Abwa, near Yathrib (an oasis village later renamed "Medina" by Muhammad) when Muhammad was six years old, leaving him a complete orphan. His father died before he was born (see **Yathrib**).

Anfāl   Spoils of war

Arkān   The Five Pillars of Islam

Aslim Taslam
     A proclamation to "submit to Islam"

Asmāʾ Allāh al-Ḥusnā
     A list of Allah's 99 names. One hadith (Sahih Muslim, Book 35, Number 6476) tells us that the person who recites them all will enter "Paradise." (Sahih Muslim's full name is Al-Musnadu Al-Sahihu bi Naklil Adli.)

Aṣ-Ṣirāṭ   The bridge where all the dead must cross. The manner of how a person crosses the bridge (governed by what a person believes in and how they conduct themselves in life); determines whether they will go to Heaven or Hell.

As-Salāmu ʿAlaykum
     A common Muslim greeting which means "peace be upon you," similar to the acronym used in the Koran or The Hadith which is P.B.U.H ("peace be upon him" i.e., Muhammad or a Muslim prophet), an utterance of respect for Allah (see **Wa ʿalaykum as-salām** for the response)

Awliyāʾ   This refers to protectors, helpers, friends, custodians, and superintendents.

Āyatullāh (Ayatollah)
     A sign from God; in the Shi'a sect, this is an honorable title given to highly esteemed religious scholars.

Baitullāh (baytu-llāh)
     A "house of God" known as a mosque, especially the Ka'aba located in Mecca; also a special manner in reciting the Koran according to intonation and rules of pronunciation

Bakr-Eid   See **Eid.**

Barakah   A blessing or a form thereof

Bashar   Human beings, man, mankind (i.e., person or people)

Burqa (burka)
                 Full body attire that is worn by Muslim women with only a small opening for the eyes, usually consisting of a dark color used for personal modesty. Its purpose is to guard men from temptation; referred to in the Koran as "Hijab" (see **Ḥijāb**)

Bid'ah sayyi'ah
                 A type of inquiry forbidden to Muslims; Bid'ah in English means innovative. It can also be applied to that which displeases Muhammad and Allah. Bid'ah Sayyi'ah is questioning the Koran and Sharia law.

Bay ah   An oath of allegiance to a leader, traditionally the caliph or imam

Caliph (khalīfah)
                 A literal successor to Muhammad; the civil and religious authority (head) over an Islamic theocracy

Dajjāl   The Muslim equivalent of the biblical Antichrist; a liar

Dār al-ḥarb *Dar* means "house," *al* means "of" and *harb* means "war"— together *dar al-harb* means "house of war" and refers to areas outside Muslim rule and, therefore, automatically at war with non-Muslim countries. In Islam, there are two main houses, *dar al-Islam* or "house of Islam" and *dar al-harb* or "house of war" (peace or war).

Dār al-Islām The house or land of Islam (see **Dar al-harb**)

Daʿwah Proselytizing for Islam

Dhikr   The name of god is spoken repeatedly as a devotional or spiritual exercise. Muslim prophets reinforce the importance of god by encouraging devotees to repeatedly recite aloud (or silently) short phrases, prayers or the name of god—a practice performed by many faiths, including some Christian denominations who use repetitious prayers—a practice specifically forbidden by Jesus:

"But when you pray, use not vain repetitions,[1] as the heathen do: for they think that they shall be heard for their much speaking" (Matthew 6:7).

The New International Version says: "… do not keep on babbling like pagans …"

Dhimmi (pl. dhimmis or dhimam)

Second class citizens who have been subjected to Islam. These are special groups of non-Muslims who are allowed to buy the protection of Muslims through a jizya (i.e., tax). It mainly includes Jews and Christians, but exceptions have been made to allow other monotheists, such as Sikhs (blending of Islam and Hinduism[2]) and Zoroastrians, to buy protection as well. Some polytheists, such as Hindus and Buddhists, whose countries have been conquered by the Muslims, have, on occasion, also been allowed to become second-class citizens by paying the jizya; however, they can only practice their religion under the strictest control of Sharia law.

Dhul-Hijja   The twelfth and last month on the Islamic calendar marking the end of the Hajj (pilgrimage); "Possessor of the Pilgrimage"

Dīn (religion) A life governed by a revelation from Muhammad with the goal of perfecting the Muslim's faith and religious practices; also means the Islamic religion

Eid (pl. Ayaad)

Celebration or recurring event/habit. There are two official holidays in Islam:

A.
B. *Eid al-Fitr (Id al-Fitar),* which is the first holiday or feast celebrated at the end of the Ramadan period of fasting and prayer; also known as the "feast of breaking the fast."
C. *Eid al-Azha (al-Adha* or *Bakr/Bakara-Eid*), meaning slaughter/sacrifice. This is the second holiday, which celebrates the willingness of Abraham to sacrifice his first-born son Ishmael in Mecca.

329

Falsafah   Philosophy or love of wisdome taken from rational Greek philosophy and was introduced as a means to interpret Islam. A faylasuf is one who studies Falsafah, a philosopher.

Al-Faraj   Signifies the anticipated return of the Shi'ite's messiah's return, known as the "Mahdi" or the "twelfth imam." Believers in this long-awaited event are sometimes referred to as the "Twelvers."

Farḍ (pl. furūḍ)

A religious obligation or action(s). An example of *fard* is praying five times a day. When a Muslim does not do the required *fard*, they can be assured of being punished after they die (see **Wājib**).

Farḍ kifāyah   An Islamic communal obligation for all Muslims regarding participation in the required jihad (military struggle against the infidels, Sûrah 2.216), who must participate and who—for special considerations—might not be obligated

Fātiḥa   This is the brief opening of each sûrah (i.e., chapter) in the Koran, which states:

"In the name of Allah, the Merciful, the compassionate. Praise be to Allah, the Lord of the Worlds ..."

This is used at the beginning of Muslim prayers *(salat)* and liturgies (see **Ṣalāt**)

Fatwā   A legal document/proclamation issued by an imam or mujtahid (i.e., "Islamic scholar") regarding an interpretation of Sharia law; it is considered binding not only on him, but also on every Muslim who follow his teachings.

Figh   The human understanding regarding Sharia law, its development through jurists *(Ulama),* and its execution through official rulings (Fatwa) regarding the observances of religious rituals morals, and laws of socially (publically and private) accepted conduct

Fuwaysiqah   To deviate or leave the right path; a wicked person

Ghāzi A holy warrior, raider; also known as a mujahid or one who has an inner struggle desiring to serve Allah

Ḥadīth/The Hadith (pl. ahādīth)
A collection of sayings written down from memory concerning sayings of Muhammad outside of the koranic revelations

Ḥāfiẓ A memorizer or guardian (i.e., a hafiz is a person who has preserved and protected the transition of the Koran by completely memorizing it).

Ḥājj (pl. Ḥujjāj or Ḥajīj)
A pilgrim or a person who has made the required pilgrimage or Hajj to Mecca at least once in their lifetime; the Fifth Pillar of Islam, according to Sunnis

Ḥākim A title applied to a Muslim ruler, governor or judge

Ḥalāl Something lawful, permitted, good, beneficial, praiseworthy or honorable under Sharia law (i.e., actions one engages in, including the preparation of food)

Ḥalaqah A coming together to study Islam

Haram Pronounced *ha 'rām*, meaning forbidden. It can also mean sinful actions, something that is sacred and not allowed/accessible for people who are not adherents or sanctified, such as a sanctuary or mosque. It also includes unlawful practices such as stealing, cheating or anything prohibited by the Koran.

Harem Pronounced *'har em* meaning forbidden place, not to be confused with haram. A harem is a place for women (wives and concubines) off-limits to all but the family and/or eunuchs.

Ḥijāb A covering; a garment used by Muslim women to cover their head and chest with the intent of preserving self-respect and modesty (see **Burqa)**

Hijrah	Alternate spellings *Hejira, Hijra* or Latin, *Hegira,* meaning to emigrate or flight. It commemorates Muhammad's flight from Mecca to Medina in 622 A.D. and year one on the Muslim calendar (**see AH/A.D.**)
Hijri year	Is Also known as Islamic New Year (see **AH/A.H.**)
Hilāl	Crescent moon
Hudā	Guidance
Hudna	Ceasefire or truce: usually until one is strong enough to resume the attack or truce during the Sacred Months. In the *Treaty of Hudaybiyyah*, we observe that Muhammad broke a treaty with the Quraish over a loophole. The Quraish, along with another tribe, attacked the Bedouin Khuza'a who were friends with Muhammad, even though the Quraish kept their part of the bargain regarding the ceasefire with Muhammad and the Muslims. During that time, the Quraish attacked the Banū Khuza'ah tribe, who were Muhammad's allies, and Muhammad used it to his advantage because he became militarily stronger than when he first had to make the treaty with the Quraish. Muhammad mounted a surprise attack on Mecca and conquered it. By breaking the treaty, the so-called *Treaty of the Prophet* became an Islamic doctrine that allows for treaties during wartime to be broken because "war is deceit," meaning that treaties are part of the arsenal of weapons to be used in winning any war.
Hufaad	(See **Khitan/Khatna** and **Circumcision**) Islamic circumcision severing the woman's clitoris (i.e., clitoridectomy).
Iblīs	Devil(s) or *Shayṭān* (Satan) or a (jinn) created out of fire, mischievous demonic beings—a genie. It was the angel, Iblis (the equivalent of the biblical Lucifer), who refused to bow down to Adam in Muslim lore (see **jinn**).
Id ul-Adha	This is a four-day celebration beginning on the tenth day of Dhul-Hijja, the twelfth and last month of the Islamic calendar; known as the "Festival of Sacrifice" when Abraham

allegedly prepared to sacrifice his son, Ishmael, to Allah in Mecca.

I'jāz   A miracle (e.g., the transmission, both in form and content of the Koran to Muhammad who could neither read nor write). Muhammad was able to memorize the Koran and then repeated it to scribes who wrote it down on anything available at the time (e.g., flat rocks, palm fronds, the shoulder bones of dead camel, etc.). This is the only claimed "miracle" associated with the Koran.

Ilāh   A deity or god(s)

Imām   A Muslim religious leader or person who leads a community and/or leads a Muslim congregation in prayer. Shi'ites designate this title as a reference to one of the twelve, bloodline successors of Prophet Muhammad, which ended with the disappearance of the twelfth imam, known as the Mahdi.

Injīl   This refers to the Islamic concept of the gospels as some kind of teaching given to *Isa* (Jesus) (as opposed to the biblical books of Matthew, Mark, Luke, and John), which contradicts the teachings of Islam. It denies the concept taught in the Bible regarding (1) the original sin of man passed down from generation to generation; (2) The need of a Savior; (3) Jesus as the sinless Son of God; (4) His death on the cross as a once and for all sacrifice for man's sin; (5) His burial and Resurrection, which proved that Jesus is indeed God the Son and—and when taken in total, (6) It is the true gospel, or as it is translated from the Greek, the "good news." Muslims believe that the real gospel has been lost and that Allah did not produce the gospels of Matthew, Mark, Luke, and John; they believe they are only made-up stories about Jesus, leaving some to wonder what Islam really considers to be the "good news." It is almost as if Muhammad was familiar with the Greek term "gospel," but did not understand what the word meant (see **Īsā** below).

Īsā (Jesus)	One of the Koran's underlining themes is " 'Isa ibn Maryam," which means "Jesus, son of Mary," allowing for His virgin birth without having Allah as a father by parthenogenesis (from the Greek, *Parthenos* [i.e., virgin plus "genesis" or origin/creation]). It seems that the Islamic concept of the virgin birth of Jesus, as contained in Islam's rejection of the four gospels of the Bible, is that God the Father had sexual relations with Mary, not unlike the mythological Greek heroes who were "demigods" (i.e., "half gods"). Demigods had one god as a parent and one human as a parent (e.g., Hercules, whose father was the god, Zeus, and his mother was a human named Alcmene). Alexander the Great also claimed that his mother, Olympia, while married to Philip II King of Macedonia, had an affair with the god, Zeus, who became Alexander's real father. The Koran also makes the claim that Alexander was a prophet of Islam (Sûrah 18:89-98). We will address this in our commentaries in Volume II *of Islam Exposed, The Koran: Selected Sûrahs with Commentary and Bible Comparisons,* as well as going into more detail in *Volume III, Science-Bible-Archaeology and Myths.*
Islām	Submission or surrender
Isrā	"The Night Journey" (Sûrah 17) where Muhammad was to have ascended to Heaven in a dream
Jāʼiz	Something allowed or permissible
Jahannam	Hell or Hell-fire
Jannah	Paradise (Hebrew, גן *(gan)* meaning a "garden"); Heaven
Jihād (struggle)	Usually, a military conflict for the furtherance of Islam, although it can mean a personal conflict within one's self.
Jihād alrahim	(see Jihād of the Womb)
Jihād aṣ-ṣaghīr	An offensive military action declared by a caliph

334

Jihād aṭ-ṭalab   An aggressive attack or jihad

Jihād ad-dafʿa

A jihad (struggle) as a means of protection

Jihād bis-saif

A type of jihad which is mostly applied to the furtherance of Islam through a Holy War or jihad by the sword (see **Jihad**).

Jihād of the Womb (Jihād alrahim)-

There is also a new jihad called "Jihad of the Womb," and it is designed to overtake a country through the Muslim birthrate.   While the Western world promotes abortion, Muslims focus on reproduction.   Think this is just a conspiracy theory? Think again. In England, the birthplace of the King James Bible and the Church of England, where the King is the head of that church, yet on Dec. 5, 2024, *Reuters* (news service) reported that *the number one name for babies in 2023 was Muhammad.* Consider this also, the Prince of Wales is next in line to be the King of England and the head of the Church of England, but even in Wales, *Muhammad is the number one name for babies!*

Jilbāb (pl. jalabib)

A conservative garment covering the entire body, except for the head, face, and hands. The *jilbab* is typically very long and loose, flowing like a coat. It does not cover the head or neck, which is usually done by wearing a scarf leaving the face—unlike the Hijab—exposed.

Jinn (a genie)

A supernatural creature a little lower than an angel who might appear ghostlike at times; can posess a person, usually evil, mischievous. A jinn is a creature created out of fire (see **Iblīs**).

Jizya

A tax demanded under Sharia law (Sûrah 9:29), which must be paid by non-Muslim males—usually Christians and Jews—in order to be allowed to live peacefully as second-class citizens who are subjected to Islamic control.

Jumu'ah Friday prayer

Ka'bah (Ka'aba)

The Ka'aba is a cube-shaped building located in Mecca. On the east corner of the Ka'aba is a cornerstone known as the "legendary Black Stone of the Ka'aba." What it is, where it came from, and its relationship with the Ka'aba (building) and Islam is steeped in speculation and mystery. The Ka'aba is constructed of stone and covered with black fabric. It is toward the direction of this mosque that Muslims around the world must face during prayer.

Ka'aba Stone

A sacred black stone contained in the Ka'aba (see **Ka'bah**)

Kāfir Non believer, infidel

Khalīfah (Caliph)

Someone who assumes the role of the head of the Islamic religion and is instrumental in pursuing a global dominance of Islam (Shi'ites have imams)

Khatīb The designated speaker in the mosque during the Friday prayer

Khimār From the word *khamr* which means "to cover:"

"And tell the believing women to lower their gaze and be modest, and to display their adornment only that which is apparent, and to draw their veils over their bosoms, and not to reveal their adornment save to their own husbands or fathers or husbands' fathers, or their sons or their husband's sons, or their brothers or their brothers' sons or sisters' sons, or their women, or their slaves, or male attendants who lack vigor [eunuchs] or children who know naught [nothing] of women's nakedness. And let them not stamp their feet so as to reveal what they hide of their adornment. And turn unto Allah together, O believers, in order that you may succeed" (Sûrah 24:31, bracketed clarification mine).

Khitan or Khatna Circumcision of both male and female gentiles.

Kitmān To deceive by withholding important information while still allowing just enough truth to be believable.

Koran The English spelling of "Qur'an;" the holiest book in Islam (see **Qur'an**)

Lâ ilâhâ illâ allâh (la ilaha ill Allah)

"There is no god but Allah." This is the most important expression in Islam, which forms the basis of the first pillar of Islam (the foundation of the Muslim life). It is important to realize that by saying this phrase with conviction, a person automatically converts to Islam. To change one's mind later and leave the Muslim faith invites death—(Sûrah 4:89; 9:11-12; 2:217; 9:73-74; 88:21; 5:54; 9:66. [Hadith]: Bukhari 52:260; 83:37; 84:57; 89:271; 84:58; 84; 64-65. [Hadith]: Abu Dawud 4346. [Hadith]: Al-Muwatta of Imam Malik 36.18.15. Reliance of the Traveller (Sharia law) 08.1 "When a person who has reached puberty and is sane voluntarily apostates [abandons] from Islam, he deserves to be killed" (clarifications mine). Three verses later [08.4], we read that there shall be no penalty under Sharia law for any Muslim that kills an apostate).

Laylat al-Qadr

This refers to the "Night of Power," near the close of Ramadan, which commemorates the time when Muhammad received his first revelation of the Qur'an from the angel Gabriel.

Madrasah A Muslim school (elementary through college)

Mahdi A guide also thought to be the Islamic messiah (see **Masīḥ**). In the Shi'a sect of Islam, it refers to the twelfth imam, and in the Sunni sect, it is believed that the al-Mahdi has not been born yet; however, both sects believe that al-Mahdi (the guide) will be revealed on the Last Day with a contrite Jesus whose job it will be to break all the crosses and confess that He (Jesus) was mistaken and is now a Muslim. If Jews and Christians have not or will not convert to Islam at that time, it will become the duty of the "Muslim Jesus" to kill

337

them. When that is done, then there will be peace on the earth.

Malā'ikah (Angel[s])

It was a *malaikah* known as Gabriel (*Jibril*), who revealed the Koran to Muhammad.

Mahr   A required payment, a dowry either with money or personal property; in some cases, one's life.

Maruna   This allows Muslim immigrants not to adhere to Sharia temporarily in order for them to be seen as more mainstream and moderate.

Masīḥ   This refers to the Hebrew word *Messiah* (מָשִׁיחַ) literally "anointed one."

Masjid al-Ḥarām

This building, the largest mosque in the world, is built surrounding the Kaʿbah in Mecca.

Mecca   Islam's first and holiest city

Medina   Formally the village of Yathrib and renamed the "City of the Prophet" by Muhammad, the second holiest city in Islam.

Miḥrāb   A niche that is cut into the wall of all mosques; indicates the direction of Mecca where the faithful must face in prayer

Minaret   An obelisk type construction adjoining a mosque where a muezzin does the call to prayer from its top

Miʿrāj   Muhammad's dream, "The Night Journey," where he ascended to Islam's seven Heavens

Muftī   An Islamic scholar and interpreter of Sharia law who has the authority to issue a *fatwa* (command, order/proclamation) based upon his interpretation of the Koran and The Hadith (see **Fatwā**)

Muḥajabah   A Muslim woman who wears a *hijab*

Mujāhid (pl. Mujāhidūn)
An Islamic warrior

Mullah   Muslim clergy who have studied the Koran, the Hadith and Sharia law

Mushaf A copy, text or process of editing the Koran

Muslim   A person who is of the Islamic religion; any individual who submits to the will of Allah

Muṭawwaʿūn (sing. muṭawwaʿ)
Police who are responsible for the enforcement of Islamic Sharia law and dress codes

Nabī   Prophets sent by Allah to guide men, even though these prophets have not been given scripture; Islam teaches that Abraham was a Nabi, as opposed to being a Rasul (i.e., messenger).

Nafs   Similar to the Hebrew word, *nephesh (נֶפֶשׁ)*, which means soul

Nakīr and **Munkar**
Two angels assigned with the task of testing the faith of those who are in their graves. Presumably, Allah doesn't know for sure what they believe in.

Naskh   The doctrine of al-Nasikh wal-Mansukh (abrogation) or the repeal, change or reversal of promises and revelations Allah originally made:

"Nothing of our revelation (even a single verse) do we abrogate or cause be forgotten, but we bring (in place) one better or the like thereof. Know you not that Allah is Able to do all things?" (Sûrah 2:106.)

There are no such passages in the Bible where God went back on (or changed) a promise.

Niqāb   A veil worn over a woman's face

Nubūwwah   Regarded by Shi'ites as the Third Pillar of Islam which deals with the office of a prophet

Nūr (light)   In Islam, it is believed that the angels were created from light, while the jinns were created from fire.

P.B.U.H.   This is an acronym meaning "peace be upon him." It is written out of respect following the name of Muhammad, but is also used for other prophets.

Prophet   A messenger from Allah

Qadhf   False accusation of someone not being chaste; being unchaste is punishable by Sharia law and can lead to a person (usually a woman) being stoned to death.

Qāḍī   A Sharia law judge

Qiblah   The direction facing Mecca where Muslims must face when praying

Qitāl fī sabīl allāh
Fight in the cause of Allah

Qiyāmah   Resurrection; the rising of the dead on the Day of Judgment

Qudsī   The classification of a Hadith believed to contain dialogue that was specifically given to Muhammad by Allah

Qur'ān   "Koran" in English means "the recitation." Muslims accept the Qur'an (Koran) as the literal word of Allah, revealed to Muhammad in a cave known as "Hira" during the year 610 A.D. by the angel Jibril or Gabriel.

Quraysh   The tribe of Muhammad; depending on the various writings and translations of the Koran (Qur'an) and The Hadith (as we can see throughout this volume), it can be spelled Qureish, Quraish, Quresh, Qurish, Kuraish, and Coreish.

Rabb (teacher or master)
Similar to the Hebrew word rabbi *(רַבִּי)*

Rajm   Execution by stoning

Ramaḍān   The sacred month when a Muslim is to be introspective, prayerful, and fast, similar to the Christian Orthodox season of Lent. It was during that period when Muhammad received his first revelations of the Qur'an.

Riba   Interest or usury; charging interest on money loaned, which is strictly forbidden in the Koran. One example would be:

O you who believe! Devour not usury [interest], doubling, and quadrupling (the sum lent). Observe your duty to Allah, that you may be successful (Sûrah 3:130, bracketed clarification mine).

Rūḥ   Similar to the Hebrew word *ruach (רוּחַ)*, which means "spirit"

Sabb (blasphemy)
It is unforgivable to insult Allah (sabb Allah) or Muhammad (sabb ar-rasūl).

Ṣadaqah   Charity or a voluntary giving above the amount required for zakat (giving to those less fortunate)

Ṣalāt (sala[t])
Obligatory participation in the five daily prayers, considered by Sunnis to be the Second Pillar of Islam.

Salām   Similar to the Hebrew word *shalom (שָׁלוֹם)*, meaning "peace"

Ṣamad   The conviction held by Muslims that Allah is "The Eternal"

Shahādah   The Muslim confession of faith: *La ilaha illa Allah. Muhammadun rasulullah*, "There is no god but Allah. Muhammad is the messenger of Allah." This is considered the First Pillar of Islam, according to the Sunnis. This can also be considered a synonym for the term Istish'hād (martyrdom).

Shahīd (pl. shuhadā)
A witness or martyr; it generally means a person killed while fighting in a *jihād fī sabīl Allāh* or "jihad for the sake of Allah."

Sharī'ah   Sharia law governing Muslims; literally means "a path to the watering hole." Sharia law is found in the Koran and Hadith. It was codified in the 14th century, mainly by a Muslim scholar named, Shihabuddin Abu al-'Abbas Ahmad ibn an-Naqib al-Misri or Ahmad Ibn Lulu ibn al-Naqib for short (AH 702-769/AD *1302–1367), in a book titled, Reliance of the Traveler* ('Umdat as-Salik wa 'Uddat an-Nasik).

Sharīf   The title used to describe the descendants of Muhammad through his daughter, Fatima's son, Hasan, whose father was also the son of Muhammad's brother, Abi Talib' (see **Shī'ah**)

Shayṭān (Shaitan[s])
       Biblical devil known as Satan (see **Iblis**)

Sheikh (Sheek or Shayk)
       An honorific title bestowed on a male to express honor sometimes inherited. He may be a tribal chieftain or proximate cleric.

Shi'ah (singular)
       A branch of Islam (Shi'ites) who believes the caliphate should ascend from Muhammad's family through his daughter, Fatima, and her husband, Muhammad's first cousin, Ali and their sons, Hasan and Hussayn (Hasan became the fifth caliph, Sharīf).

Shirk   The sin of being a polytheist, idolatry or the recurring theme of the Koran which keeps insisting that Allah has no associates and denies the Deity of Christ as seen in this verse which confuses the Trinity ("God the Father, God the Son and God the Holy Spirit,") with "Allah, Jesus and His mother, Mary."
       And when Allah said: O Jesus, son of Mary! Did you say unto mankind:

       "Take me and my mother for two gods beside Allah? he [Jesus]said: Be glorified! It was not mine to utter that to which I had no right. If I used to say it, then You knew it. You know what is in my mind, and I know not what is in Your

Mind. Lo! You, only You [Allah] are the Knower of Things Hidden?" (Sûrah 5:116, clarification mine).

Sīrah
The life or biography of Muhammad as contained in the Koran and the Hadith; it is also reflected in the Sunnah

Şukūk
Sukūk has become globally accepted as a financial system that has its basis in Sharia law. It has infiltrated many other religious, cultural, and national banking systems, despite the fact of its Islamic origin. Because of political influence and clever marketing, *sukūk* is no longer used exclusively by Islamic countries; however, it has managed to work its way into other national monetary systems such as in the United States of America.

Sunnah
Sunnah is synonymous with Sharia. Both literally mean the "way" or "path." Both concern themselves with Islamic law through the teachings and examples of conduct exemplified by the life of Muhammad, who is considered by Muslims to be "the most excellent example for all humanity."

Sunni
Largest Muslim faction; Sunni is derived from the word "sunnah," meaning an example based on the "teachings, conduct and life of Muhammad."

Sūrah (chapter)
The Koran consists of 114 sûrahs (chapters) contained in two volumes.

Tahlīl
Stating the Muslim confession of faith, *Lā ilāha ill-Allāh,* (i.e., "There is no god but Allah" [Allah— like the name Godfrey— is a theophoric name containing the word "god"]).

Taḥrīf
Forger or corruption; Islam teaches that Allah was unable to keep the Christians and Jews from corrupting the Bible, although Allah had no problem preventing the Koran from becoming corrupted.

Tajdīf
The highest of insults or blasphemy

Taqiyya (taqiyyah)

Taqiyya is an Islamic judicial term meaning "a lie," which is allowed in Islam as a permissible means of deception to further the cause of Islam, or to give cover and protection to Muslims who wish to hide their faith as a means of self-preservation and/or political cover. This is based on Sûrah 3:28, which states, "Let not the believers take for friends or helpers Unbelievers rather than believers: if any do that, in nothing will there be help from Allah: **except by way of precaution, that ye may Guard yourselves from them**. But Allah cautions you (to remember) Himself; for the final goal is to Allah" (Abdullah Yusuf Ali, bolded emphasis added).

Tawrāh

The Hebrew Torah *(תּוֹרָה)* as revealed to Musa (Moses)
This is used as an elusive speech in order to avoid a straight answer to exploit words with more than one meaning.

Tawriya

A sanctioned doctrine allowing lies under *all* circumstances, even invoking Allah's name if "technically" true.

Ulamā (ulema, sing. alim)

Leaders of the Muslim community (senior civil servants, judges, instructors, imams, in the Shi'a sect) (see **Ālim**)

Ummah (umma)

Nation or caliphate; refers to the universal community of all Muslims

Wa'alaykum as-salām (also "Wa 'Alaykum as-salaam!")

This is the usual response given to the salutation, *"As-Salamu Alaykum"* (peace be upon you) by saying, "And upon you peace" (see **As-Salāmu ʿAlaykum).**

Wafāt (death)

Barah [twelve]-wafat [death] stands for the twelve days of Muhammad's illness (poisoning), which led to his death; coincidentally, it was on the exact anniversary of the same day he was born. (Muhammad was born and died on the twelfth day of Rabi-ul-Awwal, which is the third month of the Muslim year.)

Wājib

Mandatory, obligatory (see **Fard**)

344

Warrāq   A scribe, notary or publisher/printer

Yathrib   Pre-Muhammad name of Medina, an oasis village; it was renamed "City of the Prophet" by Muhammad in honor of himself (see **Āminah**).

Ya'jūj wa-Ma'jūj (Gog and Magog)

They said: "O Dhu'l-Qarnayn! ["He of the two horns," i.e., Alexander the Great] See! Gog and Magog are spoiling the land. So may we pay thee tribute on condition that thou set a barrier between us and them?" (Sûrah 18:94, emphasis and bracketed clarification mine.)

Yawm   Similar to the Hebrew *Yom (יום)* ("day")

Yawm al-Qiyāmah

Day of the Resurrection (also the Day of Judgment) (See **Yawm**)

Zakat (Al-Māl) A tax

Sunnis consider this to be the Fourth Pillar of Islam; it includes tithes and alms, which is the duty of every Muslim.

Zakāt al-Fiṭr

Charitable gifts shared after the celebration of Ramadan

Ẓālimūn   Believers in many gods, cheaters, and people who are unfair in their dealings with others

Zandaqa

Heretics, atheists, polytheists and those who join others (gods/associates) with Allah

---

NOTES:

1   NOTE: Strong's word Number 945, is the Greek verb, βαττολογέω, which means to repeat words, similar to a person who stutters or stammers—repeating something over and over and over again.
2   Caner, Ergun Mehmet., Emir Fethi. Caner. *Unveiling Islam: An Insider's Look at Muslim Life and Beliefs*. (Grand Rapids: Kregel Publications, 2002), 170.

SOURCES CITED

Ahmed, Syed Rasheeduddin. "Halal or Not Halal?" *The Muslim Observer* (01 June 2006): n.pag. Web. 17 February 2015.

Al-Aghdadi, Ibn Sa'd. *Wikipedia, The Free Encyclopedia* (25 December 2013): n.pag. Web. 18 June 2014.

Al-Ahbar, Ka'ab (2015 May 26), *Wikipedia, The Free Encyclopedia*. Web. 06 Feb. 2015.

Al-Misri, Ahmad Ibn Naqib. *Reliance of the Traveller: A Classic Manual of Islamic Sacred Law* (Sheik Noah Ha Mim Keller, ed., trans.). Evanston: Sunna, 1991.

Al-Mubarakpuri, Saifiur Rahman. *The Sealed Nectar: The Life of the Prophet Muhammad*. Fortress Publications, 2013.

Al-Naqib, Aḥmad Ibn-Lu'lu'Ibn. *Reliance of the Traveller: The Classic Manual of Islamic Sacred Law* (Nuh Ha Mim. Keller, ed., trans.). Beltsville: Amana Publ., 1997.

Al-Ṭabarī, Muḥammad Ibn-Ǧarīr. *The History of al-Ṭabarī* Vol. 8: The Victory of Islam (Michael Fishbein, trans.), Volume VIII. Albany, NY: State U of New York, 1997.

Al-Tabataba'i, Sayyid Mohammad Hosayn. Shi'ite Islam. Translated by Nasr, Seyyed Hossein. New York: State University of New York Press, 1979.

Ali, Abdullah Yusuf, trans. *The Holy Qur'an: Translation and Commentary*. Damascus: Uloom Al Qur'an, 1934.

"Ali" (alternative title: ʿAlī ibn Abū Ṭālib). *Encyclopædia Britannica Online*. Encyclopædia Britannica, n.d. Web. 18 Mar. 2016.

Amari, Dr. Rafat. Islam: *In Light of History*, 1st ed. Religion Research Institute, 2004.

"American Peace Commissioners to John Jay," 28 March 1786. Thomas Jefferson Papers, Series 1. General Correspondence, 1651-1827. Library of Congress (March 28, 1786) (handwritten): n.pag. Web. 20 December 2014

"Ancient Hebrews." *Encyclopædia Britannica*, Volume 1. Chicago: U of Chicago (1946): n.pag. Web. 25 July 2014.

Anderson, Sir Norman. *The World's Religions*. Grand Rapids: Eerdmans, 1987.

Anderson, Stacy A. "Obama Hosts Ramadan Dinner at White House." *The Huffington Post* (June-July 2013): n.pag. Web. 4 Sept. 2013.

Andræ, Tor, Theophil Menzel. *Muhammad, the Man and His Faith* (Sheik Noah Ha Mim Keller, ed., trans.). New York: Harper & Row Publishing, 1955.

Apps, Peter. "Commentary: London's New Muslim Mayor, Already Tilting the World's Political Chessboard." Reuters. Thomson Reuters, 12 May 2016. Web. 12 May 2016

Arberry, A.J. *The Koran* Interpreted. New York: Touchstone, 1950.

Asad, Muhammad and Ahmed Moustafa. *The Message of the Qur'ān: The Full Account of the Revealed Arabic Text Accompanied by Parallel Transliteration*. Bitton: Book Foundation, 2004.

Barnes, Brooks. "Man Behind Anti-Islam Video Gets Prison Term." The New York Times, 7 Nov. 2012. Web. 2 Feb. 2015.

Beaumont, Thomas and Eileen Sullivan. "Michele Bachmann: 'Obama Is Allowing Terror Suspect Groups To Write The FBI's Terror Training Manual' " *The Huffington Post* (28 Oct. 2011): n Pag. Web. 18 Feb. 2015.

Berkson, William. *Pirke Avot. Timeless Wisdom for Modern Man* (Menachem Fisch, trans.). Philadelphia: The Jewish Publ. Society, 2010.

Berry, George Ricker. *Interlinear Greek-English New Testament,* 4th ed. Grand Rapids: Baker Book House, 1980.

Brahim Sene. "Islam: More than a Religion." *Answering Islam*. n.pag. Web. 20 Aug. 2014.

Brown, Jonathan. *The Canonization of al-Bukhr and Muslim* (Islamic History and Civilization). Leyden: Brill Publ., 2007.

"Caliph (Islamic Title)." *Encyclopædia Britannica Online*: n.pag (2008). Web. 9 November 2014.

Caner, Ergun Mehmet and Emir Fethi. Caner. *Unveiling Islam: An Insider's Look at Muslim Life and Beliefs*. Grand Rapids: Kregel Publications, 2002.

CBN News. (10 June 2014). "Historic First: Islamic Prayers Held at the Vatican."

_____. President Bush Plans to Take Part in an "Interfaith Session" at the United Nations. Geisler, Norman, and Abdul Saleeb. *Answering Islam.* 2nd ed. Grand Rapids: Baker Books, 2002.

CCC (Catechism of the Catholic Church), Paragraph 841 with footnote #330, which refers to *Lumen Gentium, the Dogmatic Constitution of the Church number 16* from the Second Vatican Council, November 21, 1964.

"Christian Leaders Ask for Muslim Forgiveness – Khaleej Times." *Christian Leaders Ask for Muslim Forgiveness – Khaleej Times.* N.p., 26 Nov. 200. Web. 09 Oct. 2014.

Constable, Pamela. "Pentagon OKs Beards, Turbans." *Washington Post.* The Washington Post, 22 Jan. 2014. Web. 09 Apr. 2016.

Coughlan, Sean. "'Oldest' Koran Fragments Found in Birmingham University. "*BBC News*, BBC, 22 July 2015, www.bbc.com/news/business-33436021.

"DANDENONG'S Mayor Has Called on Residents to Embrace a Muslim Event at Which People Will Be Forced to Cover Up." The *Dandenong Leader* [Australia], 16 Sept. 2010:

Dashti, Ali. *Twenty Three Years: A Study of the Prophetic Career of Muhammad*, London: George Allen & Unwin, 1985.

"Detroit Emergency Room Doctor Charged with Child Genital Mutilation." *WXYZ.* ABC NEWS WXYZ-TV Channel 7 Detroit, 13 Apr. 2017. Web. 13 Apr. 2017.

Dorell, Oren. "Some Say Schools Giving Muslims Special Treatment." *USA TODAY* (26 July 2007): n.pag. Web. November 15, 2013.

East Asian age reckoning. (2015, September 10). *In Wikipedia, The Free Encyclopedia*. Retrieved 13:21, October 7, 2015,

Elwell, Walter. *A. Evangelical Dictionary of Theology*, 13th ed. Grand Rapids: Baker Books, 1997.

Ernst, Douglas. "College Suspends Student Who Challenged Muslim Prof's Claim That Jesus' Crucifixion a Hoax." *The Washington Times*.

Esposito, John L. *Islam: The Straight Path*. New York: Oxford University Press, 1988.

_____. " 'Aishah In the Islamic World: Past and Present," Oxford Islamic Studies Online. Web. November 12, 2012 (subscription required).

Evans, Sophie Jane. "Saudi Arabia Sentences Maid to Death by Stoning for Adultery - but the Man She Slept with Will Escape with 100 Lashes." *The Daily Mail Online.* Associated Newspapers (UK), 28 Nov. 2015. Web. 9 Apr. 2016.

Farrell, John. "Fragments of Mark's Gospel May Date to 1st Century" (27 February 2012): n.pag. Web. 13 May 2013.

Federman, Reinhard. *THE ROYAL ART OF ALCHEMY.* (Bala Cynwyd: Chilton Book Co., 1968

"Female Genital Mutilation." *World Health Organization*, World Health Organization, 31 Jan. 2025, www.who.int/news-room/fact-sheets/detail/female-genital-mutilation.

Ford, Dana and Mohammed Tawfeeq. "Jonah's Tomb Destroyed, Officials Say - CNN.com." *CNN Cable News Network*, 25 July 2014.

Francis, James Allen. *The Real Jesus and Other Sermons* (Philadelphia: The Judson Press, 1926), 123-124. (This originally appeared under the title "Arise Sir Knight.")

Gass, Henry. "Michigan City Elects First-ever Muslim Majority City Council." *The Christian Science Monitor.* The Christian Science Monitor, 9 Nov. 2015. Web. 11 Nov. 2015.

Geisler, Norman L. and Abdul Saleeb. Answering Islam: *The Crescent in Light of the Cross.* Grand Rapids: Baker Books, 2003.

_____. *Baker Encyclopedia of Christian Apologetics.* Grand Rapids: Baker Books, 2000.

Gentilviso, Chris. "Obama Hosts Ramadan Dinner at White House." *The Huffington Post* (June-July 2013): n.pag. 4 September. 2013.

Gibb, Hamilton Alexander Rosskeen. *Mohammedanism: An Historical Survey.* London: Oxford University Press.
_____. and J.H. Kramer, eds, *Shorter Encyclopedia of Islam.* Ithaca: Cornell University Press, 1953.

Gibson, Ph.D., Shimon. *The Cave of John the Baptist.* New York: Random House, 2005.

Glassé, Cyril. *The Concise Encyclopedia of Islam.* New York: Harper & Row, 1980.

Gospel of Barnabas. Brooklyn: A&B Publishers Group, 1993

"Gospel of Thomas" (2014, December 10). *Wikipedia, The Free Encyclopedia*: n.pag. Web. 14 December 2014

Greenfield, Daniel. "Obama: 'The Future Must Not Belong to Those Who Slander the Prophet of Islam.' " FRONTPAGEMAG.com. N.p., 25 Sept. 2012. Web. 23 May 2015.

Hahnenberg, Edward P. *A CONCISE GUIDE TO THE DOCUMENTS OF VATICAN II.* Cincinnati, St. Anthony Messenger Press, 2007.

"Hajj" John Bowker, ed., *Oxford Concise Dictionary of World Religions* Oxford University Press, 2000.

Hammond, Dr. Peter. *Slavery, Terrorism & Islam: The Historical Roots and Contemporary Threat.* Cape Town, South Africa: Frontline Fellowship/Xulon, 2010.

Haykal, Muhammad Husayn. *The Life of Muhamma*d, n.p. American Trust Publications, 1976.

Hiremath, S.S., MDS, FICD. *Textbook of Preventative and Community Dentistry.* 2nd ed. Bangalore: Elsevier, 2011.

Hoft, Jim. "Fallen SEALs Father: Hillary Told Me at Funeral, 'We're Going to Arrest and Prosecute.' " (Video). N.p., (26 Oct. 2912). Web. 18 Jan. 2015

Hohmann, Leo. "Moms Declare Holy War after School Teaches Islam 'true faith' " *WND,* n.p. 31 Mar. 2017. Web. 16 Apr. 2017.

Hopfe, Lewis M., Mark R. Woodward. *Religions of the World.* Pearson/Prentice Hall Publ., 2005.

Hunt, Janin and André Kahlmeyer. Islamic Law: *The Sharia from Muhammad's Time to the Present.* Jefferson: McFarland & Co. Publ., 2007.

Ibn-Ǧarīr Muḥammad Al-Ṭabarī. *The History of Al-Ṭabarī. The Victory of Islam* (Michael Fishbein, trans.), Volume VIII. Albany, NY: State University of New York, 1997.

Ibn Ishaq and Sirat Rasul Allah. *The Life of Muhammad,* A. Guillaume, trans. New York: Oxford University Press, 1980.

"ISLAMIC LAW." *Encyclopædia Britannica,* Volume 12. Chicago: U of Chicago, 1946.

"ISIS Destroys Iraq's Oldest Christian Monastery, Satellite Photos Confirm" Fox News. *Fox News.* FOX News Network, 20 Jan. 2016. Web. 20 Jan. 2016.

Islamic Law on Female Circumcision. *Answering Islam,* n.d. Web. Nov. 2016.

Jack Van Impe Presents, episode 26, dir. Alex Rogers Kimbrough, 29 min., Jack Van Impe Ministries, June 29, 2013.

_____. Dir, Jerry Rimmer, 29 min., Jack Van Impe Ministries, October 10, 2015.

"Jewish Holidays for 632." Jewish Holidays for 632. N.p., n.d.: n.pag. Web. 8 June 2014.

Ka'ab al-Ahbar (2015 May 26). *In Wikipedia, The Free Encyclopedia*. Web. 28 May 2015.

Kateregga, Badru D. and David W. Shenk. *Islam and Christianity: A Muslim and a Christian in Dialogue*. Grand Rapids: Eerdmans, 1981.

Keller, Nuh Ha Mim. *Reliance of the Traveller: A Classic Manual of Islamic Sacred Law*. Revised ed. Beltsville: Amana Publ., 1994.

Khan, Dr. Muhammad Muhsin, trans. *The Translations of the Meanings of Sahih al-Bukhari*, Volume 6. Riyagh, Saudi Arabia, Darussalam Publ., 1997.

Kopf, Shule. "Jews rank high among winners of Nobel, but why not Israelis?" 25 December 2002: n.pag. Web. 1 May 2013.

Legacy of 'A'isha Bint Abi Bakr. New York: Columbia UP, 1994.

Liu, Joseph. "The Global Catholic Population." *Pew Research Centers Religion Public Life Project RSS*. N.p., 13 Feb. 2013. Web. 23 June 2016.

"Musa ibn Ja'far." *Encyclopedia of the Modern Middle East and North Africa. Gale Group*. 2004. n.d. Web. 18 Mar. 2016.

_____. "Terrorism." *USA Today*. Gannett (18 Feb. 2015): n.pag. Web. 19 February 2015.

Madelung, Wilferd. "'ALĪ AL-HĀDĪ". *Encyclopaedia Iranica*. Web. 8 November 2007 n.d. Web. 18 Mar. 2016.

_____. "ʿALĪ B. ḤOSAYN B. ʿALĪ B. ABĪ ṬĀLEB and ZAYN-AL-ʿĀBEDĪN." *Encyclopaedia Iranica* n.d. Web. 18 Mar. 2016.

_____. *"BĀQER, ABŪ JAʿFAR MOḤAMMAD." Encyclopaedia Iranica.* n.d. Web. 18 Mar. 2016.

_____. *The Succession to Muhammad: A Study of the Early Caliphate.* Cambridge: Cambridge University Press. 1997.

"Medina." *UK Hajj Umrah | UK Hajj Umrah Medina,* www.ukhajjumrah.travel/Destination/medina/. N.d. Accessed 22 December, 2017

Mahamud, Faiza. "Minneapolis Muslims Protest 'Sharia' Vigilante in Cedar-Riverside Area." Star Tribune, 13 Apr. 2017. Web. 17 Apr. 2017.

McAuliffe, Jane Dammen. *The Cambridge Companion to the Qur'an.* Cambridge, UK: Cambridge Univ. Press, 2006.

McCann, Jaymi. "Saudi Arabia Beheads Murderer... and Then CRUCIFIES His Body." *Mail Online.* Associated Newspapers (UK), 28 Mar. 2013. Web. 09 Apr. 2016.

McFall, Marni Rose. "Dearborn Heights Police Arabic Badge Sparks Fury." *Newsweek,* Newsweek, 5 Sept. 2025,

Memia, Michael. "Saudi Businessman Donates 10 Million To Create Islamic Law Center At Yale." HUFFPOST RELIGION. Huffington Post, 13 Sept. 2015. Web. 20 Sept. 2015.

Minor, Jack. "For Shame-Wheaton Alumni Defends Chrislam Professor." Prophecy News Watch, 03 Feb. 2016. Web. 03 Feb. 2016.

Muhammad, Bell, Richard. *The Qur'an: Translated, with a Critical Rearrangement of the Sûrahs*. Edinburg: Clark Publ., 1936.

Nasr, Seyyed Hossein. *Ideals and Realities of Islam*. London: George Allen & Unwin, 1975.

———. "Ali: Muslim Caliph." *Encyclopædia Britannica Online*. Encyclopædia Britannica, n.d. Web. 06 Feb. 2015.

———. *Ideals and Realities of Islam*. London: George Allen & Unwin, Ltd., 1975.

———. Michael. *Frontiers in Muslim-Christian Encounter*. Oxford: Regnum Books, 1987.

Newton, Jennifer for. "The 'Birmingham Koran' Fragment That Could Shake Islam after Carbon-Dating Suggests It (the parchment no mention of ink) Is OLDER than the Prophet Muhammad." *Daily Mail Online*, Associated Newspapers, 31 Aug. 2015, www.dailymail.co.uk/news/article-3216627/Koran-irmingham-thought-oldest-world-predate-Prophet-Muhammad-scholars-say.html.

"Netanyahu Seeks Support for Gaza War in Address to Congress." *Newsmax*, Newsmax Media, Inc. Newsmax Media, Inc., 24 July 2024,www.newsmax.com/us/netanyahu-speech-congress/2024/ 07/24/id/1173804/.

Palmer, Edwin H. et al. *The Holy Bible, New International Version: Containing the Old Testament and the New Testament*. Grand Rapids: Zondervan, 1985.

Payne, J. Barton. *Encyclopedia of Biblical Prophecy: The Complete Guide to Scriptural Predictions and Their Fulfillment*. Michigan: Baker, 1997.

"Pennsylvania Judge Dismisses Case of Attack on 'Zombie Muhammad.' " Fox News. *FOX News*, Fox News Network, 24 Feb. 2012. Web. 31 Oct. 2014.

"Pentagon. McDonald's Capitulate To Sharia law." *Investor's Business Daily*: n. p. 9 Jan. 2014. Web. 18 January 2015.

Pickthall, Marmaduke. *The Meaning of the Glorious Koran*, 7th ed. New York: Everyman's Library, 1993.

Rahim, Abdullah. "Jews of Yathrib." *Exploring Islam*. N.p., n.d. Web. 17 Sept. 2015.

Sachedina, Abdulaziz Abdulussein. *The Just Ruler (al-sultān Al-'ādil) in Shī'ite Islam: The Comprehensive Authority of the Jurist in Imamite Jurisprudence*. New York: Oxford University Press, 1988.

_____. *Islamic Messianism: The Idea of the Mahdi in Twelver Shi'ism*. Albany, State University of New York, 1981.

Sahih al-Bukhari. (2014 May 16). *In Wikipedia, The Free Encyclopedia*: n.p. Web. 18 June 2014.

Saint Joseph Edition of the *New American Bible*. New York: Catholic Book Publishing Co., 1970.

Sawyer, Patrick. *"Swimmers Are Told to Wear Burkinis."* The Telegraph *[UK]: 15 Aug. 2009*

Shakir, Muhammad Habib, trans. *The Qur'an*, 11th ed. Elmhurst: Tahrike Tarsile Qur'an, Inc., 1999.

Shathaya, Dr. Ghassan Hanna. "Who Are the Chaldeans?" Chaldeans onLine, 1999. Web. 16 January 2015.

Siddiqi, Mazheruddin. *Modern Reformist Thought in the Muslim World*. Islamabad: Adam Publishers & Distributors, 1982.

Sloane, J.P. "Guest Writer Dr. JP Sloane: 'Neel Kashkari & Islamic Finance 101' - Politichicks.com." Politichickscom: n.pag. (14 May 2014). Web. 17 Feb. 2015.

Sonn, Tamara. *A Brief History of Islam*. Malden: Blackwell Publ., 2004, 209.

" 'Son of God' Translation Controversy." *The Alliance For Biblical Integrity*. N.d. accessed 21 October 2017.

Sorensen, Jon. "Why the 'Gospel of Barnabas' Is a Medieval Fake." Catholic Answers, 30 June 2014. Web. 12 June 2015.

Spellberg, Denise A. *Politics, Gender, and the Islamic Past: The Legacy of 'A'isha Bint Abi Bakr*. Columbia University Press, 1994.

Spencer, Robert. "Obama's Religion-of-Peace Policy Errors." *FRONTPAGEMAG.com*: n.pag. (8 November 2010). Web. 13 December 2014.

Stanton, H. U. Weitbrecht. *The Teaching of the Qur'an*. New York: Biblo & Tannen, 1969.

Starnes, Todd. "Lawsuit: Public School Forced My Child to Convert to Islam." Fox News. FOX News Network, 29 Jan. 2016. Web. 16 Apr. 2016.

Stefanovic, Zdravko. *Aramaic of Daniel in the Light of Old Aramaic*. Sheffield: Sheffield Academic Press, 1992.

Strong, James. *Strong's Exhaustive Concordance of the Bible: With Dictionaries of the Hebrew and Greek Words of the Original with References to the English Words*. Peabody: Hendrickson Publ, 1988.

Sunan Abu Dawud, Book 37, Number 4310.

Tarakji, Leila. "Islam's Call to Prayer Is Ringing out in More US Cities – Affirming a Long and Growing Presence of Muslims in America." Web. *MinnPost*, Minneapolis Post, 6 Feb. 2024,

The Editors of Encyclopædia Britannica. "Al-Husayn Ibn 'Ali: Biography Muslim Leader and Martyr." *Encyclopædia Britannica Online*. Encyclopædia Britannica, n.d. Web. 06 Feb. 2015.

"The Star Online." *Archives / The Star Online*. N.P., 25 Oct. 2007. 18 Nov. 2014.

The Twelve Imams. (2016, January 30). In *Wikipedia, The Free Encyclopedia*. Retrieved 04:45, March 15, 2016,

THE WHITE HOUSE. September 17, 2001, " 'Islam is Peace' says President;" 3 September 2003.

Utvik, Bjorn Olav and Knut S. Vikor. "The Middle East in a Globalized World Papers from the Fourth Nordic Conference on Middle Eastern Studies," Oslo, 1998. Bergen: Nordic Society for Middle Eastern Studies, 2000.

Watt, Montgomery. *Muhammad at Medina*. Oxford: Clarendon Press, 1956.

Wikipedia contributors, "September 11 attacks," *Wikipedia, The Free Encyclopedia*: n.pag. Web. 23 August 2013.

_____. "The Twelve Imams." *Wikipedia, The Free Encyclopedia*. 22 Aug. 2015. Web. 06 Feb. 2015.

WikiIslam contributors, "Taqiyya." *WikiIslam, The Online Resource on Islam*. N. page. Web. 3 Aug. 2015.

_____. "Qur'an, Hadith and Scholars: Female Genital Mutilation." *WikiIslam The Online Source on Islam*, n.d. Web. 15 Apr. 2016

World Heritage Encyclopedia. "Yathrib." n.pag. n.d. Web. 22 February 2015.

YALE University. " 'A Common Word Between Us and You.' " *The New York Times*, 18 Nov. 2007.

_____. "A Common Word" Christian Response. Yale University, 2008: n.pag. Web. 01 October 2014.
Yuksel, Edip. "True Islam - Beating Women." *True Islam - Beating Women*. Quran-Islam.org, n.d. Web. 02 June 2016.

Zachary John. *Is the Qur'an Pure?* Based on his book: Gabriel's Faces: Voice of the Archangel (n.p. Harvard, House, 2004): n.pag. Web. 12 May 2013.

Zaimov, Stoyan. "Father" and "Son" Removed from Bible Trans-lations for Muslims: n.pag. Web. 2 July 2013.

Zawadi, Bassam. "What Does It Mean That Allah Guides Whom He Wills and Misguides Whom He Wills?" *Call-to-monotheism*. N.p., n.d. Web. 11 Oct. 2014.

Zoll, Rachel. "US Muslims: A New Consumer Niche." *Bloomberg Businessweek*. n.p. Bloomberg, 2 December 2010. N.pag. Web. 17 February 2015.

Zubaida, Sami. *Law and Power in the Islamic World*. London: I.B. Tauris & Co., 2005.

ABOUT THE AUTHOR

As a student of history and theology, Dr. Sloane has researched not only the diversity of Christianity, but he has also explored various other religions, sects, and cults in order to understand how they interact, challenge, and influence each other. It was because of his quest for knowledge that he embarked on over 30 years of higher education, graduating from a special program at Purdue University that was sponsored by the Indiana Council of Churches. He also graduated from the Institute of Charismatic Studies at Oral Roberts University, the Moody Bible Institute, and Institute of Jewish-Christian Studies. He earned a B.A., Summa Cum Laude, from the Master's University, where he attended their IBEX campus in Israel. While at the Master's University, he earned an M.A. in Biblical Counseling. At Trinity Theological Seminary, he earned a Doctorate of Ministry as well as a Ph.D., With Distinction, in Religious Studies.

Throughout the years, Dr. Sloane has appeared on such television programs as the 700 Club, Lester Sumrall Today, Richard Roberts Live, LeSea Broadcasting's Harvest, and Trinity Broadcasting Network's Praise the Lord, to name a few.

Publications Dr. Sloane appears in include, "Who's Who in the World" and "Who's Who in America." He is also featured in the "Dictionary of International Biography" and "2000 Outstanding Intellectuals of the 21st Century" (Cambridge, England).

Continued . . .

Dr. Sloane is seen here working at the site of the "John The Baptist" dig during his undergraduate work in Israel, under the direction of the Israeli Antiquities Authority and the supervision of Dr. Shimon Gibson (adjunct Professor of Archaeology at the University of North Carolina at Charlotte).

This site is located in the orchards of Kibbutz Tzuba, near the village of Ein Karem, which is also believed to be the traditional birthplace of John the Baptist (located west of Jerusalem). "From a historical point of view, the uniqueness of this cave is that it contains archaeological evidence which comes to us from the very time of the personalities and events described in the Gospels ... (in) the cave is the earliest ever Christian art depicting John the Baptist as well as the three crosses of the crucifixion."[1]

---

[1]Shimon Gibson, Ph.D., *The Cave of John the* Baptist (New York: Random House, 2005), Back Cover.

www.ingramcontent.com/pod-product-compliance
Lightning Source LLC
LaVergne TN
LVHW011216080426
835509LV00005B/156